LIFE AT THE
LIMIT

Patrick Stephens Limited, an imprint of Haynes Publishing, has published authoritative, quality books for enthusiasts for more than a quarter of a century. During that time the company has established a reputation as one of the world's leading publishers of books on aviation, maritime, military, model-making, motor cycling, motoring, motor racing, railway and railway modelling subjects. Readers or authors with suggestions for books they would like to see published are invited to write to: The Editorial Director, Patrick Stephens Limited, Sparkford, Nr. Yeovil, Somerset BA22 7JJ.

LIFE AT THE *LIMIT*

GRAHAM HILL

Foreword by Damon Hill

Patrick Stephens Limited

DEDICATION
To Bette and our children

First published by William Kimber & Co. Ltd 1969
Reprinted three times
Second edition 1976
This facsimile second edition, with additional material,
is published by Patrick Stephens Ltd 1993
Reprinted in 1994

British Library Cataloguing-in-Publication Data:
A catalogue record for this book is available from the
British Library

ISBN 1 85260 461 1

Library of Congress catalog card no. 93-79173

Patrick Stephens Ltd is an imprint
of Haynes Publishing, Sparkford,
Nr. Yeovil, Somerset BA22 7JJ

Printed and bound in Great Britain by
Butler & Tanner of London and Frome

CONTENTS

CHAPTER   PAGE

	Foreword by Damon Hill	vi
	Reflections from Brigitte Hill	vii
	Reflections from Samantha Hill	viii
One	Start Line	11
Two	1929–1954	24
Three	1955–1957	39
Four	1958	50
Five	1959	60
Six	1960	67
Seven	1961	78
Eight	1962	91
Nine	1963	116
Ten	1964	126
Eleven	1965	151
Twelve	1966	164
Thirteen	1967	183
Fourteen	1968	206
Fifteen	1969	230

FOREWORD BY DAMON HILL

It's 17 years now since my father's death, and the clear vision of him has become a little hazy. Time to read *Life At The Limit* again!

One of the unexpected benefits about my recently acquired fame (for want of a better word) as a 1993 Williams Renault Formula 1 Grand Prix driver is that a great many people I meet also knew my father and are able to tell me some of their recollections about him. There must be several more volumes of tales of his exploits to be collected and recorded from these people. Some of them can even be told in polite company.

Here is a quickie from my present employer, Frank Williams, which he told me himself.

Frank was on his way back from a Formula 2 race in Madrid in about 1968 and managed to bum a lift off Graham in his plane. It was a five-hour flight and during lunchtime. Frank had to hold his ripening bladder and also, because there were no refreshments to speak of, he was mighty relieved to find a boiled sweet to stave off his hunger. When they arrived at Elstree, Frank was waiting with the other passengers to thank my father for the lift. As he embarked from the plane, Graham pointed at Frank and said, 'Oi you. Is that your sweet wrapper?' To Frank's credit he owned up that it was. 'Messy bugger aren't you? Get back in there and pick it up!'

So that is what Graham Hill thought of Frank Williams in 1968! What would he have made of him today I wonder?

This is just one short story which sheds a little light on Graham Hill.

This book can bring him back in a small way, like touching up an old master. (He would have made a saucy remark now, but I won't.)

June 1993

REFLECTIONS

From Brigitte Hill

Life At The Limit is primarily about our father's racing career — the races he won and lost, the technical developments that he spent so many hours and days testing, his determination to get to the very top, and the people he worked with and competed against to get there.

Of course, as children, we knew very little about all this. Damon, being the boy, probably had more of an idea and natural interest than either of we two girls. I remember making the big mistake one morning of asking Damon how an engine worked. We were still at the breakfast table three hours later as I tried to come to terms with crankshafts and pistons.

When Daddy won his first World Championship in 1962 I was three years old, Damon was two and Samantha wasn't even born. The sixties for us — the height of Daddy's career — was a whirl of parties, tons of people at the house, Mummy and Daddy going away and coming back again (our Grandmother's cine films consisted almost entirely of us leaving our home at Mill Hill and then returning), interspersed with school, piano lessons, *Doctor Who*, Honey our retriever, and summer days playing in the street with our friends at Parkside. A normal childhood we thought, and in many ways it was.

It was only when I was in my early teens that I began to understand what was going on — the battle Daddy had to start up his own racing team, the triumphs and disappointments and his all-consuming passion to get the team off the ground. I even named my pony after his first car, Lola. I don't think the horse was too impressed. It was male.

Most of all I remember Daddy's sense of humour — he was so mischievous, there was always a glint in his eye — his sense of fairness, his wisdom, his honesty, his pride in us as his family, and his love and hugs.

Brigitte Hill. June 1993

REFLECTIONS

From Samantha Hill

I remember days of summer holidays and being flung into swimming pools and scrambling out for more, and Daddy being great fun acting the fool, chasing us screaming with excitement and fear.

Getting older and Damon handing over his monkey bike for me to use, as he progressed to bigger and better Bultacos — with me acting as one of the boys, trailing behind Daddy and Damon in the woods!

I remember annoying Damon when he was fixing up his car and him deservedly hitting me but giving me the perfect ammunition to start screaming just loud enough for Daddy to hear, and Damon trying hard to be nice to shut me up.

I remember playing in the car non-stop all the way to Asprey's for Mummy's Christmas present one Christmas Eve, very nearly causing Daddy to touch the bumper of the car in front just as the lights changed.

I remember the smell of Daddy's new car. I remember hours of playing backgammon.

I remember Daddy in his office surrounded by photos, leaning back in his green leather reclining chair, chewing his tongue, intent on what the person on the other end of the telephone was saying. I remember Sunday lunches and Daddy sharpening the carving knife.

I remember flying over Lyndhurst, our house near St Albans. I remember struggling to keep up when we went shooting. I remember Daddy larking about and pushing me into a cow pat.

I remember his whistle as he entered the front door. I remember him loving Ida's chocolate cake — and bringing him some Stilton cheese from the big blocks we used to have.

I remember him falling asleep in the chair.

Samantha Hill   June 1993

A TRIBUTE TO GRAHAM HILL

Originally published in the second (1976) edition

This book will give the reader a very clear picture of the sort of man Graham Hill was. In reading it he will clearly recognise the determination and perseverance which Graham put into his life both in good times and in bad.

I liked Graham as a man enormously, and we had great times together. He had a totally uninhibited sense of humour and a capacity to enjoy himself no matter what the company. His little ribald party pieces would flow out from time to time in the most reverent circumstances. Had anyone else uttered them there would surely have been a long and nasty silence but with 'Grandad' they brought the house down.

Graham tremendously enjoyed his life and the success that developed through the years. When I first met him he was a very intense man – almost frightening people away at times. He deplored dishonesty, he did not suffer fools gladly and was not afraid to show it. He did not change over the years, but he mellowed. He expanded his horizons to be much more than a racing driver. His interests and activities encompassed many facets of public life, from the Springfield Boys' Club to being on Government committees. He was a great ambassador for our sport.

He became a great personality in his own right, spreading his charm and humour as he went along. Graham Hill will be sadly missed.

Jackie Stewart

PREFACE TO THE FIRST EDITION

I am a racing driver, and have never had the time, and even if I had I don't suppose I would have had the ability, to learn anything at all about the skills of writing.

Quite often, when someone in this position is asked to publish an autobiography he very wisely gives the draft of his story to a professional writer to put it into good shape. I'm afraid that many of my readers may wish that I had taken this course, but I felt that I would rather let people see how I remember things in my own way.

Graham Hill

ACKNOWLEDGEMENTS

The publishers gratefully acknowledge the following, for pictures used in this book:

Associated Press, Victor Blackman, Maxwell Boyd, David Cairns, Michael Cooper, *The Coventry Evening Telegraph*, *The Daily Mail*, The Ford Motor Company, Max le Grand, Michael Hewett, Pascal Ickx, *The Kent Messenger*, Keystone Press, Eugene Lewis, Franco Lini, London Art Tech, Henry Manney, Official Indianapolis Motor Speedway, *The Oxford Mail*, David Phipps.

CHAPTER ONE

Start Line

At twenty-four years of age I still didn't know what I wanted to do with my life. At the time I was working in the development department of S. Smith & Sons, the watch, clock and instrument manufacturers, at Cricklewood, and although I knew that my five-year apprenticeship with Smiths and all my training was meant to prepare me for a life as a captain of industry, I never really felt that that was what I was going to be, and I never really knew what I wanted to do. The work I was doing was quite interesting—we were developing a flame heater for buses and I used to rush up and down the A1 all day on a coach, taking temperatures at various points inside and outside. Also at this time, Smiths began to develop a magnetic clutch, which was less than a success, and I was involved in that too, playing around with magnets and iron filings and generally sort of messing about.

I bought my first car a fortnight before my twenty-fourth birthday, on 31st January, 1953. It was a 1934 Morris 8 Tourer, a real old banger that I bought for £110 from a friend with whom I had been in the Scouts—the £110 I had borrowed from my parents. Incidentally, my father couldn't drive a car, and even to this day has never wanted to learn. He's the most unmechanical man I've ever known, but he doesn't seem to have suffered from it. My mother can drive; in fact she had a motor bike, a 250 Triumph, when she was only seventeen years old, which was quite something in those days. But the family never owned a motor-car; cars just weren't part of my life at all. The only time I ever got into a car as a child was when we went to the seaside once with an uncle. So I had never driven a car when I went to buy the Morris, but when the owner asked, 'Do you know how to drive?' I said, 'Yes', jumped into it and drove it across London to my home.

It was rather a zig-zag course, but I made it. I had applied to take the driving test two weeks earlier because I knew that it took about a month to come through. So a couple of weeks later I turned up for the test and tied on the L-plates which I had bought on the way to the test station. Having had no instruction, and just two weeks of driving, I then passed the test, which just shows what a farce the whole thing is. So there I was a fully-fledged motorist.

At this time I didn't know that motor racing existed. That isn't quite true because I do remember that when I was living in Hendon as a boy, we had a neighbour called Edgar Fronteras, an Italian who had raced an OM in the 'thirties; I had seen one or two motor racing photographs in his study. But it never did anything for me and I just didn't know anything about it. We used to get the motoring magazines at Smiths but I never read them.

Rowing was my sport then and kept me very busy, especially during the summer. That year, 1953, I had stroked the London Rowing Club 1st Eight in the Grand Challenge Cup at Henley. After the rowing season had finished, it was August or September, someone at Smiths threw a magazine across the desk to me and said, 'Here, look at this, you ought to do this!' And there was an advertisement saying you could drive a Formula 3 car at Brands Hatch for five shillings per lap. Well, I didn't know what a Formula 3 car was, but as I had just learnt to drive a car I thought I would like to have a go. So the next afternoon I arrived at the racing drivers' school at Brands Hatch in my Morris—while most of my fellow pupils were arriving in their Healey sports cars and the like, complete with brand-new goggles, helmets, special shoes and so on. I was a bit green and I remember that I had to borrow a helmet as I had come without one. I had decided to have a quid's worth, which was four laps, and the car provided was a Formula 3 Cooper powered by a 500 c.c. JAP motorcycle engine.

Up to this point I had never seen a racing car and the thing that struck me most about the Cooper was how small it was; it looked just like a small torpedo with a wheel at each corner. As I inserted myself into this tiny little tube, the only thing I recognised was the fact that it had a steering wheel and three pedals like my Morris. It seemed a most extraordinary thing to me, yet exciting at the same time. It was with a certain amount of apprehension that I set off down the track. The first impression I had was one of vibration and noise, the thing seemed to vibrate like mad. But it all smoothed out as I went a bit quicker; I hadn't been revving the engine fast enough to start with.

But I enjoyed it—I enjoyed it enough to want to go on doing it. I was bitten by the bug there and then. All I knew was that when I stepped out of that car my next purpose was to get back in it again as soon as possible.

Now I had no idea when I decided to go down to Brands that it was going to lead anywhere, it just seemed like a fun thing to do. Even afterwards I didn't say to myself, 'I'm going to be a professional racing driver.' I just wanted to drive a racing car. I didn't see myself as a future champion, but having driven four laps in a racing car the next step was to drive one in a race, and I had to find a way of doing it. I find that if I'm keen on something I do tend to put my all into it; I never get any pleasure out of doing things in half measures. If I do something, I want to do it properly, because that's the way I get the most satisfaction.

. . . . .

I didn't have enough money to buy a racing car of my own and the only person I knew who owned one was the man who was running the school at Brands Hatch, which was called the Universal Motor Racing Club and had about 350 members. His name was Gordon Thornton and I offered to work on his car and he accepted. I used to help him in the evenings in a garage in a mews just near the Anglesey pub in South Kensington. Every Wednesday I would go down to Brands Hatch and help him run the school, and though I was still working at Smiths they never seemed to miss me, which rather shows how important I was to the outfit.

This was, to my knowledge, the first club of its kind and the forerunner of the many clubs that are in existence today; as far as I was concerned it certainly served its purpose.

But one day I turned up at the garage to find that there was nobody there, and the car had gone. I never saw Gordon Thornton again—he went straight out of my life, and all my aspirations to be a racing driver were dashed overnight. But he was responsible for my first drive in a racing car so I'm not bitter about him walking out.

Albert Zains, who later raced in Formula 3, was also a member of the Universal Motor Racing Club. When I won the World Championship in 1962 he sent me a plaque with the Club's car badge mounted on it and the inscription *From little acorns giant oaks do grow*. It really was a nice gesture.

.   .   .   .   .

It was just before Christmas of 1953 that Thornton disappeared, and although I had been left high and dry I remembered having met a Mr. Weller who had, at one point, been interested in going into business with Thornton. I was able to track him down and we met in the Victoria pub in Paddington just before Christmas. At this time my original four laps was the sum total of my experience, but on learning that he was going to start a racing drivers' school of his own, I managed to convince him that a man with my experience would be invaluable to him and I was just the chap he was looking for. Fortunately he believed me.

My everyday motoring had also been interrupted shortly before when I had an accident in the Morris 8. As I was driving down Cricklewood Lane one morning, somebody came straight out of a side turning, just clipped the back of my car and sent it spinning around. I shot across the road, hit the kerb, and the car rolled over. The car had a canvas roof and I was trapped underneath with the whole thing sort of flattened out. Some people turned up and dragged me out, and as they were dragging me out I remember somebody handing me a cup of tea—it was almost as though they had been expecting the shunt and had been brewing up right there on the pavement. So I sat there drinking my tea and watching all the activity as the police, the ambulance and the fire engine all turned up. The firemen sprayed water all over the Morris and I was a bit peeved about that.

The little Morris wasn't all that reliable, so I used to carry my bicycle around in the back seat; now it lay broken and mangled by the kerb. Everybody was hunting around looking for the injured cyclist. So I explained that there was no cyclist, that it was my bike and that I'd been carrying it in the back of the car. Trying to explain this was rather difficult for they thought I was trying to get away with something and that there was probably a mortally injured cyclist bleeding to death beneath the wreckage somewhere.

This accident was to lead to my first brush with British justice and I didn't reckon it too much. I had to go to court where the Judge asked me what I had done. I explained that I was going along a main road and this bloke came out of a side road and clobbered me.

'Did you sound your horn?' the Judge asked.

I replied, 'No, because I was on the main road.'

A witness who had been following me said the same thing and the Judge gave him a hell of a ticking off for not blowing his horn—the poor chap had come to court to help my case and all he got was a bollicking from the Judge. The bloke who had hit me admitted that he was thinking of something else at the time and drove straight out on to the main road. Despite this the Judge found me a third to blame, which I could never understand—I suppose I was one-third responsible just for being there at the time of the accident. So I had to pay my costs, my motor car had been written off—I had no car, no money, nothing.

. . . . .

Mr. Weller put my motor racing career back on the tracks by allowing me to work for him, preparing the two Formula 3 cars he kept in a barn near Westerham, down in Kent. I left Smiths early in 1954 and so had no income, for Weller wasn't going to pay me and I needed money for fares on the Greenline bus which daily took me from my home in Maida Vale down to Westerham and back. So I went along to the Labour Exchange at Marylebone Road and when they asked me what I wanted to do, I said, 'I want to be a racing driver.'

They said, 'We haven't got any racing driver vacancies on the books at the moment. What else can you do?'

I told them I couldn't do anything else, but from time to time they used to tell me, 'Go along and see if you can do this job,' but every time I had to explain to them that the job in question was beyond me.

Anyhow, I used to sign on every Wednesday and Friday morning and get my 32s. 6d. dole money per week which paid for the bus fares. So every day I used to go down to Westerham and work all day on the two Formula 3 racing cars, a Cooper and a Kieft, among the chickens and ducks and things in Weller's barn. Now I didn't really know anything about racing cars then, but I would strip them down and try to remember how they came apart. Then I'd go off and buy new bits if they were needed, and put them all back together again.

Weller had promised me a drive in a race in return for my many hours of toil and he was true to his word. I was entered for a race at Brands Hatch on the 27th April, 1954. Prior to that meeting I had never seen a motor race in my life and here I was in my very first motor race, which must be a pretty unique experience for a driver. After practice I was very surprised to find myself on the front row of the grid for my heat.

I was a bit anxious about the start, never having made one before, but I had been told that the maximum revs limit for this car, a Mark 4 Cooper-JAP, was 6,000 rpm, so I just wound it up to 6,000 and sat there waiting for the flag to drop. When the flag did drop I slipped my foot off the clutch and, of course, I went off up the track like a rocket. I found myself in the lead— I just couldn't understand it. I thought I must have made a mistake and I looked round for everybody else. My plan had been to hang back at first and see what everybody did, because never having been in a race and never having seen one, I didn't know too much about it. I wanted to see what everybody did so I would get the hang of it. Anyhow, my lead was short-lived but I finished second in that heat. Now the opposition was a bit stronger in the final but I was running third towards the end of the race and feeling pretty pleased with myself, thinking, 'Well, this motor racing is a piece of cake,' when some silly blighter passed me almost on the line and that was that. So it was a good lesson; in my very first meeting I picked up a valuable lesson about concentration when racing.

With this invaluable experience behind me, I was now even more of an asset to the Premier Motor Racing Club, as the school was called, and in addition to being the mechanic and the only fully paid-up member, I also became the chief instructor. We started advertising the Club and got about six members. When they turned up at Brands Hatch for the first day's instruction I was able to show the chaps which was the gear lever, which was the handbrake, and which was the right way up to wear their goggles. This was pretty important stuff because we used to have chaps wearing their goggles the wrong way up, and even trying to change gear with the handbrake, with some quite startling results.

Before my second race we sent our best engine, a Norton, away to an engine tuning specialist, and this I later installed in the Kieft chassis. We were making a special effort for this race. After the start I was in second place on the second lap when the engine suddenly stopped. In putting the engine back together the engine tuner had put the key that locked the camshaft drive in upside down and during the race it slipped. So there I was out of the race with nothing to do but watch. I wandered into the middle of the infield at Brands where I started to chat to some people about the race. It turned out that among them were Colin Chapman and his girlfriend Hazel, who is now his wife. This chance encounter was to prove vital in my career.

I hadn't dared to tell my father that I had left Smiths and he thought that I was gainfully employed and working hard, for I had been leaving home early every morning and getting back rather late. But a crisis arose when I was struck off the dole after four months, for now I didn't even have enough money for bus fares. I asked Weller if he could pay me £3 per week and this is where we had a difference—of exactly £3 per week! So I found myself at Brands without means of getting back to London and I asked Colin if he could give me a lift back. 'Yes,' he said, 'you can come back in our coach.' So I got a lift and even a free meal on the way home. There was some confusion as to exactly who I was—Colin Chapman thought I was a friend of Mike Costin's, Colin's right-hand man, and Mike thought I was a friend of Colin's. So I was fed and got a lot of racing chat as well.

.   .   .   .   .

Lotus is now a publicly owned group of companies producing nearly 100 cars per week, but then the 'works' was a stable in Hornsey, North London and the only full-time employees were Nobby Clark and a boy. When we arrived back at the works Colin found they had a bit of a problem because Peter Gammon's very successful Mark 6 had been damaged and they were going to be a bit pushed to repair it in time for the next race. I told them that I had a bit of time available, like every day, and I could help. So I started to work at Lotus and Colin paid me a pound per day, which to me was a small fortune. That period was quite valuable for I gradually met the various people who were racing Lotuses at that time, and this later proved very useful.

It had become clear to me that the only way I was going to get into racing was by bartering my services as a mechanic in return for a drive in a race. One of the drivers I met was Dick Steed, and it was with him that I first went to a race abroad. His Mark 8 was the first Lotus ever to be fitted with a Coventry Climax engine and I worked right through the night mating it to an Austin A30 gearbox before driving down to Dover where I met Dick and his wife. We crossed the Channel then drove the Mark 8 on the road down to the Montlhéry circuit near Paris. On the warming-up lap I stood on the grid waiting for him and eventually he arrived with one front wheel wobbling like crazy—a steering arm had broken on the banked part of the circuit; he couldn't control the car and had to withdraw from the race. It was decided that I should stay in Paris till the replacement parts arrived and I spent a very enjoyable week there. It was then that I met Jabby Crombac who used to race a Lotus. He now runs the very successful French motoring magazine, *Sport Auto*, and has a tremendous influence on French motor racing.

.   .   .   .   .

During the winter of 1954–55 I worked for Dick Steed at his garage in Oxfordshire. I remember one day driving into Oxford in an old Alfa Romeo sports car and parking in a downhill street. When I went to restart, I found that the starter motor had packed up, so I put my foot out of the cockpit to give it a push start. I didn't realise that the cockpit was so far back in the car, almost over the back wheel, and as soon as the car moved forward the back wheel rode straight over my foot and trapped it. There I was with one leg inside the car and one outside, and the back wheel right over my foot with all my toes doubled up on themselves.

I started to ask passers-by if they would mind pushing the car back uphill and of course they weren't taking any notice, because from their side they couldn't see that my foot was trapped and so they couldn't understand why anybody would want them to push the car back up the hill. I was getting sick with pain but eventually, with some heaving and straining, one helpful man got the car off my foot, which now had all the toes sticking up vertically. The pain was excruciating for I had broken my big toe—my foot is still a bit numb in that area.

I was living with the Steeds, in their home, and working at their garage, still without pay in the hope that I would one day get to drive his Lotus, but in fact I never did. It was good experience nevertheless and I had a lot of fun because Dick used to play in the University jazz band, so we used to get to quite a few rave-ups or whatever they were called in those days.

During this period one of my ploys to meet racing people was to go to the Steering Wheel Club in Mayfair where I would soak up the atmosphere and talk racing. I used to go there with one shilling and buy myself half a pint of beer. I would stand there all night holding this half-pint which eventually got so warm that most of it evaporated—I don't think I ever drank much of it. Of course, I could never accept a drink from anyone because I didn't have the money to buy one in return. So people must have thought me a bit stuffy from this point of view, but I was obliged to stand there clasping this rather warm half-pint. I always used to walk in as if I was a member, which I never was, but in this way I got to know more motor racing people.

.   .   .   .   .

The previous August I had met Danny Margulies when he was racing his Mark 8 Lotus at Castle Combe, and in February of 1955 I went to work as his unpaid mechanic. The first trip was to Agadir in North Africa and his car, a C-type Jaguar, was shipped from London Docks and I went over to Amsterdam and joined the boat there. We had about a week's voyage down to Casablanca in this tiny little old cargo boat of about 900 tons. I remember being told that it was built for speed and for this reason it rolled like a pig. I've never been so sick as I was in the Bay of Biscay, and I had chronic indigestion for the whole trip. I remember trying to sleep in my bunk, but the ship was rolling so much my head just rolled from side to side, bang-crash on one side, then bang-crash on the other. I quite saw the point of having hammocks on a ship—they're much more comfortable and stay still while the ship rolls around them.

I arrived at Casablanca to meet Danny, Duncan Hamilton

with his D-type Jaguar and Graham Whitehead who had an Aston Martin. We borrowed an old Mark 7 Jaguar as a sort of service vehicle, then set out for Agadir, driving the racing cars on the road for 300 miles.

During this trip we saw something like a long black cloud hanging over the land ahead and then suddenly we drove straight into a swarm of locusts. These great greeny-yellow insects, about three inches long, just descended from the sky and ate absolutely everything bare. They were so thick on the road that we were getting wheelspin and it was a real squishy-squashy mess. You can imagine the state the windscreen of the Mark 7 was in—we put on the wipers and washers and all they did was smear greeny-brown squashed locusts all over the windscreen. The racing cars were open and these things were bouncing off our heads. But worse still, they bunged up all the radiators, and of course the cars started to boil. So we had to stop and tip the Arabs something to scrape all the squashed locusts off the front of the radiators. But it really was the most horrible feeling standing out there with these things zooming about and bouncing off our heads. They were sweeping the land and everything went bare in the trail of these locusts. It was terrifying to see such devastation and ruination of crops by these horrible things.

Danny raced on the twisty circuit around the town of Agadir, which must be completely different now after the earthquake of 1960. The return trip to Casablanca wasn't much more pleasant. I was being given a lift back by somebody in a DKW and we were having a bit of a dice up with one of the chaps, when a car in front pulled out to pass somebody and found a lorry coming the other way. The driver swerved back in again —and this simple movement of swinging the car out, and back in quickly, was enough to get it out of control. The car just rolled over, the driver came half-way out the window and was killed. The whole thing happened right in front of our eyes; and it could have been avoided by smoother driving or a seat belt. Back in Casablanca Danny teamed up with Duncan and Graham, and went on to race at Dakar. I had become surplus to requirements and continued back on to England by boat.

Danny gave me a drive in the C-type in April at Castle Combe—I remember that I spun it and there's a photograph to remind me. Shortly afterwards Danny and I started what was in effect a motor racing tour of Europe, with races at Spa in Belgium, Bari down on the heel of Italy, in Sardinia, and then back to the Nurburgring in Germany. Usually we would sleep in the truck, an old Commer which Danny had bought off Jack Brabham. We hardly ever stayed in a hotel—we used to sleep by the roadside, anywhere. Once we slept in a half-made haystack somewhere in Italy after driving till about 11 o'clock at night. We were asleep on the haystack when the farm workers started work at 2 o'clock in the morning. There seemed to be bullocks everywhere, then they started rebuilding the haystack we were actually trying to sleep in—there was great confusion and we had to get up and go.

When we got across to Sardinia we found that the race was from Cagliari to Sassari at the top of the island, then all the way back down again. This was particularly hazardous because the cars had hardly arrived before they sent them all back again. There were donkeys on the road, train crossings, and all sorts of hazards—a true road race. I went along as a riding mechanic to Danny and it was probably one of the last times that mechanics actually rode in a race. I took my camera with me and took photographs for *Autosport* as we were going along. I was using a Zeiss and got some rather good photographs. One of my photos taken on the Agadir trip actually made the cover of *Autosport*. It wasn't too easy bouncing around at that speed and there was no windshield on my side of the car, so my neck was in terrible shape for a couple of days afterwards. Fortunately I did have goggles and a helmet made of compressed cardboard that I had bought in a cycle shop in Cagliari. We did quite well in this race, finishing third overall, and second in our class to Eugenio Castellotti in a Ferrari.

In June we went all the way down to Messina in Sicily in the Commer. It took us six days from London, and of course we made the mistake of going down the wrong side of Italy, the mountainous West side instead of the Adriatic which had a much faster road in those days. At Messina there was a ten-hour night race around the streets and I was to share the driving with Danny. So I got my first taste of night racing and I remember all the people hanging over the walls that lined the circuit, and the headlights picking up dogs, and newspapers, and all sorts of things in the road itself. Unfortunately Danny lost it on one section of the course and went backwards into a wall. The fuel tank burst and that was that, but it had been my first experience in the big time, for Hawthorn and Castellotti and all that crew were in the race at Messina.

.   .   .   .   .

I couldn't spare the time to drive back across Europe as I had a rather important date in London—I was going to marry Bette the following Saturday. So I got myself a third-class train ticket to London. It took two whole days to get back to Victoria station and part of the time I had to sit in considerable discomfort on wooden seats, amidst whole families of Sicilians, and in the most oppressive heat.

I was rather surprised to find myself getting married because I had never really seen myself as marriage material. I shall never forget listening to myself proposing marriage, and thinking it must have been someone else talking, not me. On our wedding day my father gave me a rather powerful concoction called a Black Velvet, which is champagne and Guinness, and that set me up for the whole day. I was beaming at everyone all the time and I've never looked so happy for such a long period of time. For our honeymoon I had borrowed an old 1936 Hillman Minx from a good friend, but on the trip down to Bognor it broke down and I had visions of spending our wedding night by the side of the road. But we eventually got it going—there was something wrong with the fuel pump—and we staggered into Bognor.

Our honeymoon gave Bette a pretty good indication of what life with me was going to be like. We had chosen to go to Bognor because it was adjacent to the Goodwood circuit where the Nine Hour Race was about to be run; by some tremendous coincidence I had been put down as a reserve driver for Team Lotus. The only practice I got was when they let me do a couple of laps in the dark. I had never been round Goodwood and all I can remember is seeing corn everywhere—driving amongst the cornfields I just couldn't see where the road went. Two laps of that was all I got though I thought my big chance had arrived when one of the drivers, Keith Hall, got a bit of grit in his eye—I was accused of having put it there. Even after the race things didn't improve much for Bette—I met up with some old friends from the Southsea Rowing Club, which I had

joined whilst I was in the Navy, and we went across to the Isle
of Wight where I was shanghaied into a boat. So there I was
rowing in a regatta on my honeymoon. Anyhow we won, and
as a member of the winning crew I remember kissing Carole
Carr, the singer, and Bette getting most upset about my kissing
this lovely bird on our honeymoon.

.   .   .   .   .

To help support my new wife, I had to get a regular wage, so
this ended my career as a freelance racing mechanic. I got a
full-time job at Lotus, who were now in the racing car production business in a big way, for nine pounds per week. They
had larger premises by this time and my responsibility was the
conversion of the transmissions to racing specification, modi-
fying Austin A30 gearboxes to mate them to Coventry Climax
racing engines, buying old MG J2 gearboxes off dumps and
re-vamping them for use with two-litre Bristol engines, and the
like. I also had to modify the engines so they fitted into the
Lotus chassis, and fit the rack and pinion steering gear—
basically I did all the engineering jobs.

Two years had now passed since my first four laps and I
hadn't got much closer to fulfilling my ambition to become a
racing driver. Apart from my two Formula 3 drives, I had
driven Danny's C-type in two races, one at Messina and one
in England at Castle Combe. But I was in no way deterred
from my purpose; I knew what I wanted to do in life and
everything was just a means to that end. I think I have a
combination of my parents' qualities, and my determination I
inherited from my mother. My father is much more easy-going
and he has a very good sense of humour; I think that's one of
the important things in life, it enables you to laugh at yourself.
I think it's essential that people don't take themselves too
seriously. There was really nothing in my family background
or upbringing that suggested that I was particularly suited for
a career in motor racing, but I think the qualities I inherited
from my parents have helped me a great deal.

CHAPTER TWO

1929—1954

My life had been pretty uneventful until those four laps at Brands Hatch were to give it a real purpose. I was born in Hampstead on February 15th, 1929, so I was ten years old when war broke out in 1939, and it's the war years that I remember most of all. I can even remember clearly the day war was declared—everybody started to draw their black-out curtains in the daytime, and we all stood around talking and wondering what to expect. The sirens went and we saw an aeroplane in the sky, but it was one of ours. Eventually I went off and played with my toy soldiers.

We were living in Hendon, North West London, at the time, and I was attending the Algernon Road school. My father's business was on the Stock Exchange but he volunteered for the RAF shortly after hostilities began. We were evacuated for a couple of months in 1940 when my mother, my younger brother Brian and myself went up to Hereford where my father was stationed at the time. But we didn't like it there and returned to Hendon and spent the rest of the war in London. After any night raids and before we went to school in the mornings we would go around picking up chunks of shrapnel; all the bits had different values—a nose cone was worth sixpence, and the base of a shell was worth threepence. I can remember digging incendiary bombs out of our garden, putting my hand down the holes and pulling out unexploded ones. During the day we'd get a chance to watch a few dog fights. It was quite exciting with the fighter planes swooping about the sky and their machine guns blasting away, but the night time was bad, and sometimes we would sleep under the kitchen table as the German planes came over to bomb London. We had a Morrison shelter, one of those steel table things, that we put up in the dining room and I slept under it just once—it was so un-

24

comfortable that I preferred to sleep in my bed; but if it got
too bad, and my mother thought it was getting a bit dicey, I
would go downstairs. The anti-aircraft guns going off were a
bit shattering, and the house used to shake and rattle, which
disturbed me somewhat. Then sometimes we'd see a great
glow in the sky, and the next day we'd read in the papers that
it was the docks or somewhere that had been on fire.

Sitting up one night in 1940, I heard a fantastic noise like an
express train, and I remember the cat leaping up in the air, its
hair standing on end. Then there was the most almighty
explosion that shook the house, broke the windows and burst
the doors open. An enormous bomb had fallen about a mile
away and wiped out rows and rows of houses. Nobody ever
discovered what it was, but it was thought to be the biggest
bomb that had ever been dropped in England. People talked
about a mysterious red thing in the sky, and secret weapons.
It was obviously larger than a normal bomb and it had done
so much damage that the pundits thought it must be so large
that no plane could carry it.

We never slept in the underground stations—we got used to
the bombing and just hoped we weren't going to be hit. We
actually had incendiary bombs fall alight on the roof of our
house, but we'd just go up and knock them off. Houses close
to ours got bombed and burnt, and we'd have shells, and
shrapnel and broken slates raining down on our roof. We were
all very glad when it finished.

The bombing raids lessened; then after a lull the flying
bombs started. I remember the first one very clearly—I was
lying in bed and I heard this thing sounding like a motor boat,
chugg-chugg-chugg. Then I heard the engine stop and I
thought, Crumbs! It's crashing! Then a short time afterwards
we heard a great explosion. It was weeks before we found out
what it was, and by then they had started coming over in great
numbers. They were really frightening because you'd hear
them and wait for the engine to stop—when the engine stopped
you got your head down. But you'd hear these flying bombs
coming and you'd be thinking, Keep going! Keep going!
Somebody else can have it! But when the engine stopped there
really was a breathless pause. During the day you could
actually see the bombs and some would be going a lot faster
than others. When they were really going fast you knew they

were going to continue for some time and would disappear into the distance. Others would come over very slowly and you'd think, Hello, very dodgey! And you'd watch them stop and go straight down to the ground with about a ton of explosives. We even saw the fighters trying to catch them up—they were too dangerous for the pilots to try and blow up in the air while they were chasing them, because they'd then fly straight into the explosions. Instead they would come up alongside one of the flying bombs, get one of the fighter's wings under one of the bomb's wings, toss it over and bank it, and the whole thing would turn around and go back the way it had come.

.   .   .   .   .

When I was thirteen years old I went to Hendon Technical College, and the following year I joined the Boy Scouts; I remember these as among the best years of my life. St. Mary's 8th Hendon was a very active Scout group, and I used to spend five or six nights a week at Scouting. The main activities were gym on Mondays, band practice on Wednesdays (I played the drums) and parade on Fridays, with camps at Easter and in the Summer. We had never been a church-going family but the Scouts had a church parade one Sunday every month, and on top of that I actually became a server at St. Mary's Church, Hendon.

.   .   .   .   .

In 1946, after leaving school at sixteen years of age, I was apprenticed to S. Smith & Sons Limited, the instrument manufacturers. The only reason this came about was because my father knew the manager of one of the Smith plants at Cricklewood and, because I had some sort of mechanical bent, it seemed like a good idea. There was an 'entrance' examination, and every year thirty of what they considered to be the brightest pupils were sent off to a college that Smiths ran near Cheltenham. The head of this College was a Swiss, called Professor Indermuhle. The years I spent there gave me a very good basic training in engineering practice. The standards were very high and cleanliness was instilled into us in no uncertain manner. The machine shop had a parquet floor and in the middle of this were work benches, lathes, surface grinders. The parquet flooring was kept polished like a dance floor, despite all the dirt, the iron filings and turnings. Cleanliness in instrument making is vital, but the sense of cleanliness in engineering that they instilled into every boy that went there was a marvellous asset that automatically brought with it a feeling of pride in our work.

I lived in digs, paying thirty shillings a week for lodging out of a pay packet of £2 2s. 6d. which gradually rose to £3 5s. od. during the five years of my apprenticeship. I bought my first motor bike, a 1936 Velocette costing £65 whilst I was at Cheltenham; I bought it from a friend and the first thing I did was to ride it straight out of his driveway and into a parked car. So my first experience of a motorised vehicle resulted in my first accident. I bent the handle bars a bit but didn't do myself any damage on this occasion. By this time I had a girlfriend in London and I had been cycling home every weekend from Cheltenham.

We had to work on Saturday mornings and then I would set off in the afternoon and cycle the 100 miles to London to visit my girlfriend. I would take her out on Saturday night but was so bushed by all this cycling that more often than not I would fall asleep. Now this wasn't much fun for her and on Sunday I would cycle all the way back to Cheltenham, so my weekends weren't really much fun for anybody—but I got very fit. I decided to get a motorcycle and make everybody happy. Well, the next stage was that I spent so much time repairing my motorbike that I hardly ever got to London. So from my girlfriend's point of view I was better off cycling, even though I was quite useless when I arrived.

Shortly after I bought the motor-bike I got into a rather ugly scene in a pub, and I picked some fellow up and hurled him across the bar. I did myself a mischief in this exertion and I got a hernia—a lump appeared and it was all very painful.

Eventually the doctor said that I would have to go to London and have an operation, and so I got on my bike—it was the winter of 1947 which was the biggest, nastiest, snowbound winter we've ever had and all the roads were closed. Anyway, there was I with my hernia setting off on my motorbike across the snowbound Cotswolds to get to London. I practically paddled most of the way astride my motorbike and the very next day I went into hospital. I shall always remember being shaved for the operation by a couple of nuns—they were stropping away with the razor and I thought: That's funny, it doesn't seem to be doing much. And of course they had forgotten to put in the blade. I think they were just as embarrassed as I was by the procedure. I was a bit naked for a while.

My motor-bike ended its career one particularly misty night when I was going home to London across the Cotswold Hills. There was a lot of very low cloud about and apparently some fellow's lights had failed and he had stopped on the side of the road. I don't remember anything about it, but it seems that in a bank of cloud I rode straight into the back of his car. All I remember is waking up at the side of the road, realising I had had an accident, and hearing very large lorries thundering past my ear. I could hear somebody saying, 'His leg's broken, his leg's broken,' but I had obviously given my head a bit of a knock as well. My left thigh was broken and I spent three months in hospital in Cheltenham and another month or two at home where I had to walk around with my leg in an iron support fastened to my shoe and ending in a hoop in my crutch—very uncomfortable. In hospital they had drilled and pinned my leg and hung weights on it. Altogether they didn't make a very good job and it ended up half an inch shorter and quite bent. I'm quite bandy in that leg, and subsequently my pelvis dropped on one side to compensate for the shortened leg and gave my spine an S-bend—I've had back trouble ever since. This 5-month absence put me back a year at the College.

At one stage during my four year stint at Cheltenham I used to hitch-hike backwards and forwards to London. Now this was a less tiring method than cycling but it wasn't nearly so reliable and I was often late. So often in fact that eventually the good professor banished me to the Cricklewood plant in London. I was sentenced to night work in the automatic shop. This was a dark, dirty, smelly, oily place with sawdust on the floor and so much oil in the atmosphere that it was dripping off the electric lamps. I remember I used to cycle to work every night to feed bars of metal to these ever hungry automatic machines, and eventually my clothes even got to smell of the cutting oil. We would get one break, about four o'clock in the morning, when I used to scoff a piece of toast. Fortunately my father knew the manager of this plant and some pressure was discreetly brought to bear, and the Swiss professor was persuaded to have me back after two or three months in this dungeon.

.   .   .   .   .

To replace my wretched Velocette I bought a 500 cc 1947 Matchless competition model. I had in fact done a couple of scrambles with the Velocette and got my first taste of competition —I actually won a silver spoon for third place in a scramble. But I never raced the bikes on a circuit. Rowing was to become my sport—in 1949, when I returned to Cricklewood after completing my stint at Cheltenham. I had a cousin who rowed for the Auriol Club at Hammersmith and I did a bit of rowing there before I went into the Navy to do my National Service in June of 1950.

My call-up had been deferred until I finished my apprenticeship at the age of 21, and then I joined as an ERA—short for an Engine Room Artificer. I spent six weeks in basic training at the Victoria Barracks in Portsmouth where we were taught how to march and handle a rifle, and generally to obey orders, which we did with the utmost difficulty. I was made a section leader I think it was, and every day I had to march my section, about 40 or 50 chaps, through the streets of Portsmouth down to the dockyard where we were trained in the Naval workshops—a very motley procession. At the end of the basic training I was given the rating of Petty Officer and sent on a six week Petty Officer's course at HMS *Royal Arthur*, a concrete battleship at Corsham near Bath. There we did assault courses, lectures— I had my first taste of public speaking—and learnt how to command and all that jazz, and I must say I enjoyed it very much.

It was here that I was introduced to rum. As a Petty Officer I was entitled to a tot of rum every day. Now a tot is an eighth of a pint: not only was it a lot in volume, but it was neat rum, whereas the chaps below the rank of Petty Officer got grog, which is two parts of water to one of rum. Well, as you can imagine, we all got as high as kites never having touched this highly potent stuff before. We'd knock this stuff straight back and then cough and splutter; tears would come pouring out of our eyes. But we had to drink it there and then when it was issued at about 12 o'clock, just before lunch, because we weren't allowed to save it. Well, of course, everybody got drunk as lords, and we'd laugh our way through lunch, with such hilarious happenings as our spuds jumping off the plates—it was the funniest thing I've ever seen—everybody was jabbering and joking, lunch was just a scream. But gradually we got less girlish about it and began to really look forward to lunch. You weren't allowed to bottle the rum, so if someone did you a favour, you'd ask him to come round to your mess at around 11.30 a.m. and have 'sippers'. If you saved somebody's life you might be entitled to 'gulpers'—and if this amazingly generous offer was ever made you could watch the poor bloke stand there with tears in his eyes as his tot was seen to be gulped down somebody else's throat.

The people who have been in the Navy for years have little rum rats in their bellies. By about 11.30 they're watching the clock and licking their lips waiting for the tot to set them up for the day. The system does have hidden advantages—for instance, after your tot you'll eat any old rubbish that's put in front of you. It also livens up lunchtime and everyone talks louder than normal, with less intelligence, and vociferous arguments break out. But after lunch the effect wears off and everyone crashes their swedes and goes to sleep; a deathly hush descends over the ship.

It's quite a good way to carry on, because half an hour's kip after lunch must be good for the digestion. The effects of the alcohol could possibly be quite bad, I've no idea really, but it seemed worth it at the time.

I actually bottled my tot once, which is strictly against Admiralty orders, but I wanted to give some friends a taste. It took a great effort to actually pour it into a bottle—a great deal of determination and strength of character was needed to make this sacrifice for a friend. If you are teetotal and don't take your tot you get an extra 3d. per day—at 3d. per tot it must have been the cheapest liquor that ever was.

My next posting was to the Chatham Barracks and from there I used to ride home to London on my motorcycle. I joined the London Rowing Club at this time and Bette took up rowing as well. I would come up and row at the weekends and sometimes in the evenings—I rowed in pairs, and in fours, but I used to concentrate mainly on eights for that was where the club strength lay.

.   .   .   .   .

I was eventually assigned to a ship, HMS *Swiftsure*, which was a 10,000-ton cruiser. The ERA's mess was some 25 feet long and perhaps 15 feet wide and about 28 people used to mess in this space so you can imagine it got a bit crowded—28 people eating and sleeping in this small area. We were assigned to the Home Fleet and I got one or two reasonable trips during the year I served on this ship. We went down to the Mediterranean and made courtesy visits to Gibraltar, San Remo, and spent a week in Monte Carlo—of course, I never realised that seven years later I'd actually be racing there. We also went to Tangiers, a very interesting city, where I saw my first exhibition. It really was a rather amazing experience for which I'm ever grateful to the Navy. That was one of the few things that National Service did for me, opening my eyes to the extra curricular activities.

Back home we made courtesy trips around Britain and I visited all sorts of exciting places like Dundee, Scarborough and Glasgow where we were given the freedom of the city, which really meant we could travel on the buses for nothing. The trip to Glasgow started badly for just after we had tied up the tide went out and the ship settled onto the mud. The water intakes got blocked up and all the machinery had to be stopped because it needed water circulating for its cooling, so the whole ship was plunged into darkness. The cooling systems got clogged up with bleeding eels and mud and it was a particularly horrible job to get it all cleaned out.

The ship was powered by steam turbine engines and the boiler room was an awe-inspiring place to be in—it rather gave you an idea of what hell might be like, especially when we were steaming at full power. I have, in fact, in my possession a certificate stating that I'm capable of being in charge of a boiler room while steaming at full power, which might be a useful thing to have if anybody ever gets a steam-powered racing car to work. I also spent some time in charge of a propeller—fortunately for all concerned there were three more —I then had 20,000 horsepower at my fingertips which is considerably more than I've ever had since.

When we were based at Inverness in the north of Scotland, the Captain asked for volunteers to go out in a submarine during exercises. In my ignorance I volunteered to go aboard this sub, the *Sea Scout*, for the day, a tiny little boat of only 600 tons. I had got used to the 10,000-ton cruiser which was fairly ponderous in its movements—when you got into a rough sea it would rise and fall very slowly, it would take about a week to go up and a week to come down. Well, this tiny little submarine bobbed up and down like a cork and the moment we put our nose out of the harbour I was sick; whereas I hadn't been sick at all so far during my short term in the Navy, I was sick as a dog aboard this thing in a few minutes. I brought up the slippery fried egg I had had for breakfast and rushed below into the lavatory and spewed my heart out. They have a system of levers and things in submarines to get rid of the waste, but I must have pulled the wrong one, because I got everything back again. This didn't help me at all, and it didn't help the balance of the sub as far as I could see.

`In this exercise we were going to be dive-bombed and we had to look out for 'enemy' aircraft. When they were spotted we started to crash dive and we all leapt below and there were crashings and clangings and shouted orders, running around and what seemed to be general confusion, as I stood in one corner and watched the whole thing. The next minute we were hit by a smoke bomb. The hatch wasn't shut yet, which didn't seem to help because we were diving under the water—I was a bit worried about all this. The whole submarine filled with smoke and everyone was coughing and spluttering and their eyes watering; I wasn't terribly impressed by the fact that we'd been hit. We got below all right, but according to the rules of the game we'd obviously been sunk.

They didn't have too many submarines so they must have reinstated us as a member of the enemy force because we started to play again. The bombing stopped, so we lay near the bottom somewhere, suspended in the middle of the sea stock-still, while the destroyers searched for us. We could hear them coming by the swishing noise of their propellers getting louder and louder, and we all stood motionless and nobody moved and nobody spoke because the destroyer's detectors could pick up the slightest sound. Even the spanners were rubber-covered so that if you had to use them they didn't make a clink when they touched the metal. This applied especially to the wheel spanners which they had to use all the time on the valve wheels. Anyway, the noise of the propellers got louder and louder and obviously they were somewhere overhead. The next minute there was the most almighty explosion—it was shattering. They'd dropped something about the size of a hand grenade, but when this went off it was as if somebody had been on the outside of the submarine hitting it with a gigantic great hammer. It was only a tiny little grenade, so I couldn't imagine what it would be like if they dropped the real thing —depth charges.

So we'd been knocked out of the game again. Then I was given a chance to look through a periscope and observe the ships of the enemy. I must say that at that point I was pleased to be in the submarine, despite the recent shocks. The surface ships looked just like sitting ducks up there on the water line —you could put the old periscope's crossed sights on them and bang! dead centre! Then I realised that right where I was looking, right where I would aim to fire a torpedo, was where I would have been aboard a ship, just below the water line in the engine- or boiler-room. It was rather a dismaying prospect and I immediately thought that I wasn't really in the right service. I was below water in either case, and I certainly didn't like the sitting duck idea.

.　　　.　　　.　　　.　　　.

I left the Navy in June of 1952 after two years' service, and I'm sure that everything I learnt in that time I could have learnt in one year. We were resented slightly by the old hands, the regulars, who had taken years to get where they were—and here were we civvies coming into their Navy with their rank without appreciating the finer points of naval history and discipline. We were also overcrowding them a bit for there were six of us National Service ratings in the ERA's mess which already had twenty-two people in it. But although they didn't show it, perhaps they welcomed us also because we brought a breath of fresh air into their set-up. Service people are forced to lead a rather confining life and to have had us young men from the civilian world living with them in their mess must have provided some diversion.

I wasn't shot of the Navy quite, for I was on a three-year reserve; for three weeks every year for the next three years I had to go back. When I left in 1952 I grew a great big moustache, rather like a wartime RAF flying officer's affair. I can't remember exactly why I did this; I think it was because I was being a bit bolshie at the thought of having to go back into the Navy in a year's time—and I knew that moustaches weren't allowed. You can get permission to stop shaving and grow a full beard, but you're not allowed to grow a moustache. For good measure I had taken my Naval suit and turned the jacket into a rowing club blazer. When I turned up for my three weeks training wearing my rowing club blazer and a bloody great moustache they had an epileptic fit. Questions were raised in the House and it turned out eventually that nothing could be done about my moustache which pleased me immensely. They really used to go puce with rage seeing me walking around with this great fungus growing right across my face. I did this for three years and rather enjoyed doing it because I felt that I was getting my own back on the establishment for pinching two whole years of my life.

.   .   .   .   .

When I returned to Smiths I joined the car heater development section, but at the time my big interest in life was rowing. The training was very severe and we used to row every night of the week and on Saturday afternoon and Sunday morning as well. Seven days a week, and we used to do weight training on top of this. I was courting Bette fairly regularly at this stage, and on Sundays we would have lunch down by the river and walk in the park in the afternoon. By the time Sunday evening came I would be dead beat, but it was worth it for I really enjoyed rowing. It taught me a lot about myself, and I also think it's a great character-building sport. You have to have a lot of self-discipline and a great deal of determination. You not only get to know about yourself, but you get to know about other people—who you would want to have in a boat with you over the last quarter mile of a race when you're all feeling absolutely finished. You get to know the sort of people who are going to keep rowing their guts out and the sort who will let you down. With seven other fellows relying on you, you just can't give in. I think it's a particularly good sport, quite apart from being very healthy exercise; it's very good for your competitive mental outlook and I think that I learnt a lot while I was rowing which has helped me in my motor racing career.

We were reasonably successful in a number of regattas in

1952 and I was in the Club's 2nd Eight at Henley that
year. The following year I stroked the London Rowing Club
1st Eight in the Grand Challenge Cup at the Henley Regatta
—but we were knocked out in the semi-final by a very good
Parisian crew. We had done quite well and we got over the
course in the fastest time that any Club crew had ever achieved.
I just love Henley, but unfortunately it clashes with the races
at Reims every year. Invariably it is the French Grand Prix,
which is a particularly drawn-out meeting with practice Wednesday through Friday and the race on Sunday, so I have to
miss the whole of Henley every year. I managed to get back
one year and thoroughly enjoyed it. Henley was exactly the
same as I remembered it from ten years before. It is very
English and hadn't altered a scrap—which pleased me immensely, for I am a traditionalist at heart. It was raining so
much on that occasion that all the lawns in the Stewards'
Enclosure had turned to something like creamed spinach, and
everybody in their with-it gear was walking about in bare
feet with their shoes over their arms and their trousers rolled
up—a marvellous sight.

It's significant, I think, that in both the sports in which I've
excelled I have been sitting down. In fact, I was even facing
the wrong way in one of them. I am one of the world's worst
runners and have never been able to put one leg in front of
the other at all rapidly. I couldn't run fast to save my life and
I was always last at the schools sports; the only thing I was any
good at were the javelin and the discus; my running was hopeless. When I played football or cricket, I used to keep goal or
wicket—I think I must have pretty good anticipation to compensate for lack of speed. And, of course, good anticipation is
vital in motor racing, as it is in everyday motoring.

.   .   .   .   .

I had a break from rowing on Coronation Day, June 1953.
We had a lot of medical students rowing at the London Rowing
Club and some of them from St. Thomas' Hospital persuaded
me to go mountain climbing with them on Coronation Day,
because they reckoned that the thing to do in England on that
day was to get as far away from the crowds in London as
possible. As Sir Edmund Hillary and the Sherpa, Tensing
Norgay were scaling the dizzy heights of Mount Everest, we

would mirror their efforts here in Great Britain and go and climb Snowdon.

I had never been climbing in my life before and didn't know the first thing about it; when they instructed me to go out and buy some boots with special rubber soles from Lillywhites, telling me that these were what the climbers on Everest were using, I did as I was told.

We drove up to Wales and slept in a farmhouse the night before our epic climb, but when the big day came I noticed that everybody else had boots with little iron crimpons and I was the only one with these rubber-soled boots. I imagine they're marvellous when you're marching through snow, but it hadn't snowed on Snowdon and I was stuck with this rather slippery pair of boots. Anyway, we set off with our lunch strapped to our backs and walked for miles and miles. They said we were going to the Sloping Buttresses which meant nothing to me, but is apparently a particularly difficult climb. After marching cross-country for hours the going started to get steeper and somebody announced, 'We'll have lunch on the terrace.'

Well, I thought, that sounds lovely; the idea really appealed to me as I was famished by then. The going got pretty stiff and we started climbing what seemed like sheer rock faces to me. It was coming up to lunchtime and I began to think: Well, I don't see any terrace around here.

Eventually we all arrived at a little ledge which was just wide enough to sit down on with your legs drawn up underneath you like a little gnome. Well, that was it; that was the terrace. I sat with my back pressed hard against the mountain, my feet just hanging over the edge, looking down this sheer drop, supposedly enjoying lunch on the terrace. It was ridiculous; I was too petrified to eat. Then as I was trying to make sandwiches it began to hail—as fast as I cut the bread, the sandwich filled up with hail. That was novel, making hail sandwiches. Next someone passed me a great round of cheese, and of course, I let it slip. And this lovely great big cheese that was going to be everybody's lunch went bouncing down the rock face with ever increasing bounds until it smashed to pieces hundreds of feet below. You can imagine how popular that made me. So that was lunch on the terrace, hail and wind and the cheese bounding down the mountainside as it slipped from my frozen fingers.

After lunch, we set off up the Sloping Buttresses which were steeply inclined rock faces. The wind was getting pretty strong by then and we split up into two parties with me on the tail-end of one. We were roped together and I was hanging onto the end of the rope unable to get any grip on the rock with my rubber soles. The other lads with their crimpons could stick their boots in any old nook or cranny while I was slipping and sliding all over the rock face.

They said my wearing the boots was a very good experiment, but I wasn't at all impressed with being used as a guinea pig. Anyway, they suffered for their sins, as every few minutes they had to haul me up on the end of the rope. At one point I was left straddling a razor-edged piece of rock that formed the top of a ridge for what seemed hours—the others had all disappeared around a corner and I was way up there all by myself with the wind really whistling around me. I didn't fancy that at all—I was scared stiff.

Despite all this drama we eventually reached the top and set off for a café. Now that was a bit of an anti-climax—I really felt I had achieved something, climbing Snowdon on Coronation Day—and then we just walked into a café. That just ruined it for me and, to cap it all, we got inside the café and were told that it was closed. There was nothing to do but return by an easier route. But I must say it was good exercise and an experience I shall never forget. I'm quite certain that I will never do it again, so it was my first and last climb—to the top of Snowdon on Coronation Day while the Queen was getting crowned at Westminster Abbey.

The following winter I was to get pretty close to meeting the Queen, although fifteen years were to elapse before, surprisingly, I actually got invited to lunch at Buckingham Palace. Just a few months after the Coronation I made a bold attempt at storming the Palace. I had a friend with a lovely old 1926 bull-nosed Morris and was persuaded to go to the Oxford *v.* Cambridge Varsity Match at Twickenham. Three of us went in this old banger without a roof, and parked it on the pavement quite close to the football ground.

When the match was over we rushed out to avoid the crowd, and drove the car off the grass verge just as Princess Margaret and the Duke and Duchess of Gloucester came by with their police escort. We tagged ourselves onto the end of this royal cavalcade and, lo and behold, we had a straight run right through from Twickers to Buck House! Along Kensington High Street we went, with policemen waving us on and saluting the two royal cars and the dirty, scruffy old bull-nosed Morris bearing three chaps in duffle coats and cads' caps. The Morris was wide open so we were able to wave back to the crowds standing by the side of the road in a rather regal fashion.

We had a fantastic ride and thought, well, we're going to finish up having afternoon tea at the Palace. So we stayed right with the cavalcade as it went into the Mall, around the roundabout, and straight into Buckingham Palace. We started to follow them in through the gate, but of course, we got pounced upon and turned out. It was a good try, but next time I entered the Palace, I had been properly invited.

Looking back, I used to enjoy life to the limit before I got into motor racing. Although I had no contact with racing before I actually started driving, a lot of the things that I had done were to prove very useful as I later developed into a racing driver. My engineering training was particularly important because it helped me to get jobs as a mechanic, and later my understanding of engineering principles was invaluable to me as a driver. The self-discipline required for rowing, and the 'never say die' attitude it bred, obviously helped me through the difficult years that lay ahead before I began to achieve my real ambition.

CHAPTER THREE

1955–1957

During the latter half of 1955 I worked all day at Lotus and spent the evenings working on other people's racing cars, still hoping that they would give me a drive. Colin Chapman was racing himself at this stage and although he was very fast he didn't always stay on the road; we would spend a good many evenings repairing the works cars having already put in a full eight hours in the factory. But it was Colin who gave me my first real chance in racing—at the beginning of 1956 he lent me the bits to build up my own Mark 11 Lotus sports-car. The arrangement was that he supplied the car and remained the owner of it, while I prepared the car in my own time and raced it independently. All the starting money, prize money, and bonus money if any went to Colin. It wasn't a great business deal on my part, but at least I was doing what I wanted to do and was grateful for the opportunity.

I learnt that Colin's wife, Hazel, also had a pretty good business mind when I bought an old 1929 Austin Chummy from them. I paid Hazel £25 for the car, even though I knew it was not a runner, and I had to tow it away because there was something wrong with the propshaft. But it was already a car with quite a history, and wore on its windscreen a little sticker to indicate that it had been over the Grossglockner, a mountain pass in Austria, one of the highest in Europe. Actually, Colin and Hazel had to get out and walk beside it for the last couple of miles—it got a bit breathless at that height. It was to serve me well for nearly three years, but the car did have certain drawbacks. It had virtually no brakes to speak of and I used to help it stop by running the nearside wheels along the kerb. But the lack of brakes meant that I developed a fantastic sense of anticipation for I had to drive about two miles ahead all the time. Many's the time I had to turn right when the fellow in front suddenly indicated that he was turning right. I couldn't get stopped in time and couldn't swing into the lane of traffic on the left, so I just had to go round beside him. The starter didn't work either, so I had to run alongside the car with the door open and the ignition on, pushing it till it got up a bit of speed, then lean in, flick the lever in and out of gear and when the engine started I'd jump in and off we'd go. I drove the Chummy for about three years, putting in oil, water and petrol in about the same quantities. It devoured oil at an astonishing rate, and water used to go straight in and out.

One day I thought I should give it a bit of a service, so I took the drain plug out of the gearbox and nothing came out, no oil at all. So I put some oil in and, of course, it just came straight out again. The back axle was the same—I undid the plug and not a drop came out. I couldn't quite see where to fill it so I just squirted a bit up through the drain hole and screwed the plug back in. But it didn't really need transmission oil at all; a most extraordinary car.

In fact it was fairly reliable and it served me pretty well all the time I owned it. I still had it when we started Speedwell Conversions in 1958 and had left it outside the workshop one night and walking back to it later I suddenly thought, Lord, there's some villain sitting in my Chummy. So I rushed up and found all the fabric roof was torn and had caved in, and there was fur everywhere. Some poor cat had jumped from a great height off a nearby building and landed on the roof. Of course, it had gone straight through and from a distance the fabric hanging down had made a shape like the back of somebody's head. So that meant a new roof. Shortly after I sold it for £25, the same amount I had paid for it nearly three years earlier. About three months later the police came along and asked was I the owner of a car with this particular registration number—the poor thing had been abandoned in Chelsea. The new owner had thoughtlessly abandoned my beautiful little old car—I wish I owned it now, it would be a pleasure to have it renovated.

.   .   .   .   .

I entered the Lotus Mark 11 that Colin had lent me in the *Autosport* Championship series of races. I was reasonably successful with the car which had been painted bright yellow and was nick-named the Yellow Peril. This made it rather con-spicuous, so my mistakes were easily observed and remembered. Even today, when I go to address a motoring club there's always someone with a good memory in the audience who wants to put the World Champion in his place and asks, 'Do you remember the occasion at Brands Hatch in 1956 when you spun four times on four consecutive laps?'

If I ever happen to forget it there will be plenty of people around ready to remind me. Eventually I got black-flagged by the RAC steward in charge of the meeting and had to come in. I asked, 'Can't I continue slowly?'

And he said, 'No—there must be something wrong with the car for you to keep spinning like that, and it would be dangerous to continue.'

I was bitterly disappointed, but I had to retire. Really, it was a valuable lesson well learnt for it's a fact that when you've made a mistake and spun off, or left the road somehow, you have then broken your rhythm, become rattled, and there's a very good chance that you will make the same sort of mistake again. You have to play yourself back in again very carefully for a couple of laps. The tendency is to try and make up the time lost and go at it like a bull at a gate post—and that's no way to go motor racing.

I was leading the *Autosport* Championship before the start of the final event of the series at Oulton Park. I could have won the Championship which carried a lot of kudos in those days, but a con rod bolt broke in this final race. It was my own stupid fault because I had over-tightened the bolt myself whilst preparing the engine and during the race it just snapped. So that was another lesson learnt the hard way. I had been using a modified Ford 100E engine in the Mark 11 and this unit gave all of 40 bhp! I didn't have a transporter for the car and had to drive it on the road to the circuits. So I had a hood made and Bette and I used to climb into the racer, pull the hood over our heads and drive to the meetings.

.   .   .   .   .

I first went to Le Mans in 1956, as a mechanic and reserve driver for Lotus. But it wasn't until 1958 that I was to drive in this classic. As a reserve driver I had to practice but I had to wait until the regular drivers had finished practising by which time it was always dark. Then I was allowed two laps which prevented my getting a lap time; the first one would be with a standing start from the pits, and at the end of the second one I would have to slow down and come back into the pits. So I never got a time over a flying lap and never knew how fast or slow I was, but I fulfilled the practice requirements just in case something happened to one of the regular drivers and I would have to drive in the 24-hour race in his place.

Colin didn't actively discourage me from racing but he didn't like his staff going off to race every weekend. He was trying to run a fast-expanding business with about thirty employees, and by 1957 I was in charge of an ever-growing department. I remember one of the people who came to work with me was Keith Duckworth, who is now the most brilliant designer of racing engines in the world—he designed and built the Ford Formula One engine, and the Cosworth Formula Two unit, both the best engines in their class of racing. He formed Cosworth Engineering with Mike Costin, who was Colin's right-hand man and chief development engineer. Jim Endruweit, who ultimately became Racing Manager at Lotus, also joined my staff, coming straight from the Fleet Air Arm with, I remember, a most impressive box of tools.

·   ·   ·   ·   ·

When the 1957 season came round I felt I was becoming too useful to Colin in the factory for him to provide another racing car for me. So once again I was bartering my services as a mechanic. As I had been reasonably successful the previous year, and was getting fairly well known, I was able to get quite a lot of drives, twenty altogether, between March and September that year. I drove a tremendous variety of cars. I had three wins in four races driving Doctor Manton's Mark 11 Lotus with an 1100 cc Coventry Climax engine, and I raced similar cars belonging to Harley Deschamps, Jack Richards and Peter Lumsden, all of whom shared their racing car with me out of pure kindness. On reflection remarkably generous gestures. Tommy Atkins gave me what must have been my first race in a big single-seater, an old 2-litre Connaught that he had linered down to $1\frac{1}{2}$ litres and entered for the Formula 2 race at Goodwood on Easter Monday. I remember being on the starting grid towering above all the little Coopers and

Lotuses in this huge Connaught which made a fabulous noise but just didn't go. It had a Wilson pre-selector gearbox and at the start I managed to stall it on the grid right there in front of 55,000 people. Eventually I got away and didn't see another car for the whole of the ten-lap race finishing an embarrassed last.

I also raced Tommy's DB3S Aston Martin after a rather trying testing session at Goodwood. Everybody had told me what a great car the Aston was but it felt just terrible to me. I lost it and spun going through Fordwater, which is a very fast right-hand corner—almost flat out—leaving tyre marks 180 yards long. Very frightening. Tommy then got Roy Salvadori to try the car, for Roy was the Aston Martin king in those days. He came in with an ashen face after just one lap and announced that it was diabolical. Apparently the mechanics had put the front shock absorbers back on without filling them up with oil. And I had been thundering around trying to get in a good lap time with effectively no front shockers—I didn't know too much about suspensions in those days.

Another rather hairy sports car I drove a few times was John Ogier's Tojeiro-Jaguar. So I was getting a lot of drives in a wide variety of cars at that time. This led to a rather remarkable outing at Brands Hatch.

I was down to drive a Tojeiro Jaguar for John Ogier in one race and a 1500 cc Willment sports car in another race. I had two races that day; I quite often used to race two or sometimes three times at a particular meeting in different cars. There was a combined practice session for the sports cars and they were going to be divided up into two races—for 1500 cc cars and for the over 1500 cc cars. I went out practising in John Ogier's Jaguar which had a 3½-litre engine and was a big heavy sports car. I was flogging into Kidney Bend after coming off the bottom straight at Brands Hatch (this was in the days when we used the club circuit; the international Grand Prix circuit hadn't yet been built), when suddenly the front right-hand wheel fell off—and of course that was the wheel that we wanted on that particular corner—off it came and I went careering across the grass on three wheels. I came to a grinding halt and then ran back to the paddock and jumped into John Willment's car and continued practising in that—having explained to John Ogier that his car was parked out in the field minus a front wheel. On my third lap I was going along the straight past the time box when the same front wheel fell off. Fortunately, I was able to get it to a halt before clobbering anything. The wheel did stay up inside the body but gouged a great patch in the paintwork and bulged the body somewhat.

It certainly was the most unlucky coincidence that within fifteen minutes I could drive two racing cars and have the same wheel come off on both of them. Most extraordinary.

I was very fortunate that nothing worse happened. The stub axle had broken on one car; the hub carrier on the other.

.   .   .   .   .

I get quite a lot of letters from people who want to get into motor racing, but very few of them indicate that they want to make an effort to find a way for themselves—they always want, or expect, some sort of help beyond what they're going to get. In my replies, I usually try to explain that if they want to get into racing badly enough, they will find a way. It's difficult to get into racing without money, but I managed to, and I believe it's still possible—with sheer determination, application and some ability. But it's up to the person to make his own way, and to realise in the beginning that nobody's going to help him. The moment someone realises that he's on his own, and that he's going to have to make his own opportunities, then he's one rung up the ladder. If I can get this across to any enquirer I feel that I've helped him. Anybody who ever went to a racing driver's school had exactly the same opportunity as myself.

I think the school idea is a good one because it will get you into a racing car at comparatively little cost, and you can very quickly prove to yourself whether or not you're cut out for motor racing. Either way it's useful, because if you have an inkling that you'd like to race, you can try your hand at a school and if you realise it's not for you, then at least you won't go through life regretting that you've never tried, and you will be able to devote all your thoughts and energies into some other pursuit. On the other hand, if you go reasonably well at the school and feel that motor racing is what you want to do, it will add to your enthusiasm; if you realise you have some talent for racing you will make a bigger effort. The schools are much better run nowadays, and some of them even enter their most promising pupils in a few races. They are expensive; gone are the days when you could get four laps for a quid, but it's a much faster and cheaper way of establishing your ability than buying a racing car or converting your road car.

When I started as a racing mechanic I saw it as the only means I had of getting into racing. I had no money, so I couldn't buy my own car, and I knew no one who had money who'd be prepared to buy me a racing car. Starting this way not only put me in a position to barter my services as a mechanic for a drive, but I was also learning about racing cars. It was a difficult, drawn out process, but I don't think that was a bad thing in itself. It gave me an acute sense of values, and I really appreciated what I was going to get from racing. I think if things come too easily at first, you're not prepared to fight so hard later, so I think having things a little difficult initially could make you a better racing driver eventually. But they were hard times, although this doesn't seem to matter if you have an aim, and I was fortunate in that Bette backed me to the hilt. When we were first married I was earning £9 per week at Lotus, and we were paying £5 per week rent for our flat in Hampstead, so Bette had to carry on working as a secretary to help support the household. It's a tremendous asset to have someone who is a part of your life and who's with you and not against you. It's really vital in a sport like ours where there are plenty of pressures anyway, and you don't want any extra load.

It should be easier to get into motor racing by the very same method I used. There are many more racing cars now, so there must be many more opportunities to drive. The whole sport is more professional and there are more teams looking for new talent.

When I started practically everybody was an owner-driver and quite naturally they were only interested in furthering their own racing careers; most of them couldn't spare the effort to help anybody else to get into racing. But the sport was getting more professional all the time, and by 1957 there were people about who were buying and entering cars for other people to drive, making it their business to find the best available drivers. John Ogier, Tommy Atkins and John Willment whom I drove for then, all became very successful entrants. These men were fairly rich from businesses outside racing, but they would put a lot of money into buying the best available racing cars, preparing them well, and employing good drivers. This way they were almost assured of success and they got a fair return on the capital they tied up in racing. Some teams were, and are, able to make money out of motor racing.

Some of the people I drove for in 1957 actually paid me, and usually the arrangement was that the driver got about 50 per cent of all the monies received for the car. Bette kept an account book of all my earnings from racing in that year and it's quite fascinating to see how it all added up. When I won the 1100 cc class in the British Empire Trophy in Doc Manton's Lotus Eleven, the car earned a total of £255. We had been paid £30 starting money by the organisers, and £20 by Esso, with whom Doctor Manton had a contract; we got £150 for first place in our class, £20 bonuses from both Esso and Dunlop, and £5 bonuses from Ferodo and Champion. My share for the meeting was £125 and that was the best that I'd ever done up to that point. The idea of becoming a racing driver started to make sense—financially as well!

By August of 1957 it was pretty clear to me that Colin wasn't going to give me any sort of drive. His attitude was understandable, because he was having to give up racing himself to concentrate on designing and building cars, and for much the same reasons he didn't want one of his staff to be dashing off every weekend.

I had raced John Willment's 1500 cc sports car a couple of times and John was planning to build a Formula 2 car of his own and he invited me to join in on the project. I was to help build the car and when it was completed I was to be the driver. It seemed a promising deal to me, and I accepted. When I told Colin in August he immediately said: 'Well, if you are going to leave, I want you to come and drive for me.'

For two years I had wanted to hear these words, but I had already arranged to drive for John Willment and I could not back out now, even though Lotus was obviously the better bet.

The Willment Formula 2 project was never completed but John very kindly had a word with John Cooper, and got me a works Formula 2 drive with the Cooper Car Company, my very first works drive. I was to be third driver to Jack Brabham and Roy Salvadori.

I had a very pleasant shock when John Cooper came up to me in the pits at Silverstone and said 'Now, about terms—will £100 do?'

I nearly fell over backwards. I didn't know that much starting money was offered to anyone, let alone to me. So I gulped hard, said 'Yes, I think so'—and tried to appear as though this sort of offer was an everyday occurrence. I felt on top of the world. After Jack and Roy had tried all the cars I was left with the third one—I wouldn't say that it was an old nail, but those two obviously knew what they were doing.

In the race Roy and Jack rushed off into the lead and I was tooling around doing my best until coming through Maggots curve I hit a great streak of oil and disappeared up a service road backwards. I regained the track just after Salvadori had passed me, thus lapping me, and taking things quite easily because he had the race well sewn up. Naturally I began to catch him, and you can imagine his surprise when all of a sudden he saw this new team-mate of his appear in his mirror. Of course I was trying to overtake him because I was now a whole lap behind.

At my first attempt to get by he shut the door on me. So I tried the other side and again he shut the door. Now this seemed to me rather unfriendly behaviour from a team-mate, but it had not become obvious to me that Roy had not seen my car off the track when he had lapped me, so when he began to shake his fist and wave his hands in the air, I thought, what strange behaviour! Then he started to indicate with his fingers that I should be second, or at least I thought that was what he was trying to say.

After the race Roy came storming up to me—'What do you think you were playing at?' and pointed out that he was the senior driver.

And I said, 'Look here, old chap, I was a lap behind' or words to that effect—and of course that altered the whole picture. I was redeemed.

Team Lotus had been at this Silverstone meeting, but Colin was obviously none too pleased to see me driving for 'the enemy'. A few days later Reg Tanner, who was competitions manager for Esso, brought Colin and I together for a meeting at the Steering Wheel Club, and there it was agreed that I should drive for Team Lotus for the remainder of the 1957 season, and for 1958. So within the space of a few weeks I had left Lotus, joined Willments, had my first works drive for Cooper,

and returned to Lotus as a works driver. Esso offered me a
£1,000 retainer for 1958, and of course I was delighted. Such
a large sum of money, it was just unbelievable. I celebrated
by going out and buying my first brand new car, an Austin
A35.

There were just two meetings left in 1957 that had been
postponed earlier in the season because of the petrol rationing
caused by the Suez crisis: one was at Goodwood; the other was
the Gold Cup Meeting at Oulton Park. At Goodwood I drove
the Lotus Formula 2 car, a front-engined device with strut type
rear suspension and certainly the ugliest car that Colin Chapman has ever designed. I had a fantastic dice with Jack
Brabham, it really was a right old ding-dong. The Climax
engine didn't appear to be giving all its power—I heard this
strange flatulent noise and then saw the end of my exhaust pipe
swinging around in the breeze. But on the very last lap I got
into the lead at Madgwick Corner and going into Woodcote,
the last corner, Jack came by me with all four wheels on the
grass, straight across my bows, off the track on the other side,
and then sliding back onto the track again. Of course, I had
backed right off the throttle thinking there was going to be the
most almighty shunt, but Jack came back on the track again,
right in front of me and won the race. A typical Brabham
carve-up and he pipped me to the post with a desperate
manoeuvre that deservedly paid off. A most exciting race and
I was pleased to have done so well, even though I had lost.

The Oulton Park meeting I remember as being my first drive
in a Lotus Mark 15, the new big sports car with the 2-litre
Coventry Climax 4-cylinder engine. This was an enlarged
version of their 1½-litre Formula 2 engine, but in this larger
form gave 170 bhp and was being used in Formula 1 races, so
it was in effect a Grand Prix engine. Cliff Allison was our number one driver for Team Lotus, and when we arrived at Oulton
Park, his car was ready but mine was still being built back at
the factory. So we put the one car through scrutineering then
rushed it to the paddock, removed the scrutineer's 'passed'
ticket and the racing numbers, and wheeled it back to the
scrutineering bay with my numbers on and got another
'passed' ticket. Cliff practised it with his numbers on, then it
was whipped around the back of the pits where they were
exchanged for my numbers. Then I went out and practised,

and nobody ever twigged that there was in fact only one works Lotus 15 there.

On race day I turned up nice and early, but my car wasn't there, and it still hadn't arrived half an hour before the start of the race. With about 15 minutes to go Mike Costin appeared having driven the racer from London to Cheshire on the road. We just had time to fill it up with fuel and slap on the numbers and spare scrutineer's ticket and I took my place on the grid.

I was way up near the front row somewhere with this brand new car that had never been scrutineered or practised. Of course, all this was cheating like mad, but I rushed off and was doing rather well when a spark plug blew out of the cylinder head taking the last couple of threads with it. But I had led the race and set a new outright lap record with a sports car. Stirling Moss equalled my time later in the day with an Aston Martin sports car so I was in pretty good company.

By this stage I doubt if I had been in forty races, so I was relatively inexperienced. It was less than 3½ years since I had first raced a car, and I think very few drivers have signed on to a works Grand Prix team after such a short apprenticeship. To me it had seemed like a long hard struggle, but really it was hard rather than long.

CHAPTER FOUR

1958

Nowadays I regard Formula 1 Grand Prix racing as the ultimate. It is the most difficult form of racing and the most satisfying at which to succeed. It's the top of the tree as far as I am concerned. I do other races simply because I enjoy them and they fill in the gaps between the Grands Prix.

When I was getting into racing I didn't aspire to be a Grand Prix driver, or any other sort of driver; I didn't want to count my chickens before they were hatched. As I saw it, my future was very much in the hands of those people who were giving me rides. So I had to be completely flexible, making myself available to drive anything, anywhere, as well as helping in the preparation of the cars. I never went to a race I was not competing in—if I went off just to watch a race it meant that I wasn't really furthering my own racing career. I even used to begrudge going to the pictures, although I usually enjoyed the film once I was there; I had a terrible feeling that I was idling away a whole evening when I could be doing something more useful. Even today, I don't like going to the pictures for this same reason.

Because I wasn't taking too much interest in racing outside my own activities, the Grand Prix drivers were not my heroes —I was probably past the hero-worship age by the time I started racing anyway. Even when I signed on to drive for Team Lotus to drive in the Grands Prix I did not feel that I had fulfilled any ambition. I had simply joined a team whose programme included the World Championship Grands Prix, and so I was going to be a Grand Prix driver.

My first Grand Prix was at Monte Carlo in May of 1958. Bette and I drove down there in our Austin A35; I remember we did the journey from Calais to Monte Carlo in thirteen hours, which I thought was a pretty good time for such a small car. My team-mate was Cliff Allison and we were both driving the old cigar-shaped Mark 12 Lotuses. We had 2-litre Coventry Climax engines, bored-out versions of the Climax 1½-litre Formula 2 engine, so they were a bit over-stressed. 1958 was the first year that Lotus had competed in Grand Prix racing and, although our front-engined Mark 12 cars were of quite an advanced design, we were at a disadvantage to both the more powerful 2½-litre Ferraris, Vanwalls and BRMs, and also to the rear-engined Coopers which were using the same Coventry Climax engines as ourselves. A Cooper entered by Rob Walker and driven by Stirling Moss had already won the first Grand Prix of the year in the Argentine.

At this time Colin himself was very much involved in the development of his first real road car, the Lotus Elite. This was a brilliant and very original design, with an integral body and chassis made of fibreglass, but the problems of getting it into production were enormous and consumed most of Colin's time so that the Grand Prix programme suffered. But it was the Elite that started Lotus off as a car manufacturing company—it was a beautiful little car and is now regarded as a post-war classic.

At Monaco only sixteen cars are allowed on the starting grid so one has to qualify for the race. Only the sixteen fastest cars in practice are allowed to start. Jo Bonnier, who was driving his own Maserati 250F, and myself, tied for the last two places on the grid with a time of 1 minute 45 seconds for the lap.

In those days the race used to be a hundred laps of the 1.9-mile circuit, which was very hard work in the front-engined cars of that period. The heat from the radiator and the engine would seep back through the cockpit and you had the exhaust system alongside you, so it was pretty uncomfortable. I was driving as fast as I could, but I had to think of my engine—a stretched-out 1½-litre is obviously not as reliable as it was in its original form. With an overstressed engine, you can't go bouncing off kerbs or making rough gearchanges; you try to drive as smoothly as possible and, above all, you don't over-rev the engine.

When the race started I was last but by the seventy-fifth lap I found myself in fourth place, and I hadn't overtaken a soul. Twelve of the other cars had dropped out and there I was running fourth. A piece of cake, I thought; my first Grand Prix, and running fourth already. Then my back wheel fell off.

As I turned into Portier, the corner that leads back onto the seafront before the tunnel, the car suddenly spun around and the revs went soaring up. I thought it had jumped out of gear, so I started fishing around like crazy with the gearlever, trying to find the right gear, revving up in each gear and dropping the clutch. Nothing happened and I thought it was a bit strange, so I looked out and I noticed that the rear wheel was alongside the cockpit. I climbed out of the car and promptly fell over. I was suffering from heat exhaustion and was as weak as a kitten. I had to get the marshals to help me to pull the car back off the track. And that was the sad end of my first Grand Prix.

That night I paid my first visit to the Monte Carlo Casino where Colin Chapman, Cliff Allison and myself devised a system, if it could be called that. We each put £25 into the kitty and then just backed the colours. Colin stood on one side of the table, myself on the other, and Cliff passed money to us as needed. We'd follow one colour until we lost and then the chap on the other side of the table would double up on the other colour. Well, the doubling-up system worked well all evening until all of a sudden we had a run of colours against us. We kept doubling up, putting on two £1 chips, then four, then eight, until eventually we reached the point where we had to find 128 to put on our chosen colour.

Cliff had to run round from his side of the table with everything he could lay his hands on; I was digging deep into my pockets for the last chips; and even then we couldn't quite make the 128 between the three of us. Still, it was quite a major operation to get what we had together, stack it into a neat pile, and plonk it on the red before the little ball started rolling.

Fortunately it came up red and I've never seen such a look of relief on Colin's face as I saw that night; he had gone almost white at the thought of all that money going on a 50–50 chance —for it really was big money to us in those days. When it came up red, we could not get the chips off quick enough. We'd only won about a tenner each on the system, but nearly losing everything had been rather a nasty shock.

When it was agreed that it was time for us to go, I got all the money I had won and, for a final fling, plonked the whole lot on red again. I thought if I win it will be great, and if I lose, I will have had my evening's fun and lost nothing, but it came up red again. What the hell, I thought, let's leave it on once more. By then, Bette was getting a bit worried and she was pleading with me to take it off. But I wasn't listening and she went off to enlist help in dragging her gambling-crazed husband away from the tables. By the time she got back with Jack Brabham I had won twice more and was busily scooping up about £120 worth of chips off the table, while Bette and Jack and other friends were trying to drag me away. . . . I scrambled all the chips together and cashed them to record my first big win at the Monte Carlo Casino.

I first gambled when my parents took me to Epsom when I was fourteen years old. I backed five winners in six races, much to my parents' dismay—they thought that I was hooked on a life of gambling.

Since then I have made some big losses, but I think, all in all, I must be about even. I find it enormous fun, although I wouldn't go out of my way to go gambling. In London I do sometimes drop into a club and have a bit of a flutter, but I've got no great love for it. I think the only way to approach it is to put aside as much as you can afford for betting and say to yourself, okay, I'm going to spend this and as long as you are strong-willed enough to stick to this original amount, you can't go very far wrong.

Some years later I used to get my hair cut at the Westbury Hotel in London and my barber followed the horses. He once gave me a red-hot tip and in an impulsive moment I put £50 each way on this nag. And blow me if it didn't come up at some ridiculous odds; I won over £700. Naturally, I told all my friends of this extraordinary bit of luck and they insisted that I should in future pass on my barber's information.

The next time he gave me a tip I told them about it. They backed it and then, of course, it didn't win. This happened two or three times more, and they all lost heavily every time I had a haircut. Eventually they suggested that I could do without haircuts as it was costing them a bomb!

.   .   .   .   .

In 1958 I was also racing Formula 2 and sports cars for Lotus; I drove a Mark 15 in the May meeting at Silverstone and I just managed to win. I had built up a comfortable lead when the brake fluid started to leak away and all of a sudden I had no brakes. I was still in front as I completed the last lap, but Roy Salvadori and Keith Hall were catching me at a great rate. They drew level with me going into Woodcote. As I had no brakes, I went into the corner a whole lot faster than they did and much too fast for comfort. I crossed the line in a hairy old slide, just a hairsbreadth ahead of them to win. But I still had the problem of stopping a brakeless vehicle. I got the speed down enough to complete my slowing-down lap in safety, but when I got back to the pits I just could not stop and I unfortunately ran into my mechanic, luckily without injury—he got the message very quickly.

As I was racing on all the Grand Prix circuits for the first time I had a few more frights in store. The first time I went down the straight at Spa-Francorchamps in Belgium, where the car was able to reach its true top speed, I was absolutely scared stiff. The car kept going faster and faster, and the road seemed to get narrower and narrower, until I just backed off the throttle in a blue funk, went back to the pits and had a bit of a think. I decided that I wasn't cut out to be a Grand Prix driver after all, that Brands Hatch was really more my mark. I was pretty dejected about the whole thing. Then I got back into my car and in a few laps I got the hang of it, and eventually it didn't worry me at all. It was just a question of acclimatization to the higher speeds.

On a very fast circuit like Spa and Reims the cars are able to reach their true terminal velocity, whereas almost everywhere else a corner looms up well before you reach the absolute maximum of the car. At Spa the 2-litre Lotus was probably doing about 160 mph, about twenty or thirty miles an hour faster than I had ever done up to that point. I didn't finish at Spa, nor in the Dutch Grand Prix at Zandvoort which preceded Spa, due to some mechanical ailment or other.

An even less pleasant high-speed occurrence befell me at Reims a couple of weeks later. We were running the new Mark 16 Lotus for the first time. This was the so-called Vanwall-shaped car, because its shape was very similar to that of the Vanwall which had a body designed by the same aerodynamicist, Frank Costin. To get the driver further down in the cockpit so that his head did not stick out into the airstream, Colin had re-routed the drive line. There was a universal joint between my ankles, where the drive came from the engine, then the propshaft passed diagonally under my left knee to another universal joint just by my left thigh. Then there was a short shaft straight into the gearbox which was alongside my left hip.

On this occasion, the gearbox got so hot that the solder which held the gearbox oilfiller cap in place simply melted. As I was flashing by the pits at something like 160 mph the filler fell off and boiling oil splashed down onto my thigh. At that moment I didn't know what had happened but my immediate reaction was to get as far away as possible from the source of this intense pain. I tried to get right out of my seat. By then I was going into the very fast and difficult right-hander at Gueux, just past the pits, which was flat out in the Lotus. A photographer took an extraordinary shot of me at the time, half in and half out of the cockpit in the middle of a 160 mph corner. I remember it was reproduced in *Motor Sport* without comment.

That particular French Grand Prix at Reims, which was won by Mike Hawthorn in a Ferrari, was quite a significant one, for it was the last race of Juan Manuel Fangio. I am often asked if I raced against him and my answer is 'No—but I was once in the same race!' I have met him many times since and I admire him enormously. He has only to walk into a room and you sense his presence; all the drivers say that they feel this. The thing that strikes you most about him when you meet him is his eyes—steely blue and very piercing.

He was a tremendous driver and nowadays he is a marvellous ambassador for motor racing. He is still an international figure and is recognised wherever he goes. He will arrive completely unannounced at a motor race and yet, when he walks down the pit road amongst dozens of other people, the crowd in the stand opposite will stand up and cheer him. One of my big regrets is that I cannot speak Spanish and so I am unable to communicate with him except through an interpreter.

But it gives me a little bit of pride to say that at least I was once in the same race as Fangio, even if it dates me a bit.

I had to retire in the British Grand Prix at Silverstone in July; I was in something like fifth place at the time and doing better than we'd done all the year, having a great dice with Harry Schell in the BRM, when the gearbox packed up again.

I had to start from the back of the grid for the German Grand Prix at the Nurburgring and this time an oil line split and the engine oil came out, not onto me but onto the exhaust pipe, creating a great thick cloud of white smoke. I couldn't see a thing and I tried desperately to remember which way the road went as I slowed down to a stop just on the edge of a steep drop. I walked back to Adenau Bridge and watched the tremendous scrap between the Ferraris of Pete Collins and Mike Hawthorn and Tony Brooks in the Vanwall. After a bit I noticed that Collins was missing but it was only when I had hitchhiked back to the pits that I learned that he had been involved in a serious accident. He died later that evening. The prizegiving was a miserable affair for everyone, for Peter was extremely popular and had come to typify the driver of that era.

Cliff Allison and I were very much the new boys of Grand Prix racing and we weren't often invited to mix with the established drivers. There was a definite code in those days, a sort of rank consciousness which I don't think exists today. People like Pete Collins and Mike Hawthorn were always very pleasant to us and always had something to say, though it was usually taking the mickey. It didn't really bother me for I didn't really exepct to be accepted into their environment just because I happened to be in the same race. The people who dominated racing in the fifties were mostly pretty wealthy fellows with a lot of time to spare. Nowadays we are much busier, racing practically every weekend of the year, and all the drivers are thrown together for much more of the time and so we get to know each other better. The newer drivers seem to be accepted very quickly and I am quite sure that there is less consciousness of rank.

In 1958 there was a Portuguese Grand Prix, held at Oporto, and by then things were very tense in the Ferrari and Vanwall camps, for Mike Hawthorn and Stirling Moss were having a great tussle for the World Championship. But all this was a bit over our heads. We were just concentrating on driving as fast as we could and finishing the race.

During practice Cliff lost control of his car just in front of the pits, where the course crossed some tramlines, for it was a road circuit in the truest sense of the word. He went between a lamp post and a brick wall and wrote his car off, and knocked himself out for a few minutes. Mimo Dei offered him a spare Maserati from the Scuderia Centro Sud and Cliff accepted it. We rang Colin Chapman and I scribbled out a release from Team Lotus on a piece of paper. I am sure it can't have been very legal, but there it was. Cliff and I were the only representatives of Team Lotus there, and Cliff had to be released by somebody.

The race was a bit of a disappointment for me. I got a bit sideways at much the same point as where Cliff had had his accident and when I went to turn the steering wheel onto opposite lock to correct the slide, my hand got caught against my thigh. There just wasn't enough clearance. So I couldn't do anything about the slide and I went straight into the straw bales and finished up parked on top of them, right in front of the pits—very embarrassing.

The night after the race our Portuguese hosts gave all the drivers, mechanics and entrants a great party—wine is about as cheap as water in Portugal and probably a great deal safer.

When we got back to Lotus, I told Colin that I just could not control the car because the cockpit was so cramped. He simply got the mechanic to take a hacksaw, cut out the dashboard, move it up two inches, and weld it back on again. The trouble is I have very big legs, probably because of all my cycling and rowing, so I always have this problem. Eleven years later, when I was driving for Lotus again in 1969, they built me a Formula 2 car and exactly the same thing happened in the first race of the season at Thruxton. Trying to put on opposite lock correction, my hand hit my thigh and I lost control. This time there was no damage except to my pride.

The Italian Grand Prix at Monza in September was to prove my best performance of the season. I finished fifth and won my first point in the Championship. I actually coasted over the line having run out of fuel on the last lap. The race was not without incident because my car had run out of brakes earlier and I had stopped three times to top up the radiator and had also survived a small fire, which fortunately extinguished itself.

One of the things that sticks in my memory about the Moroccan Grand Prix at Casablanca was that we stayed in a very smart hotel which had self-opening doors. I had never encountered such doors up to that point and I was frightfully impressed that the doors should fly open when you stood on the mat in front of them. We were entertained rather royally in Casablanca and we had a few amusing evenings. In those parts they were able to provide some entertainments which one doesn't see elsewhere.

It was at Casablanca, the last Grand Prix of the season, that Moss had the almost impossible task of winning the race and setting the fastest lap in order to get enough points to win the World Championship from Hawthorn—and even then it would only work if Mike did not finish better than third. Stirling did his bit all right, but so did Mike, finishing second and taking the Championship.

Mike had won one Grand Prix and been second five times, whereas Stirling had won four, but under the system then operating Mike scored more points. And so Mike Hawthorn became the first ever British World Champion racing driver. Had the present points system been in use, Stirling would have won the title in 1958 and also in 1957, but that's the luck of the game.

·   ·   ·   ·   ·

In between motor races I was working at Speedwell Conversions, a company I had formed with Len Adams, John Sprinzel and George Hulbert at the end of 1957. We had each put up £25 which gave us a working capital of £100. We operated from a mews garage in Golders Green. George was the development engineer; Len Adams the salesman; John Sprinzel attended to the administration side and raced an A35; while I did all the bolting-on. We concentrated on Austin A35s and Morris Minors; we polished up the cylinder head, fitted bigger valves and stronger valve springs, and modified the combustion chambers, so as to make the engine more efficient and more powerful. We also fitted anti-roll bars and anti-wind-up kits to the suspension and harder lining for the brakes. In fact, we did all the modifications that people with A35s or Minors might want, to give them a fast, but relatively cheap, motor car.

I used to race the Speedwell A35 occasionally and it was a great deal of fun. At the Silverstone May Meeting I remember I was getting up to more than 90 miles an hour on the back straight into Stowe Corner, which in any other sort of car required a lot of braking. But in the A35 I could keep my foot hard on the throttle pedal and throw the car into the corner flat out; as I came out of the corner I would have another look at the speedometer and I was amazed to find that it was never showing more than 75 mph—about 15 mph got scrubbed off in the corner. I won my class in this race and was pleasantly surprised when the British Motor Corporation sent me a cheque for £200. It came right out of the blue; I did not know it, but they were giving bonus money to people who raced their cars successfully.

On another occasion I drove the A35 at Brands Hatch and I was in third place leading the 1000 cc class while just ahead of me Les Leston and Ron Hutcheson were having a great dice in 1500 cc Rileys, battling door handle to door handle. On the last lap I was right behind them up the hill into Druids and they were so busy trying to out-fumble each other that I was able to slip through on the inside. The crowd went wild at the sight of this little A35 slipping through like a tiny minnow as the two Rileys battled with each other. I managed to hang on to my lead for the rest of the lap and won the race.

A few years later when the Speedwell business centred around Minis, I took one to a race at Brands Hatch. It was well tweaked up, but for good measure we added some nitro-methane to the fuel. Nitro is an explosive which is used a lot in drag racing and also at Indianapolis, but it is against the regulations in British racing.

On the grid, I was eager to get going, for nitro-methane fumes are suffocating and make people's eyes water. I looked out at the one-minute board and everyone on the grid was coughing and crying—luckily, no-one twigged.

I went off the startline in a great cloud of smoke, the tiny Mini tyres spinning furiously. Then I started passing the other cars and when I finally nipped past a 3.8 Jaguar I could see the poor driver's eyes were out on stalks, all but popping through the windscreen—he just could not believe that a Mini could pass his Jaguar on the straight. Fortunately, the engine blew up and so I did not have to face the embarrassment of a scrutineer's analysis of the Mini's fuel. I think that everybody realised there was something a bit fishy going on, but we all enjoyed it while it lasted—although I most certainly wouldn't have done it later.

CHAPTER FIVE

1959

The 1959 season didn't get off to a very brilliant start. My new team-mate, Peter Lovely, and myself walked around Monte Carlo watching everybody else practising for two days while we waited for our cars to arrive. The transporter had broken down in the middle of France somewhere, but it arrived eventually, just in time for the last practice session. I was able to qualify, but poor Pete didn't have a chance—he had never raced at Monte Carlo before and his carburettors fell off before he had done many laps. He decided that if Grand Prix racing was going to be like this, he would be much better off selling Volkswagens in Seattle. So he went back home and he must have made a million.

Ten years later he came back to Lotus and bought the car in which I won the 1968 World Championship at Mexico. He paid a good price for it and raced it in the States with a Cosworth-Ford engine. If he had stayed on in 1959, he might have won a couple of World Championships, but he probably did very much better financially selling Volkswagens.

My race at Monte Carlo didn't last too long, for after about twenty laps I glanced in my mirror as I flashed down the hill past the night clubs and I could see nothing but a great white cloud of smoke. Good Lord, I thought, somebody's on fire.

As I went round the right-hander at Mirabeau I turned my arms and a great flame shot up from under my armpits. Bloody hell, I thought, it's me.

I started to get the thing stopped. I was very anxious to get out of the car fairly quickly, but from that very narrow cockpit it wasn't all that easy. I put my hands out onto the rear wheels and started to lever myself out. But as soon as my foot came off the brake pedal the car started to roll forwards, my hands slipped as the rear wheels turned and I slid back down into the cockpit.

I did this a couple of times and then I thought, hell, this is no good, so I let the car roll downhill a bit and parked it against the kerb. Then I leapt out. By this time the flames were getting pretty high and I was rather impressed by the fact that the flames were coming from underneath a 25-gallon fuel tank. I took a few rapid steps to put some distance between myself and the car. Then I realised that if I didn't put the fire out, I wouldn't have a car for the Dutch Grand Prix. So I rushed back again, put my arm down into the cockpit and bent over double, struggling to remove the fire extinguisher which some thoughtful mechanic had wire-locked into place and was only about the size of a matchbox anyway.

When I got it free I unscrewed the knob, directed it towards the fire and a tiny little jet of nothing came out. The flames were getting higher and higher but then a Frenchman came rushing up with a great big fire extinguisher. Saved, I thought, but he just stopped in his tracks and started reading the instructions on the side of the extinguisher whilst my poor car was going up in flames. I grabbed the thing from him, struck the red knob and put the fire out.

Apparently an oil pipe had worked loose and then rubbed against the red hot rear disc brake, causing a hole and starting an oil fire right under the fuel tank.

There and then I promised myself that in the future, at the very first sign of a fire, I would stop and get out.

My very next race at Zandvoort, for the Dutch Grand Prix, put the resolution to the test. I got on to the second row of the grid, behind Jo Bonnier who was to win the race for BRM, and Brabham and Moss both in Coopers. Beside me on the grid was Jean Behra in a Ferrari, and at the start of the race I suddenly found myself just behind Behra and ahead of Stirling Moss. I was slightly overawed but I kept trying to get past Behra because I felt I was much quicker through the twisty section. Behra, however, wasn't having any of it and when we got back onto the straight he just spurted off into the distance. Then I would catch him up at a twisty bit and so it went on.

Finally I thought: Let's be a bit smart about this; obviously Behra doesn't want to be passed by a completely unknown driver like me but if I let Stirling through, things might be different, I might be able to nip through with Stirling.

So I waved Stirling through and you can imagine how much

pleasure it gave me to give Stirling that signal. And the very next lap Behra saw Stirling in his mirror, politely moved over and, as Stirling slipped through, so did I.

After this great bit of tactics I was all set to follow Moss to greater glory. But as I put on the brakes at the end of the straight, the cockpit filled with smoke.

Oh blimey, we're on fire again, I thought and I stopped immediately. When I got out of the car I couldn't see any fire, so I lifted the bonnet and had a look around. Then I became aware that the crowd was wildly cheering and clapping me and I began to think that this was great stuff. What I didn't realise was that in my great haste to get out of the car I had ripped my overalls from top to bottom, and as I was bending over the engine, the crowd was seeing much more of me than they had anticipated when they paid their money at the gate.

In my ignorance of the real reason for their acclaim, their cheers only spurred me on to greater efforts and finding nothing wrong, I put the bonnet down, climbed back in and rushed back into the fray, having left the engine running all the time.

It didn't take me long to find out what was wrong—the next time I put my foot on the brake pedal, there were practically no brakes. Apparently the inboard rear brakes had got so hot that the seal had melted and the fluid had gone straight onto the hot discs and created all that smoke. But I continued driving on with just the front brakes and finished, although well down the field. Innes Ireland who had replaced Pete Lovely drove a fine race to finish third for Lotus in his very first Grand Prix.

.   .   .   .   .

For Le Mans, I was to drive a Lotus 15—this was a Series Three 2½-litre car and was basically a development of the Mark Eleven. The car actually belonged to Derek Jolly, an Australian, who was to be my co-driver. I wasn't too happy about the car—every time we went over one of the slight bumps on the straight the whole car would vibrate like crazy. I rather had the feeling that it was the half-shafts creating an out-of-balance feeling. It certainly vibrated badly, and if I wasn't happy, Derek wasn't too happy about it either.

In the race, Derek put it into a sandbank for a while and then I had a front wishbone break on the suspension. This led to a hell of a row between Colin and one of the mechanics as to whether the car should be withdrawn or not. In the end, it carried on but then the gears started giving trouble and the engine over-revved and broke. So it was out anyway.

The Belgian Grand Prix was cancelled that year, and so the next Championship race was the 45th French Grand Prix at Reims. This was the hottest race we ever did. The temperature was so high that a lot of drivers were giving up from sheer heat exhaustion. Apparently, the first bloke to come into the pits was Masten Gregory driving for the Coopers—John Cooper and his father, Charles Cooper; he came in after ten laps and said: 'I can't go on, it's too hot.'

Well, of course, John Cooper's eyes popped out of his head —'Too hot?' and he threw a bucket of water over him. 'Get back in and drive,' he said.

But eventually Masten became ill from heat exhaustion and was forced to retire. My own car packed up of its own accord, so I didn't have to withstand the terrible heat problem for long.

To make matters worse, the road had just been tarred and stoned before the race, so that all the tar melted and all the stones were loose—they were coming off the back wheels of the cars and hitting the drivers in the face, smashing wind-screens and breaking the mirrors—all in all they were inflicting all sorts of injury. So we not only had heat problems, but we were being literally shot-blasted with the stones.

This was the beginning of the end for drivers to compete in two races on one day, because after that race a lot of drivers were absolutely flaked out and yet, shortly afterwards, they were supposed to jump into a Formula 2 car and go out and race again. I am sure that it was this race that led to the banning of drivers competing in World Championship events from racing within twenty-four hours of that event or racing on the same day.

I drove the Lotus Mark 15 for the Sports Car race at Aintree in 1959; it turned into a real old ding-dong between myself and Jack Brabham which lasted right up to the last few minutes of the race, when it began to pour with rain. It rained so hard that I couldn't see in my mirrors to check where Jack was. I thought he was right on my tail right up to the finish, but in fact he had aquaplaned off the track and just disappeared. I was left driving madly around in all those terrible conditions, thinking he was right up my chuff. But anyway I won the race quite convincingly.

The German Grand Prix was held on the Avus circuit, which was my first time there. It is situated in Berlin and half the track is in East Berlin and the other half in West Berlin. So we could only race on the Western half. Originally the Avus had been a length of autobahn, or dual carriageway, with the track linked at either end by a banked turn, but one of the banked turns was the wrong side of the frontier. So, instead of the banking, at one end there was a hairpin. The two tracks run within twenty yards of each other, but there is a great bush-lined centrepiece, so you can't actually see the cars on the other side, though they aren't too far away. At the very end, coming back on the back leg, there's a bit of a right hand kink which is very fast, absolutely flat out in fact, after which you suddenly come face to face with what appears to be a sheer brick wall. I remember on my first lap of practice, coming round this bend and standing on all the brakes. Cor blimey, I thought, what's this? I've taken the wrong turning! In fact, of course, it was the banking—brick or cobble-lined and looking like a vertical wall. The first time round, I went so slowly that I was slipping down it, but by the time I got going, I got the hang of it and I was going round it at full bore—the 'g' loading was fantastic.

The surface is terribly bumpy and you go rushing onto the banking and everything gets twice as heavy—the car settles right down on its springs and your hands get forced off the wheel and onto your lap; your head gets forced down onto your chest and you can't hold your head up. All you can see is wall; the sky vanishes and you are just held there by centrifugal force. One moment you don't know where you are going and the next it all smoothes out and you're off the banking again and down a long, long, long straight. Tony Brooks driving a Ferrari won the race at about 140 mph average, which was fantastically fast and it remained the fastest road race until quite recently.

In the event, which was run in two heats, my car packed up on the first one and that was my German Grand Prix. Altogether, the Avus is not a nice circuit. Jean Behra had been killed on it, driving in a sports car race the day before, and Carel de Beaufort had an extraordinary accident in the same race. He went over the top of the banking and just disappeared from sight—straight over the top and down the other side onto a wooded sloping bank. It must be 50 feet high or more. He went straight down, snapping off little trees, charging straight through a wire fence into the paddock and rejoined the race. It was not until three or four laps later that the timekeepers suddenly realised that the car they had last seen disappearing over the top of the banking was in fact re-circulating. There was a frantic flurry at the start and finish line and they rushed out and black-flagged him, because they felt that if he had been over the top of the banking he or the car couldn't possibly be in a fit state to go on running! This is where he earned his name, the Flying Dutchman. A remarkable performance.

. . . . .

The Portuguese Grand Prix that year was held in Lisbon, a very nice circuit outside the town—a true road circuit. Right at the start of the race I suddenly discovered that my fuel tank was leaking and as we were busy pouring fuel in at one end, fuel was running out of the other. There wasn't much we could do about it, so I started in the race. One part of the track goes up a long, uphill straight and then goes through a cutting— you do a right and a left through the cutting and then continue onto another part of the track. It's very difficult to see anybody in this cutting once you're into it and as I was pressing on, and had got halfway through the cutting, the car just suddenly spun round like a top and stopped bang in the centre of the road. Apparently, the fuel tank which had been leaking had suddenly opened up and deposited all the fuel onto the track and onto my rear tyres, so I had spun. It didn't eem to take very long; I was just sitting there very briefly and had just come to a stop when Phil Hill came round the corner going at full bore. I remember seeing his eyes growing as large as saucers and his arms straightening out as he realised he couldn't avoid a collision. I just had to sit there, sideways across the road, watching him crash straight into me, all four wheels locked up, tyres smoking.

Fortunately he hit my back wheel so that all the rear suspension took the brunt of the blow rather than the cockpit. The car, of course, spun round and tweaked my neck, as you can imagine, with such effect that I passed out.

Eventually when I got out of the car I was seeing two of everything—I could see two Lotuses, two tracks and four cars going by when there were only two. I had upset an optical nerve. I could just make out two Phil Hills getting out of his cars—his radiators had been stoved in—and staggering off to the pits. Both of him just walked across the track and disappeared. Anyway, I got myself back to the pits and that was the end of that race. Not a great success. That evening at the prize-giving I apologised profusely to Phil Hill for my rather untidy parking, and we've often laughed about it since.

I hadn't achieved very much in the whole Grand Prix season and I was pretty fed up by the time we got to the Italian Grand Prix at Monza.

As I was being pushed to the starting grid I noticed that there was rather a lot of slack in the steering, the wheel itself was turning almost a quarter of the total lock without shifting the front wheels. The steering column clamp was obviously loose, and to cap it all the fuel tank was leaking again, it was with some trepidation that I started that race, but after a lap and a half the quill shaft between the clutch and the gearbox broke in half. I must admit that I was very relieved to be able to coast to a stop.

A couple of weeks later I was racing at Snetterton in the same car and dicing for the lead with Ron Flockhart in a BRM. At last I seemed to be in a Formula 1 race with a chance to win. But the quill shaft broke again in exactly the same spot and for exactly the same reason. Either it was the wrong material or it had been wrongly heat-treated, but anyway it was one of the same batch. Well, that for me was the end—I had just about had enough. I had endured so many failures and so much disappointment and I didn't see any end to it. In two whole seasons of Grand Prix racing, I had finished once and scored just two World Championship points and I didn't want to face another season of constant failures.

I told Colin that I had been approached by BRM and that I wanted to leave; and I told him why.

CHAPTER SIX

1960

My first race for BRM was at Buenos Aires in January, 1960, when I drove a front-engined car in the Argentine Grand Prix. I had already tried the car at Goodwood, but only briefly. My team-mates were Jo Bonnier and Dan Gurney, which made it a strong team. The front-engined car was a lovely car to drive and nicely balanced, but it wasn't really quick enough. I thoroughly enjoyed driving for BRM but there were some snags.

I began to realise that things were not quite the same as at Lotus when I asked for two pounds more pressure to be put in the front tyres of my car because it was under-steering a bit. The mechanic said to me: 'Well, you'd better ask Mr. Berthon' —he was the designer.

I thought that this was a bit strange, but being new I thought, okay, I'll ask Peter Berthon. When I told him that I would like to have two pounds more in the front tyres, he refused, and gave me the impression that the car had been specifically designed to run at this exact pressure and I ought to drive it as it was. Of course, this came as a bit of a shock as it was the first of many little differences that I had at this point. I suppose it was partly because BRM felt that it was a bit cheeky of me to move into a team and start telling them how to set up their cars straight away, but it was only a question of tyre pressures and I thought this was very much in the driver's department.

When I went to BRM I did very much better financially. I was getting a bigger retainer than I had done in the past, and a bigger percentage of the starting money. When I decided to leave Lotus, in an effort to persuade me not to go Colin showed me all the designs for his new Formula 1 car, which was the first rear-engined Lotus. But I really didn't feel that I wanted to stay; I had had just about enough. Even the exciting prospects of this new car weren't enough to attract me, and I thought a clean break was necessary.

Of course, it's very difficult to say whether this was the right decision or not. There's no doubt that Lotus have been the most successful team ever in Grand Prix racing and, in fact, they started to become successful very shortly after I had left them. A very nasty coincidence! It was certainly from this point that Colin started to spend more time on Formula 1 and, after the Lotus Elite production was established and his factory was built, he was able to realise what motor racing was going to do for him. I think it was then that he started to take a decisive interest in Formula 1 and, of course, the first rear-engined Lotus was a very successful car. When I left, Innes Ireland became the Number One driver and he had a very successful year.

The new Lotus was down at Buenos Aires, entered for its first Grand Prix. It was showing terrific form and you can well imagine my feelings at the time. I had jumped out of one team to join another and now I was finding myself being left behind by my ex-Number Two driver—it was a pretty galling experience. But I didn't have any regrets; I had made my decision and that was that. I tend to look forward rather than backward; there is little point in dwelling on the past.

In the Argentine Grand Prix, both Bonnier, who was leading, and I went out with broken valve springs.

.   .   .   .   .

We brought out the first rear-engined BRM for the next meeting—and what a pig it was. I remember testing it down at Goodwood and it really was terrible. So at the Easter meeting at Goodwood, Jo Bonnier elected to drive one of the old front-engined cars and I was left with the prototype rear-engined one; this was a real beast and I have a photograph of me cornering at Woodcote with both inside wheels off the ground. During the testing beforehand I found that every now and then the car would suddenly take a dive and dart straight into the infield, out of control.

At Zandvoort in 1960 BRM did particularly badly and we had a very high-powered meeting afterwards in the Bouwes Hotel. Ernest and Sir Alfred Owen, their sister Jean Stanley (who is married to Louis Stanley), Peter Berthon, Raymond

Mays, Tony Rudd, Jo Bonnier, Dan Gurney and myself were all there and I remember telling Sir Alfred that the only way to get anywhere was to put Tony Rudd in to run the racing and allow Peter Berthon to concentrate on the designing. Tony Rudd should be in charge of all the racing and the development. This did not exactly make me frightfully popular; I had only been in the team five months and here I was telling them how to organise themselves. But I felt it had to be said.

Raymond Mays was, and still is, the Racing Director, and he is concerned with the arrangements with the organisers and drivers, with the starting money and travel arrangements and so forth, in fact all the administration. I always got on very well with him. Mr and Mrs Stanley turn up at practically all the Grands Prix and have given the team a lot of support. Louis Stanley has made quite a name for himself as author and commentator on Grand Prix racing from the inside; he has also, of course, been responsible for the Grand Prix Medical Unit, which must be one of the most advanced in the world and attends most of the international races.

The BRM had been having valve spring trouble with the 4-cylinder 2½-litre engine and as a desperate measure Peter and I agreed that I should take some of the valve springs away to be re-heat-treated and shotpeened by Speedwell. We were fairly successful, but in the re-heat-treating the valve springs were distorting and did not always turn out successfully. However, we managed to get some that were a bit better than before and a few of them did last a race or two.

The Monaco Grand Prix came soon after the Easter meeting at Goodwood and at the start of the race it was raining. Then the track began to dry, leaving wet patches under the trees. As I was coming out of the Gasworks hairpin and into the straight, I attempted to overtake somebody under the trees. I got onto a wet patch with my inside rear wheel which started spinning like crazy while the outside wheel, still on the dry, locked the differential; it turned the car sharp right and I went straight into the timing box. The steps were completely written off, stranding the timekeepers up above, and I was left with a battered car surrounded by pieces of wood. Fortunately, I wasn't hurt.

When I got back to the pits I discovered that my watch was missing—in the force of the shunt the strap had broken and the watch must have flown off. I walked back to the remains of the car and then I suddenly spotted my watch lying in the middle of the road. Just at that moment a car came along and ran right over the top of it, right in front of my eyes. There it was, all bits and pieces, springs, gear wheels, broken glass, all over the road—shattered and mangled by an unknowing driver.

The next race at Zandvoort was pretty good for me, because I had a tactical dice with Stirling Moss. He had had a puncture in the beginning of the race and pitted for a wheel-change. Towards the end of the race he was catching me hand over fist in his Cooper, gaining about two seconds a lap. I had one of my first experiences of having to work out what is happening in a race. I knew that I had twelve laps left and twenty-six seconds in hand; I reckoned that I should be about two seconds in front of Moss at the finish. In fact, I ended up about one and a half seconds in front and in third place—it was a very close call, but it certainly gave me a good exercise in keeping cool under pressure. It is very difficult to remain cool and calm under that sort of pressure, when somebody is catching you and there is nothing you can do about it. Of course, it is a bit demoralising to have someone catching you up so quickly. But to have held off Moss and kept the place I needed, without his overtaking me or my making a foolish mistake, was very satisfying.

It was in this race, the Dutch Grand Prix, that both Gurney and Bonnier crashed, which led to the meeting at the Bouwes Hotel which I have already described.

    .   .   .   .   .

I had a few diversions from BRM. Early in the year I did a record run for Speedwell on the Jabbeke Motorway, where we got a specially streamlined Austin Healey Sprite to do 132.206 mph over the flying kilometre. It was my first and last effort at any speed attempt and although it wasn't very fast, it was quite quick for a Sprite.

For 1960 I had a very nice arrangement to drive for Porsche in the long-distance sports car events and for Formula 2 in this country and abroad. I thoroughly enjoyed driving the Porsche. It was entirely different from the normal run of British cars—such as Lotus or BRM—and it felt a lot different. It had a super engine, very smooth and reliable, which fairly purred along. I am not sure that the roadholding was as good as the British cars, but the car felt solid and always seemed as though it was one unit and not a collection of parts. I liked driving for Porsche, although they didn't pay me too much.

My first Targa Florio was in this year and I drove the Porsche with Eddie Barth, an East German who had come over to West Germany. It is customary to go down to Sicily for the Targa Florio about a week early to do some practice in ordinary road cars. This is because the circuit itself is forty-four miles long and extremely difficult to remember. I was very tired when I first arrived and they said: 'Right, we'll take you out to look at the circuit.'

They took me round in a Porsche and showed me the circuit —I thought they were joking—I just couldn't believe them. It was a twisty mountain road with drops and broken edges, with stones lying around, very narrow, slippery and rough. Anything less like a racing car circuit I had yet to see.

The next day I set about the business of learning to drive round the Targa and you can imagine the confusion during the first few laps. The only way you can begin to learn is to keep going around and around and then gradually you pick out landmarks—two trees means a slow right followed by a long, fast left; a house on a corner with a blue door means a fast right. There are altogether a thousand corners and many of them look the same, so you've got to be very careful not to make a mistake and arrive at a very slow one thinking it is a fast one. This is easily done, especially when you start mixing it with somebody else. With a car in front, you start to concentrate on getting past it and then you suddenly realise that you are lost; you have forgotten where you are and so you have to back off until you can pick out a landmark again.

The track surface changes all the time—it's shiny black tarmacadam which becomes like ice in the wet and is terribly slippery in the dry. Then, of course, you get other hazards, like donkeys, horses, people and even cars. During practice life goes on just as normal in the villages that we are rushing through—in fact, we do try to go through them slowly—and you get workmen returning home from the fields, and their mules with great bundles of grass over their backs. You can come round the corner and find them all across the road. One year a little boy ran out from the side of the road and went straight into the side of my car. Luckily he only broke his leg, but it was a horrible experience. And with all these animals wandering round the track, herds of sheep, goats and so on, they leave their cards on the road; you can come ear-'oling round a corner expecting a nice dry road and the next minute you're right in it, wheels spinning, opposite lock, correcting a dirty great slide!

One year we arrived to find that they had suddenly decided to paint the white line down the middle of the road—there were blokes on their hands and knees with a pot of paint marking dotted lines while about eighty drivers were learning the circuit. It was an impossible, dangerous task. It takes over an hour to do a lap of the circuit and when we got round the next time the blokes had moved on a bit. And, of course, nobody took any notice of the paint being wet; drivers were running over the white lines, getting them on their tyres and leaving white dashes everywhere. You've never seen such confusion! But they didn't stop—they just kept on painting their white lines. I admired them; they were brave men all right and they had an exciting week. Every year, a week before the race, the authorities get terribly keen, mending the road and filling the holes in. They send out gangs of men pouring hot tar onto the road and shovelling a lot of loose stones on top of it. The first couple of cars to pass over it just tear it up, throwing the stones everywhere and making the road twice as slippery.

I have never won the Targa Florio, but I'd love to for it's a classic, one of the oldest motor races in the world and completely different from anything else. The local people are very keen and enthusiastic; they line all the roads with complete disregard for their own safety. There is no question of crowd control out in the country—they just like to get as near as they can to the cars on the road, which of course makes the race doubly dangerous.

The BRM was a good car at Spa, going well and handling quite nicely. I was up in second spot, due to the retirement of one or two others, when the engine packed up and I coasted into my pit. Now the pits at Spa are situated on either side of the finish line and my pit happened to be on the far side; so when I went into my pit, I had crossed the start and finish line and therefore started the last lap. If I had stopped before the start line and then crossed it after the winner I would have qualified as a finisher—in third or fourth place—but as I had crossed it, obviously I had to do another complete lap to cross it again, even though it was only ten yards behind me. So I was officially retired and that taught me another lesson—read and understand the regulations.

The whole meeting was a disaster. Stirling Moss had had a serious accident in practice—a wheel came off and he hit a bank and was flung out of the car on a very fast corner. And then in the race itself two people were killed: one the young and up and coming Chris Bristow, and the other Alan Stacey. Bristow had been having a particularly good season and he was having a great battle with Willy Mairesse when he went off the road at a very, very fast right-hander. He didn't stand a chance. Stacey was a very courageous driver who had a false right leg from the knee downwards—not many people realised this. Going through Malmedy Corner it appeared that a bird hit him in the face; he lost control of the car and was killed.

This is an example of the hidden dangers in motor racing. If you do get hit in the eye or hit hard in the face, it is always very difficult to remain in control of the car. Apart from being temporarily blinded, the sheer force of hitting at 150 mph or so a bird which might weigh a pound or two is probably enough to knock you unconscious, and could even kill you.

So it was a very tragic race. Spa is quite a frightening place and we always treat it with a lot of respect.

A week later I raced at Le Mans, sharing a Porsche with Jo Bonnier. We had something go wrong with the engine and stopped at the pits. The mechanics lifted the engine out in ten minutes flat, stripped and pored over it on the pit counter to decide what was wrong, reassembled it and put it back in the car again. And off we went. It was a very impressive display of mechanical skill. However, the Porsche was retired at 08.55 Sunday morning after nearly seventeen hours' racing, due to valve train trouble.

From there we all went off to Reims for the French Grand Prix. This turned out to be a disaster for me. For the first time ever in a Grand Prix, I had got myself on the front row of the grid. When the time came for the start, with thirty seconds to go, I tried to engage a gear and I found that I couldn't depress the clutch. So there I was, sitting on the front row trying to find a gear and planning that when the flag dropped I would jam it into gear, open the throttle and hope that I didn't stall it.

Toto Roche dropped the flag in his usual fashion, whilst I was trying to get into gear without stalling the engine; cars were going by on either side of me, some of them running onto the dirt and raising clouds of dust. The poor chaps coming up from the rear just couldn't see me sitting there in the middle of all the dust and tyre smoke and Trintignant, who had started from the back row of the grid and was now doing about 70 mph, caught my back right-hand wheel and, of course, spun me round so that I was facing the grandstand! I did not realise that I was now minus my rear right wheel and I was still trying to get into gear for the engine was still running. I was not going to be put off by a tiny little bump on the back like that!

Slowly it dawned on me that I wasn't going to get a gear in. I looked round for a push and then I saw that I hadn't got a rear wheel! I had, in fact, crossed the start line, though not under my own steam, but Toto Roche was very kind; he paid BRM the full starting money.

The British Grand Prix at Silverstone turned out to be probably one of my finest races and also one of my biggest disappointments. But before the race all the Grand Prix drivers were put into Mini-Minors, which had just come onto the market, and we were to do a demonstration lap as a publicity stunt. We all got together and decided that we'd all be in reverse gear at the start and, when the starter dropped his flag, we'd all shoot off backwards. It was terribly funny. Of course, everyone had to be sure that everyone else was going to play the game. Although it wasn't going to be a race—it was supposed to be a demonstration after all—we went round eyeballing each other and thinking: Well, I wonder if I can trust that blighter, I wonder if he's going to shoot off forwards. Anyway, everyone played fair and it worked very well. Then, immediately we stopped going backwards, selected first gear and tore off. The demonstration, naturally, turned out to be a high-speed slip-streaming act—a race—and the cars got dented and bashed as we went down the straight about four or five cars in a line, each touching the one in front. We were going into corners three abreast; it really was most exciting and why there was not an almighty shunt I just don't know!

But to get back to the British Grand Prix: I got myself on the front row of the grid after making a very good practice

time. But I stupidly stalled on the line and poor Tony Brooks
—who was right behind me—shunted me up the rear. I got a
push start and set off at the back of the field. Naturally I was
a bit narked at making such a stupid mistake, for I had got
myself on the front row and here I was at the very back about
thirty seconds behind everyone else. However, I drove probably one of my best races ever and reached sixth place by lap
twenty. By lap thirty I was fourth and on the thirty-eighth lap
I got into second place, only about five seconds behind the
leader, Jack Brabham, who was having a very successful year.

By now I really had the bit between my teeth and eventually
I managed to get by Jack and take the lead on the 55th lap.
The race was 77 laps in all. I drew out a lead of about a second
to a second and a half and I was maintaining this quite well,
although Jack had the pressure on.

Jack was beginning to hot things up when I noticed that the
brake pedal pressure was beginning to disappear. I had an
idea of what was happening, because this had occurred before.
The rear brake was, in fact, a single disc working off the gearbox and of course this had to cope with the two rear wheels.
As it was out of the airstream, it tended to get too hot; as a
result of this, the seal melted and fluid could escape past it.
As we had had this problem before I had a clue as to what the
trouble was now—but it was still a bit worrying. I realised
that when there was no more fluid left, my foot would go down
a lot further and I would have no rear brakes at all; I would
then lock up the front and go straight on somewhere!

There were another five laps to go as I came into Copse
Corner. There were two cars in front, one of them, I remember,
was Phil Hill in a Ferrari. I had to make a decision. Jack,
behind me, was only a second away. Either I could go by the
two cars and get into the corner before they did, or else I could
sit behind them, Indian file, and lose time—perhaps sufficient
for Jack to pass me before the corner. I decided to overtake
them under braking, thinking that if they were between Jack
and myself it might hold him off a bit. But I arrived just a bit
too quickly and the brakes weren't up to it; I spun, went off into
the ditch and that was that.

It was a tremendous disappointment to me and I remember
walking back to the pits feeling pretty dejected; but I got a great
reception from the crowd which helped to disperse the gloom.

However, it was for me a tremendous race and I was delighted to have done so well. It rather offset some of the disappointment of not winning the British Grand Prix, which I have never won. I probably came nearer to it that day than I ever have since.

But I made a mistake. I took the wrong decision for I knew that my brakes were dodgy. I took the chance and it didn't pay off. The brake problem was not generally known at this time so I came back to the pits and said I had made a mistake —which was true, for I had.

> On lap 54 [a contemporary report said] the ugly BRM shot in front. A cheer rippled down the grandstand and those even with short memories could recall when the green BRM was the only green on the grid, or even remember how the mention of the make would make the crowd at Monza Autodrome burst out into laughter. But the BRM was to have only 17 laps of glory and the formidable and tireless fiend who hovered malevolently over every BRM ever made materialised at Copse Corner six laps from the end; and Graham Hill, a military and very British figure with a long nose and heavy moustache, walked back to the pits carrying his helmet and dutifully acknowledging the cheers in a reticent manner.

That race, in fact, clinched Jack Brabham's World Championship title for the second year running.

.   .   .   .   .

I was racing at Roskilde Ring, near Copenhagen, one weekend at the beginning of September, very close to the time when Bette was expecting our second child—Brigitte, our eldest, had been born in 1959 and was quite the prettiest baby—the nurses said she was the most beautiful baby they'd ever seen and naturally I proudly agreed, although she was the first I'd ever seen! I was driving a Lotus for Reg Parnell on this very difficult little circuit. Reg thought he would have a bit of fun and he got the commentator to announce that he had just picked up a newsflash that I had become the father of twins. Everyone came up and congratulated me and of course the press at the meeting picked the news up and released it all over the place. Directly I got home—I had discovered by then, of course, that it wasn't true—messages started coming in from all over the world—cards, cables, flowers, little twin sets, everything for twins. We had a terrible time persuading everyone that we really hadn't had twins. So Reg's practical little joke grew into something he hadn't quite anticipated—though he thought it was terribly funny.

Damon, in fact, was born the next week-end when I was racing at Snetterton, in Norfolk, with Dan Gurney and Jo Bonnier. Bette rang me up at 8.30 on the morning of the race to tell me that I was the father of a son and I was naturally delighted; she says that my first reaction was to ask if that was all she'd woken me up to tell me, but I don't think I was quite as callous as that! Dan and Jo were also delighted and it certainly made our day. The morning after the race I went straight to the hospital to visit Bette and our new baby boy. Imagine my horror upon finding him a bright yellow with little slit eyes—for all the world like a Chinaman. I immediately protested to the Sister that there must have been a mistake and this couldn't possibly be our baby; Brigitte having been so beautiful, I just couldn't believe that this ugly little China-man could be in any way connected with us. Eventually I was persuaded that there couldn't have been a mistake and, when his eyes opened properly and the yellowness disappeared, he grew into a lovely baby too. When our third child, Samantha was born, she was a spitting image of Brigitte and just as beautiful, much to my relief. Damon was christened not long afterwards at St Paul's Church, Mill Hill, and a large motor racing contingent turned up for the occasion.

CHAPTER SEVEN

1961

The Tasman Series of races in Australia and New Zealand in January and February of each year has become one of the most enjoyable aspects of my motor racing life. I don't really like to be away from my wife and family for two months on end, so usually I do the New Zealand Grand Prix and then fly back to England for three weeks and return to Australia in February. 1961 was the first year that I went down under and I finished third in the New Zealand Grand Prix driving a $2\frac{1}{2}$-litre BRM. On that occasion I had time to do a bit of sightseeing in the South Island when Innes Ireland and myself went to stay with a friend called Ian Duncan at his sheep station in Canterbury. He flew us there in his own aircraft, a little Cessna. This was my first flight in a light aircraft and we also got some idea of what a beautiful country New Zealand is. It is roughly the size of the British Isles but it has everything in the way of scenery. Alps, plains, fiords, beautiful inland lakes, thermal geysers and thousands of islands dotted around the coast. The population is only two and a half million people—together with 64 million sheep!—and there are still parts of the country where nobody has ever been.

Everything is inclined to happen slowly to someone who is used to the hustle and bustle of London and it tends to be a little quiet socially, but it really is a beautiful country. The hunting and fishing are probably the best in the world. Innes was a keen shot and Ian Duncan organised some deer stalking for us, which was an entirely foreign pastime to a Londoner like myself.

We went scrambling up the mountains—I was carrying a .303 rifle which was really hard work—and when we got to the top, Innes peered through his telescope and spotted a deer about five miles away down the other side of the mountain. Having just climbed to the top of this mountain, I wasn't too keen to go trudging down again. 'You two go off and chase the deer,' I told them, 'and I'll just hold the fort here.'

So they disappeared and after about half an hour a storm blew up with a great deal of thunder and lightning. And I was right up there amongst it all. I didn't fancy holding a rifle with all that lightning dancing around me, so I put that down pretty smartly and got well away. The rain was pouring down and I got absolutely soaked, for there was no shelter at all. I found a large flat rock and stood there holding it over my head, like Atlas, with my back to the side of the mountain.

The storm blew away eventually and left me drenched, cold and miserable and all alone. The only human beings for miles were Ian and Innes and I had no idea where they were. As the clouds cleared I spotted them in the distance but then they disappeared from view again so I started to walk round the mountain. I hadn't gone very far when I came face to face with a couple of deer, magnificent great beasts with tremendous sets of antlers. They just stood stock still staring at me and I stood stock still staring back at them. There I was, face to face with these deer, and my rifle slung over my shoulder. Very slowly I started to unsling my rifle but as I got it halfway off, the deer just picked up their feet and trotted off round the side of the mountain.

They didn't seem to be moving all that quickly so I went scrambling after them, clutching my rifle as I slipped and slid, hoping to get a shot at them. I galloped along in this ungainly manner but the deer just trotted gently out of sight. Very soon afterwards I heard two shots and that b—— Innes had shot them both—my deer!

The next thing we had to do was carve up the beasts and then set off home with legs, antlers and so on all strung about our necks. The skins alone weighed a ton and we dragged these along behind us. We arrived back at the homestead very bedraggled and very weary; somehow it was not at all as I imagined the return of the happy hunter.

Nowadays shooting is one of my great passions. The year before last, 1967, Alan Mann, Dickie Attwood, John Whitmore and myself hired a grouse moor up in Sutherland in the remote North of Scotland. A couple of us flew up there in a private plane piloted by me, but as there wasn't an airfield I had to ring up and notify the Town Clerk of Dornoch before I took off.

He cycled out to some common land with the wind sock under his arm and hung it out alongside a pathway. When I arrived over Inverness beacon, I called up Lossiemouth Naval Base control to check on the weather. I had flown up at about 8,000 feet above the cloud in beautiful sunshine, but their weather report was rather pessimistic, giving a cloud base of only a hundred feet. So I took a wee peep at the map and decided to let down over the sea on a radial off the Inverness beacon, hoping, of course, that I would in fact arrive over the sea. This worked out perfectly and I came out alongside a lighthouse, breaking cloud at the reported hundred feet. Then I had to fly up and down the coast at about 50 feet looking for the landing strip, but I did eventually find it and landed. Alan Mann was there to pick me up and we then drove about 30 miles to a lonely little lodge in the heart of the Highlands. I only had two days so one day we went grouse shooting and the next deer stalking.

We had brought a Snow Trac from Switzerland especially for the stalking and this meant that we could go and shoot deer anywhere, whereas normally one is obliged to stick to pony trails. I don't think the gillie was any too impressed with our motorising the moors but he helped me to stalk my first stag. I brought him down with a good shot and I was rather pleased, but on the way back the tracks came off the Snow Trac and there we were stuck up on the moors with a useless machine, so we had to leg it back—what a slog. It was some time before we could get it repaired. When my two days were up I went back with Dickie Attwood to pick up the plane and fly back for a race at Oulton Park. To our horror we found that there had been some cows grazing on the common and they had used the aeroplane as a back-scratcher. The plane was full of dents.

All in all, that one stag must have cost a fortune—we had hired the moor for five weeks and, due to my racing commitments I had only shot over two days; then the aeroplane had had hundreds of pounds' worth of damage done to it by those bovine Scottish beasties. My stag must certainly have been the most expensive one ever shot.

To go back to New Zealand in 1961, this also saw my first introduction to water skiing. But all I managed to do was to emulate a submarine and get myself towed along under water;

I never actually emerged to get on top of the water. I broke innumerable ropes and eventually they all gave me up. It was not until a couple of years later, when I returned to Sydney, that I was eventually taught to ski by a friend with whom I used to stay. He very kindly taught me to ski with his own boat in the Middle Harbour, which is apparently where all the sharks normally congregate. It's a sea water lake with just a narrow entrance under a bridge at one end. The sharks come swimming through the entrance and then can't find their way out again. So you get a lot of very hungry sharks in there. So my friend was teaching me to water ski in these shark-infested waters and, of course, I kept falling off and would have to hang around in the water till the boat came back. On one occasion he had a dog in the boat with him, yapping away, and if there's one thing that attracts sharks it's a dog. You can imagine the incentive to stay up and every time I went down, I went down fighting. It certainly taught me how to ski and even though I am not one of the world's great water skiers, I can manage fairly adequately.

Sydney is one of my favourite cities—in February it's always nice and warm and the air is always clear because it's right on the sea. On my first trip there I actually lived on a boat in the harbour and that was fabulous. I like the Australian people very much—they are inclined to be a bit abrupt and off-hand, perhaps even a trifle rude, but I think it's because they do not warm to people particularly quickly. This suits me fine because I don't like people to be gushing. The Australians are a bit wary of being upstaged by the English and they are inclined to use attack as their method of defence. They try to needle you with a few acid remarks. Once they realise you are not going to bite back or be supercilious, they couldn't be friendlier. My tactic was usually to say something like 'Speaking as a Pommy bastard' and then I was in. They call all the English Pommy bastards, rightly or wrongly.

The Australians are pretty keen on their beer and I must say it didn't seem to taste too bad, though I'm not sure I would drink it in England; it's terribly fizzy, full of gas and ice cold —of course on very hot days it's ideal. They serve it in all sorts of odd glasses, 5-ounce, 7-ounce, 9-ounce—it's frightfully confusing. I didn't care for their pubs very much, they look a bit too hygienic, all tiled. They seem solely designed for the purpose of drinking beer. Until recently, there were laws which stopped the serving of beer after six o'clock and there was always a rush hour before this, called the six o'clock swill. Everyone poured out of the offices and straight into the pubs. To facilitate the speed of serving they have things like milkmen's crates for the glasses. The chap whose round it is plonks his crate down on the counter with all his pals' glasses in it and the bartender fills them up with a thing like a miniature petrol pump. The chaps knock it back, put their glasses back into the crate, and the next fellow goes for more. It's a sort of conveyor belt way of drinking beer. I couldn't understand why they didn't all have bigger glasses, but apparently a larger glass takes longer to drink and therefore the beer gets warm. I remember going in and asking for a pint of beer and being thought very uncouth. I was very surprised. After all, over here it's thought to be manly to order a pint—and that is 20 ounces. And the Australians are very hot on manliness.

Sydney's heat is great for water skiing, but it was no joke to drive in it. In 1961 we were still using methanol fuel instead of petrol and it was so hot that the jolly stuff was boiling in the fuel tanks so everything had to be packed in dry ice, including the cockpit. It was 110° in the shade at Warwick Farm and I wasn't looking forward to the race at all. After just nine laps my fuel tank split and I dropped the lot on the track, causing me quite a moment. My race was over and I really was quite glad. Some of the drivers had to stop because of heat exhaustion and burns, mainly on the feet and legs.

The next race was on an airfield circuit at Ballarat and both Dan Gurney and I won our separate heats in our BRMs. We were to be the main contenders for the final on the next day. When the mechanics turned up on race day they couldn't find Dan's car in the hangar, where all the cars were being prepared. Somebody had stolen it and Dan seriously thought that I was the joker. There was a big hunt and we eventually found it tucked into some straw bales way over on the other side of the track. Some hooligans had got in during the night, driven the car off down the track and crashed into the bales. Fortunately the damage was only superficial and Dan was able to race and win, his only victory in a BRM. In fact, it was the last time he drove for BRM.

.   .   .   .

In March I teamed up with Stirling Moss to drive the Camoradi Maserati Birdcage at Sebring in America. The car was called the Birdcage because in fact it resembled one—it had a tubular space frame with millions of tiny little tubes all strung together in diagonal form—the most complicated chassis I think I have ever seen. Into this they had stuck a Maserati Formula 1 engine, slightly de-tuned, and away we went. It had the most enormous brakes—the one good thing about the car was the stopping power, they were fantastic brakes—but I wasn't all that enamoured of the road-holding of the car. Stirling started at the back of the race, because the starter failed, and then set up fastest lap, but it all came to nought when the car stopped, suffering from suspension failure.

I remember another year at Sebring, in 1963, I drove with Pedro Rodriguez in a Ferrari. He did very well at the beginning, going off like the clappers of hell at the start and was leading, but unfortunately he made an off-the-track excursion— Sebring is a bit of a flat, slightly uninteresting circuit insofar as it's on an ex-airfield. You go rushing round the actual airstrip among old World War II planes that are scattered all over the place. Some of the runways are so wide that they practically disappear over the horizon and the track is marked by straw bales—the circuit looks very much like a temporary affair and very immediate post-war England type standard. It doesn't seem to have improved with the years, though they have put up the odd stand or two. But drivers go there regularly—I've been there myself for several years.

Pedro was in the lead for quite a way, but then he made his off-track excursion and brought the car in. When I drove away, I found the exhaust pipe was missing and the thing was making a terrible din; every time I backed off great flames shot through the cockpit—a most alarming experience.

The next thing was, we had no clutch. Then we had trouble with the brakes and the car gradually began to fall to pieces during the course of the race. It's a twelve-hour race and goes on into the night. I was down to do the last stint of the day, in the dark, and I had just an hour to go when all of a sudden the lights started to go dim and flicker. Then the engine started to misfire and I suddenly realised I had no dynamo. I immediately switched everything off, the lights, the lot, because I realised that otherwise I wasn't going to last the race.

I decided to have a go at following another competitor. The trouble was finding the right one for my speed. I was racing round the circuit in the dark with absolutely no lights at all and I began to get a little worried because I thought the organisers might try and blackflag me. Directly I came into the pit straight and passed the start and finish line where the time-keepers are, I would switch the lights on and as soon as I was out of sight I would turn them off again.

Well, of course, the marshals around the circuit began to get wise to the fact that there was a car circling without any lights, because they would hear the engine noise and then this great black thing would go whooshing by, spurting flame, but without showing a proper light anywhere. It got a bit difficult when I lost the tail of one car and had to wait for another car to come by; obviously I needed a car that was going fairly quickly so I could still motor on round. I made a couple of off-the-track excursions at the Esses—I went charging off into the boondocks but I managed to find the circuit again after a lot of banging and crashing about. Each time I came past the pits I was just hoping that the battery was going to last—I could see the time creeping up towards ten o'clock when the race was due to finish.

The lights were getting weaker and weaker and eventually, as I was going past the pits all that could be seen, apparently, was just a glow from the filaments. There was a big argument going on as to whether I should be blackflagged or not, but ten o'clock came before they could agree. I just saw the chequered flag and then the car ground to a halt on the slowing-down lap—it just stopped; there wasn't any juice left in the battery and the engine had run out of sparks. Anyway, we came third and got away with it.

I had a few outings with Pedro at Sebring, driving a Ferrari loaned to Luigi Chinetti who was the Ferrari concessionaire for America; he always got Pedro Rodriguez to drive for him and I co-drove with him on several occasions.

· · · ·

The 1961 season was the beginning of the new 1½-litre Formula 1. The change of formula had been announced late in 1958 and had been vigorously opposed by the British constructors who were just starting to become successful in Grand Prix racing. Coventry Climax had built full-size Grand Prix

engines of 2½ litres for Cooper and Lotus in 1959 and 1960 and
Jack Brabham had won the World Championship both years.
But now all the British constructors were back to square one
and had to rely on the Coventry Climax 1½-litre engine which
produced little more than 140 bhp against the 170 or more of
the Ferrari V6. I had been at the RAC meeting when the new
Formula was announced and there was a lot of booing and
protesting, but it was too late, it was already a fait accompli.
There was nothing much we could do about it.

BRM weren't really prepared for it, for some reason or other
which is beyond me; in fact, BRM didn't have an engine at all.
It looked as if we were going to be a bit pushed. Even before
the end of 1960 I started dashing around to buy 1½-litre
Coventry Climax engines wherever I could—they had suddenly got a bit scarce. I bought one from Gordon Jones who
used to run a Formula 2 Cooper and another one from the New
Zealand racing team, who had also been racing in Formula 2.
I spent a lot of my own money, but at least I was sure of having
an engine and, of course, BRM ultimately repaid me. They
built up lighter versions of the 2½-litre rear-engined chassis and
installed the Climax engines in these for myself and for Tony
Brooks. My old team-mates, Jo Bonnier and Dan Gurney, had
both gone to Porsche who were entering Grand Prix racing for
the first time. Porsche had been very successful in Formula 2
racing in 1960 with their flat four 1½-litre engine and they were
to run these same cars in the 1961 Grands Prix whilst at the
same time developing an eight-cylinder engine.

But that year the Ferraris won virtually everything. Although
our chassis and roadholding were better than the Ferraris, we
just didn't get a look in, they had too much power for us. The
British contenders were really battling for fourth place, because
Ferrari entered three cars for Phil Hill, Taffy von Trips and
Richie Ginther. There were only two major exceptions: the
victories of Stirling Moss at Monte Carlo and the Nurburgring.
Both these are circuits where driving skill and roadholding are
both at a premium, and sheer power does not outweigh these
other two necessities. Stirling was driving the Lotus with a
1½-litre Coventry Climax engine and he really gave us two
magnificent drives.

My season did not go very well. At Monte Carlo, which was
the first of the Grand Prix events, I failed to finish.

Innes Ireland had a hell of a shunt in practice coming out of the tunnel. He had a different gearchange system from the normal layout on his car and he changed down instead of up —a mistake easily made under pressure and sometimes with dire results. Anyway, he got the wrong gear and the car spun round, hit the wall and chucked him out.

He was in some considerable pain—he's one of those very unfortunate people who are allergic to painkilling drugs so he just has to grit his teeth and take it. I visited him in hospital that evening and I must say he looked a bit secondhand, but he made a very quick recovery despite the parties in his private room at St. Thomas' Hospital that he insisted on throwing for his visitors every night.

The race itself developed into a furious battle between the Ferraris and Stirling Moss in his Lotus, with Stirling the victor by seconds from Richie Ginther. A classic race on a classic circuit and one of Stirling's greatest. In the meantime I had dropped out pretty early on with fuel pump trouble, although the car was going quite well.

I came eighth in the Dutch Grand Prix; went out of the Belgian Grand Prix; took a sixth place in the French Grand Prix and I did not finish either the British or German Grands Prix.

Reims that year was won by a newcomer, Baghetti, in a Ferrari, much to everyone's astonishment, when he outfumbled Dan Gurney on the last lap at the hairpin. I finished sixth and picked up one Championship point—it was the first Grand Prix that I had finished that year.

At the Nurburgring I had a bit of bad luck. I was doing fairly well at the beginning and was quite well placed when, coming down to the first corner after the pits following the first lap, I tried to take Hans Herrmann on the inside going in and he closed the door on me and I had to brake hard. The car got slightly out of control, slid across the track and bumped into Dan Gurney who was trying to get by me on the other side in another Porsche. Herrmann and Gurney were both driving for Porsche at this time. As I hit Gurney the force of the impact on the front wheel broke the steering on my car and I went out of control, flew straight over a bank and right over the top of a cameraman's camera bag. Fortunately, I landed the right way up but it was rather a nasty old moment and, of course, it put the car out of the race. I had a lonely walk back to explain why, in fact, I was walking instead of driving, which was a bit embarrassing.

Stirling won a magnificent victory over Ferrari in that race, with the underpowered Lotus, and he really had a great day —it was a typical Stirling Moss performance.

In the meantime, Tony Rudd had been busy building a new car to take the BRM V8 engine. It was the first time that Tony had been given a chance to design the whole chassis and suspension himself. We had many long discussions together about the way the car should behave and we had high hopes for it. The chassis had actually been ready in May but it was not until the beginning of September that the new engine was ready. The Italian Grand Prix at Monza was on the 10th of September and prior to that we took the new car down to Monza to do some testing.

In 1961 the combined circuit was being used; the very fast road circuit and the super-fast banked circuit. This banking is terribly steep—I tried once to run up it and failed; I could only just get to the top when I took my shoes off and my bare feet gave me a bit of extra grip. The cars could go round this absolutely flat out, and that was probably over 160 mph. The surface itself is made up of huge concrete slabs, supported every few yards by large concrete stanchions; over the years the slabs of concrete have sagged between the supports and the surface is now a series of hollows and ridges. The ripple board effect is very damaging to a car at high speed. The centrifugal force, which tends to throw the car out of the corner, acts almost vertically and forces the whole car down onto the road. Suddenly the car becomes twice as heavy and all the springs are fully compressed; the chassis is riding on the bump rubbers— little rubber doughnuts at the ends of the shock absorber plungers which prevent any metal to metal contact. With no suspension, the car gets literally hammered every time you hit one of the ridges and the whole car jumps about on the banking in the most alarming fashion. One moment, the back end seems to be shooting out and up to hit the guard rail at the top of the banking; the next moment it is the front end that is going. The driver gets a tremendous pounding, too, and you get to the point where you can hardly see. You hang onto the steering wheel like grim death. The cars are not really designed to take this sort of treatment and you get a lot of failures and some very hairy moments. Fortunately, they no longer use the banking for the Grand Prix events.

Anyway, we went out to Monza to do some testing before the 1961 race and although it didn't tell us too much about the car's roadholding it was a very good test for the engine; you could run it at full power and full speed for quite a while. It was a beautiful, smooth engine and it was rather nice sitting there on the straight with it fully wound-up and it made a sharp contrast to the rather rough four-cylinder engines that we had been using.

One afternoon I was flogging around the banking when suddenly I felt the most terrible searing pain in the back of my neck. I leapt forward in my seat—which isn't too easy when you are going round the banking at 160 mph. I yanked myself up with the steering wheel and looked behind to see flames belching forth from around the engine. They were being swept back by the slipstream but they certainly gave me a hell of a fright.

I switched everything off immediately—the ignition, the fuel pump, everything. The fuel injection unit pumps petrol out at 100 lbs per square inch and if there is a leak and the pump keeps on pumping you're in dead trouble. In fact, this is precisely what had happened, for a fuel line union had come loose and fuel was being sprayed at full pressure all over the engine and exhaust pipes. I was trying desperately to get the car stopped, which wasn't easy from that speed. It seemed to take forever, especially taking off the last twenty mph or so. You have to keep cool and stay with it right until the end; if you start levering yourself out and you take your foot off the brake pedal, you're off again at undiminished speed.

Anyway, eventually I got it stopped and off the track. I leapt out and the engine was blazing away merrily. I started to gather up great handfuls of earth and threw it all over the engine to try and kill the flames; I was a bit worried in case the whole thing blew up. When I realised that I wasn't having much effect with this action, I took off the top of my overalls and the long woollen vest that I wore underneath and I started beating the flames out with these. This was before the days of fire-resistant Nomex overalls and underwear, and I always used to wear long woollen underwear which was then the best available solution. Although it was terribly warm in hot weather, I had always persevered with it.

There I was, in the middle of nowhere, with nobody around for miles, all on my own, tearing my overalls off and trying to beat the flames out with a woollen vest. I must have looked a right Charlie standing there, beating my car with my vest, naked from the waist upwards. In the end, I stuffed the woollen vest down onto the engine right over all the flames and got it out. I remember thinking to myself that if this thing goes up I'm going to get some pretty good burns.

The main thing was that I had got the fire out but I was a bit annoyed at the time because nobody had turned up— obviously I was due at the pits and nobody had come round to see what had happened, though eventually they did arrive. I let it be known that I was a bit peeved that they hadn't got there sooner and that, when they did arrive, they hadn't got a fire extinguisher. I remember I had a pretty good row with the team manager about it. The car wasn't too badly damaged but obviously we couldn't do very much with it at the race, so we withdrew it and I drove the Climax-engined car.

It was a pretty frightful race for, on the second lap, Jimmy Clark and Taffy von Trips collided at the end of the back straight. The Ferrari went straight up a sloping bank and into the wire fence holding back the crowd, killing a number of spectators and Taffy himself. It all happened just in front of me—it was quite terrible and I drove straight into a great cloud of dust and just missed Taffy's car which had bounced back into the road. Jimmy luckily escaped unscathed. Of the five Ferraris that had started the race, only Phil Hill's finished and this gave Phil his second win of the season and secured the World Championship for him. He is still the only American ever to have won the title. I retired from the race with a dropped valve around lap ten.

The last Grand Prix event of the season this year was the United States Grand Prix at Watkins Glen in October. The Ferraris did not compete and I was going better than I had done all that year with the V8 car. In the latter part of the race I was running second when I had to make a pit stop with magneto trouble and I lost almost a lap. Even so, I did manage to finish fifth, my best result in a Grand Prix that year, my only other placing being a sixth in the French Grand Prix at

Reims. Tony Brooks, who put on a tremendous burst of speed towards the end of the race, came in third, so BRM looked like being quite well set for the next season.

During 1961 I did quite a lot of racing in England, which was something I can't do much nowadays because the international calendar is so full. But at this time I was driving quite regularly a 3.8 Jaguar saloon and also the new E-type Jaguar which had only been announced in March of that year. John Coombs and Tommy Sopwith were the two main protagonists in the grand touring world and they were always battling against each other. They each had an E-type from the works and Salvadori was to drive one for Coombs and I was to drive one for Sopwith. The first race with the E-type was at Oulton Park and I had a very good race with Roy until eventually he faded away with some sort of brake trouble and I won the E-type's first race on its first outing. We had managed to head off Jack Sears in a 250 GT Ferrari and Innes Ireland in an Aston Martin DB4, so it was an impressive debut for the new car.

I won a few races with the E-type but although Jaguar made a lightweight racing version, they didn't develop it nearly enough and eventually it was out-classed by the Ferrari GTOs. I really used to enjoy the saloon car races at that time and Roy Salvadori and I used to have some great dices together. I must have won my share because John Coombs eventually asked me to drive for him. The big cars were a lot of fun, much less sensitive than single-seaters and much more forgiving. We used to slide about a lot and now and then in a really fierce battle the door handles would rub together, so the crowds loved it.

CHAPTER EIGHT

1962

Every year in January the BRSCC* put on a Racing Car Show and in 1962 Guards Cigarettes laid on a Championship, a Scalextrics Championship for those little electric cars that are operated with a push-button. Bert Lamkin, who was the Paddock Marshal at Brands Hatch and also an electrical engineer with the Post Office, laid out a fabulous circuit and there were heats and run-offs for the first prize, a little silver guardsman and £100. And I was lucky enough to win it— £100 for playing Scalextrics. I thought it was pretty good value and in fact I won it for two years running—and then they stopped doing it. Pretty mean! It certainly was a lot of fun. You need much the same sort of ability to run a Scalextric car as the real thing; you need to have the judgment and the concentration, just a split second's lack of concentration and you're off the track, you're going too fast and you dive straight off. Really, it's almost exactly the same as motor racing and in much the same way you can very easily get rattled under pressure.

1962 was also the year that I began with the Monte Carlo Rally. This year I was to drive for Rootes in a Sunbeam Rapier with Peter Jopp as my co-driver and navigator. I found it an enjoyable car to drive; it had a super overdrive on three of the gears, operated by an electrical switch, which gave us seven gears. We were able to ring the gearchanges quite easily with a little switch on the steering column.

Unfortunately, what spoiled our chances in this rally was more a mistake of the team manager than anyone else. The first difficult section was a pass beyond Chambery where all the cars from all the capitals of Europe converge onto a common course; everyone from different parts of Europe eventually congregate at Chambery and from then on into Monte Carlo follow

*British Racing and Sports Car Club

the same route. The first pass out of Chambery is the Col du Granier which is very difficult. About half an hour before the first cars set out, all the teams send out a spotter car to make observations. It goes out over the route and then it comes back on another road to report to the team manager as to what sort of condition the pass is in. The main problem is whether or not to fit studs. If the road is dry the studs are bad—they don't dig in, you don't grip and you slide a good bit more than if you are using ordinary tyres. But on ice, boy, they just dig into the ice and you have almost the same sort of driving power as you get with a cogwheel, it really grips the ice; in fact, you probably get more grip with some of these spikes than you do with a standard tyre on ordinary dry roads. They are ideal for braking; you can really stop on ice with these things.

Our spotter went over just before sunset and the message came back: 'The track's dry, you don't need spikes.' I was fairly new to rallying, and if the team manager tells me that, that's what I do, but apparently all the other members of the team, a lot more experienced than me, decided to go against the team manager's decision and they all fitted spikes. They were absolutely right, because when we got up to the pass and went hurtling into the first bend on an apparently dry road, we went round the bank like a wall of death ride, just straight up the bank and round it. Cor, blimey, I thought, what's happening here? And I suddenly twigged it: the sun had gone down, it was dark, and the temperature had dropped quite suddenly. The road, which had just been damp before, was frozen solid. We had sheet ice for the whole of the Col du Granier without a spike on the car. We had a very treacherous drive over and did it in about fifteen minutes when the rest of the team were doing it in eleven. Of course, going up you got very little traction and no grip; going down the other side was terrifying and I am amazed that we didn't lose more time. The trouble was, we lost so many points that it virtually put us out of the running for the rest of the rally. We did eventually finish in tenth place which, under the circumstances, I didn't think was too bad. The car ran beautifully and I thoroughly enjoyed the whole thing.

·   ·   ·   ·

My first race abroad with the new V8 Type 56 BRM was the Brussels Grand Prix. I had missed the Tasman series because we were testing the new car. The Tasman races were still run for the 2½-litre cars and we wanted to get on with developing our 1½-litre. In any case, we had not got an engine which was really reliable enough to last the whole series out there. The Type 56 had run in practice the year before, but this was to be its first race.

The Brussels circuit was a fairly new one in the park where they had held the World Fair. It was a good circuit and we did very well—I was quickest in practice and I won the first heat, which was most encouraging first time out in the car. The race sticks in my mind because I was at that time suffering very badly with my back and I was wearing a steel corset; I remember walking around very stiffly all the time and I had to get in and out of the car very carefully.

In the second heat something went wrong with the starter motor and we couldn't start on the starter. I got away after a push start, but I was then blackflagged and disqualified. Although the regulations translated into English allowed a push start, the French version apparently did not. The race officials were very sympathetic but there it was. It seemed bloody ridiculous to me to disqualify somebody for such a fiddling reason. A penalty of one minute would be preferable rather than robbing the spectacle—not to mention the team. The Easter meeting at Goodwood scored our first win for the car and also my first Formula 1 victory ever. Goodwood was very pleasant at this time of year—was, because there is no longer any motor racing there—and we used to stay at an old pub which was a lot of fun.

The race was marred by the shocking accident which befell Stirling Moss. I saw the whole thing. I was comfortably in the lead and was virtually going round to finish, because a lot of the opposition had dropped out. Stirling had had some problems with his car and he had made two pit stops. He was two laps behind me and coming up to unlap himself in his efforts to get back into the hunt. As we were going through Fordwater I saw him behind me in my mirror—the next corner is a bit of a right kink before you get into St. Mary's and as I was going into the right kink I was braking on the left of the road. Stirling suddenly flashed by me on the outside, on the grass, and just went straight into a bank. As he passed me, or drew level with me, he was already on the grass and out of control.

I backed off and watched the whole thing; he just went straight across the track, the car went over a bump and a flame shot out of the exhaust pipe—I never quite understood what that was—and he didn't seem to be making any effort to correct; there were no violent manoeuvres to stop the car going straight on. Normally when you brake on the grass there are bits of grass and dirt flying up as you lock your wheels up, but there didn't seem to be any of that either; he just went head-first into the bank. It was a terrifying sight and it gave me a fearful shock.

The next time round I looked very anxiously to see whether Stirling was up and about, but I couldn't spot him; in fact, it took a long time for the marshals to get him out of the car, because he was trapped by the tubular chassis which had collapsed around him with the force of the crash. They couldn't extract him. There was petrol everywhere; the batteries might spark and set it off and they couldn't use hacksaws either because of the danger of sparks. The whole thing was pretty fraught and of course poor Stirling was in a bad way. It's always a tremendous shock to see a friend have an accident and, with Stirling, it was difficult to believe that it had really happened. I was very worried to know how he was and my lap times dropped terribly. But I had enough lead and I won the race, though what had happened to Stirling, of course, really took the gloss off everything and everyone was dreadfully worried.

I personally think that something went wrong with the car; there's no doubt in my mind from the way he went past me that he was well out of control when he flashed by; the car was going so fast that one would suspect a throttle stuck open, but this seemed unlikely because there were no skid marks—if your throttle sticks, the first thing you do is press hard on the brakes: of course, he would have been braking here in any case, but I think there would still have been some skid marks. There were no marks, and there didn't seem to be any effort to slow down either. The wheels were certainly not locked. It might have been brake failure or steering failure, though I don't think there was any evidence of this.

I am pretty sure though that something went wrong, because there was no question of his trying to pass me—it's just not a place you can pass anyone, even a very slow back marker; you more or less have to follow in single-file round the corner and he wasn't ever in an overtaking position. The other inexplicable thing was the flame that came out of the exhaust pipe. I don't know what happened, but I am positive that it wasn't a driver's error.

.   .   .   .

The *Daily Express* May meeting at Silverstone was a damn good one. On the BRM we had been having a bit of trouble getting the exhaust pipe to pass through the suspension and so we were running on stub exhausts at this time. We had fitted them sticking up in the air and slightly slanting towards the rear. I could see them all in my mirrors, four on either side of the engine. In practice I broke the lap record made by a 2½-litre car and it looked as though I was the fastest. Richie Ginther, the American who had been in the Ferrari team, was now my team-mate on a second Type 56. I was also racing a Jaguar E-type and a 3.8 saloon, so I was going to be fairly busy.

In the Formula 1 race, Jimmy Clark got a pretty good lead and I was lying about fourth having a bit of a ding-dong with Surtees and with Richie. Then Richie had a bit of a shunt—I am not quite sure what happened, but he went off at Club Corner. Anyway, that left myself in front of Surtees and behind Jimmy who was about twenty-five seconds in the lead. Then I noticed that the exhaust note had changed and the engine began to feel a little bit flat. Looking in my mirror I suddenly saw that one of the stub exhausts was slightly out of line; then it disappeared altogether. Looking at the other side, I noticed another one doing the same thing. I began to lose exhaust pipes one by one. They were the megaphone type of exhaust pipe and the ends were breaking off, thus reducing the length of the pipe and of course affecting the engine performance.

The note was changing all the time and the engine was getting flatter and flatter. On one side I was reduced to just two, and one of those was falling off; on the other side I had three left. I was losing pipes all round the track and losing power at the same time.

Anyway, it began to rain towards the end of the race and I began to catch Jimmy. By the last lap I was only two or three seconds behind and coming up fast. Going through Abbey I could see that I was really gaining on Jimmy and the finishing line at Silverstone is only just at the exit of the next corner, the very fast Woodcote Corner right in front of the grandstand.

I came up fairly fast approaching Woodcote and he obviously saw me in his mirror. I was going to go through on the inside but as soon as he realised what I was up to, of course, he shut the gate on me and closed right in, which, incidentally, is exactly what I would have done in his place. So I whipped the BRM round to the other side and went straight round the outside of him. Unfortunately, the track—it had stopped raining—was only dry on the proper line and I had to go right onto the wet. I crossed the finish line in a great big broadside, all sideways on, and I pipped him by just about a car's length or less. Of course, it was a fantastic finish and I must say one of the most thrilling finishes I've ever had. To beat Jimmy Clark and Lotus at the same time made it doubly a pleasure. I must say, even though I had won, I did feel a tiny bit sorry for Jimmy—it must have been very disappointing having had the race in the bag only to be pipped on the line.

In the race, with six laps to go, I had been seventeen seconds behind, which is normally a hopeless position, but with the last lap to run, I was only four and a half seconds behind. Apparently Masten Gregory got slightly in the way on that last lap which lost Clark a bit of time (so I really ought to buy Masten a drink one of these days) but even so, four and a half seconds is a lot to make up on Clark on the last lap. We were very chuffed at BRM.

And the exhaust pipes—I had just one left on the right-hand side, and two on the left; three out of eight. But it had been enough.

.   .   .   .

The first Championship race in 1962 was the Dutch Grand Prix at Zandvoort, where we set the pace in practice. I set the fastest lap and went round in 1 minute 32.6 seconds which, apparently, equalled the lap record held by the $2\frac{1}{2}$-litre car of the previous Formula 1. So already in 1962, right at the beginning of the season, we were equalling the lap speeds set up by the $2\frac{1}{2}$-litre engines which had about 270 hp, whereas we were now running with about 180 hp—or some 90 hp down. Of course, our cars were lighter and they had better tyres, but it was amazing that we were able to make that sort of speed.

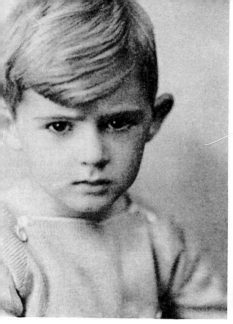

A RATHER SERIOUS LITTLE BOY –
I used to hate having my picture taken.

PETTY OFFICER GRAHAM HILL, RN.
I am actually cleanshaven and smiling.

BETTE AND I ENJOYING A PARTY AT HOME – thank God I've trimmed my moustache since then.

EXPERIENCING A
MOMENT ON MY
1936 350 CC
VELOCETTE during
the Gloucester
Grand National
Scramble, 1948.

OUR 1929 AUSTIN
CHUMMY,
before and after a
of a tart-up.

ONE OF MY EARLY RACES IN A 500 CC COOPER NORTON –
the owner's wife was having a baby that day and that's how I got the drive.
From little acorns . . .

A BLACK LOOK – OBVIOUSLY I DIDN'T WIN!
British Grand Prix, Silverstone, 1959.

THE 1960 BRITISH GRAND PRIX ALL OVER AGAIN.
Jack Brabham and myself battling it out at a Lord's Taverners charity meeting at
Brands Hatch.

IT SEEMS A BIT ROUGH HERE!
Aquaplaning puts me into the bank at Snetterton in my brand new BRM, 1962.

WOT A SHOWER – THE BRM TEAM, 1960.
Left to right: Jo Bonnier, myself and Dan Gurney.

A BURST OF ACTIVITY IN THE PITS AT LE MANS –
I bring in Colonel Ronnie Hoare's Ferrari for fuel and tyres; Jo Bonnier is about
to take over and we finished second. Le Mans 24 Hour Race, 1964.

NOT SURPRISINGLY, I LOOK REASONABLY PLEASED –
I have just won the Indianapolis '500', 1966.

JIMMY CLARK AS ONE OF THE FAMILY.
A very pleasant welcome as Jimmy and I return from one of our many races abroad.

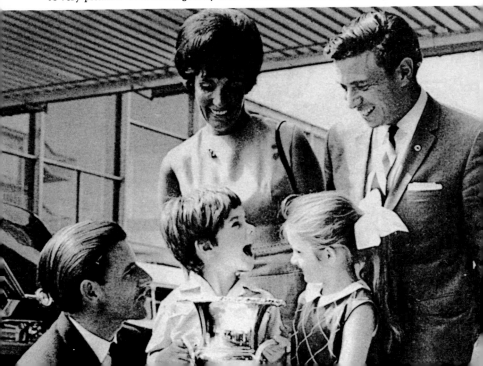

A BIG HUG FOR THE WINNER –
Bette and I after I had won the Spanish Grand Prix, 1968.

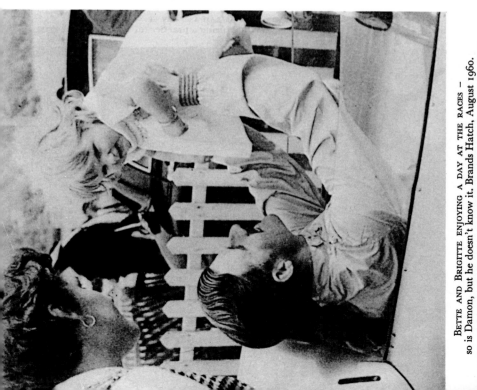

BETTE AND BRIGITTE ENJOYING A DAY AT THE RACES –
so is Damon, but he doesn't know it, Brands Hatch, August 1960.

Sir Alfred Owen happily shakes hands with a privet hedge — myself on the winner's rostrum after winning the South African Grand Prix and clinching the World Championship, 1962.

Things are never as bad as they seem!
Tony Rudd and myself in earnest consultation during a practice for the US Grand Prix, 1965.

GETTING MY CAR BACK –
pushing the car onto the circuit after taking to the escape road. Note the tyre marks. Monaco Grand Prix, 1965.

OUR FIFTH MEETING!
Princess Grace, Prince Rainier and myself after I had won the 1969 Monaco Grand Prix.

A DRAMATIC FINISH –
myself (right) just beating Jimmy Clark to the finish line. Silverstone, May 1962.

I SAY, SOMEONE'S LOST A WHEEL!
A Formula 2 race at Crystal Palace, 1968.

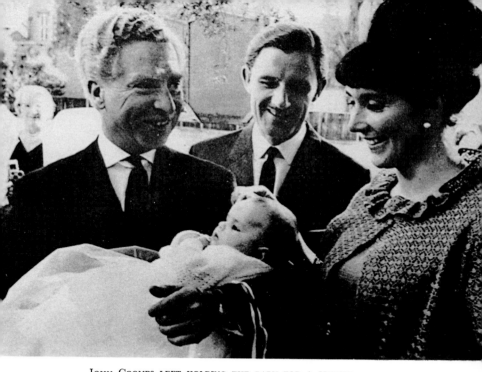

JOHN COOMBS LEFT HOLDING THE BABY FOR A CHANGE.
Samantha's christening with proud parents.

'OKAY, INNES, YOU DRIVE, I'LL NAVIGATE!'
s Ireland giving me a lift back to the pits during practice for the Belgian Grand Prix at Spa.

MOTOR RACING IS A FAMILY AFFAIR –
Samantha, my new mechanic, fits a wheel nut on for me – back to front.
Daily Express Trophy Race, Silverstone, April 1968.

MAKES YOU WONDER WHY WE DO IT?
Colin Chapman and myself just before the start of the British Grand Prix, 1968.

A MAGNIFICENT SHOT OF MY CAR EMERGING FROM THE TUNNEL AT MONTE CARLO.
Note the lights marking the kerbs – it's the first time I've ever seen 'em. Monaco, 1968.

A FABULOUS FAMILY WELCOME FOR ME AT LONDON AIRPORT
After winning the 1968 World Championship in Mexico. Brigitte is wearing a
genuine Mexican sombrero from the 1904 revolution.

THE MOMENT OF IMPACT AFTER THE REAR WING COLLAPSED.
The car turned left into the barrier at around 150 mph. Spanish Grand Prix, Barcelona, 1969

'WAIT FOR IT, STEWART!'
Jackie and I filling in time during practice.

THE CAR IN THE FINAL STAGES OF DISINTEGRATION, FLYING BACKWARDS WITH THE
UNDERSIDE SHOWING.
My arms can just be seen at the front end of the car.

AMERICAN GRAND PRIX, WATKINS GLEN, 1969.

THE CAR ENDED UP UPSIDE-DOWN
and I was thrown forwards a further twenty yards.

JUST COMING IN TO LAND –
a two-point landing for my Lotus after one of the many bumps at the Nurburgring.
The German Grand Prix, 1969.

BIG BROTHER IS WATCHING YOU.
The BBC closed-circuit television link-up for the Fordsport annual presentation party which enable
me to say a few words of thanks on this very amusing occasion. The Carlton Tower, London, 196

Things looked pretty good for the Dutch Grand Prix and our luck held. I won my first World Championship event after four years of Grand Prix racing. The car went beautifully—I had absolutely no problem with it at all. I am not sure what happened to everyone else but we won the race quite convincingly and we were naturally all delighted. It was a repeat of the first Grand Prix win that BRM had ever achieved, with Jo Bonnier in the Dutch Grand Prix of 1959. That was the only Grand Prix they had won to date and here they were, three years later, winning in Holland again. Everyone was tickled pink and the future certainly looked good for us at that stage.

There were celebrations after the prizegiving and a tremendous party in the Hotel Bouwes. Zandvoort is a very friendly circuit; it's a small seaside resort and we all stay more or less in the same hotel. There is a lot of fun in the lounge and the bar and there's always a pretty good cabaret. Most of the GP Circus congregates there the night after the race and we always have a damn good party; this year I remember the hotel owners getting a bit upset when two or three drivers had a race to climb the columns in the lounge, which were about two storeys high. We then decided we'd all go for a swim. About thirty of us left the hotel—which was right on the seashore—and just undressed on the beach and dived in starkers. It was a terribly funny sight because the lights were shining from the hotel and, as we were all running down the beach to get into the water, all you could see was the light shining on rows of bobbing white bottoms. We tried to get into a nightclub afterwards without much success—perhaps we were a bit damp.

The only cloud on the BRM horizon at Zandvoort had been the appearance during practice of a new Lotus. Colin Chapman had turned out what was the first racing car to appear this year with a completely monocoque chassis, which did away with all the tubes. It was rather like an eggshell or an aircraft fuselage and I must say it was the most beautiful-looking car and, of course, extremely functional. It was a bit shattering to find this thing appearing at the race, but I think they must have had some sort of problem, because it was not to show its true potential at first. But even then we could see we were in for some trouble. The car looked right, which is always a sure sign.

The 1962 Monaco Grand Prix was the first time I had ever been there, of course, with a chance to win the race. We did fairly well in practice, in fact I was on the front row of the grid with Jimmy Clark in the Lotus 25—Jimmy having got pole position with the monocoque car which had first made its appearance at Zandvoort.

In the race itself there was a multiple shunt immediately after the start. The starting grid in those days was on the sea side of the pits and we used to roar off for about two hundred yards and then stand on the brakes to go around the Gasworks hairpin—a potentially dangerous situation.

There has nearly always been a bit of banging and shunting at the hairpin. A lot of teams chop the noses off the front of their cars and cut them back almost to the radiator so that they don't have an extended nose—which can get in the way when you're right up close behind another car. If your nose cowling gets clobbered it can close up the air intake and then you have to come in because the car overheats; sometimes the hole is a bit small in the interests of streamlining and this isn't necessary at Monte Carlo due to the slower speeds involved. My car was the one which I had run at Zandvoort, but with its nose shortened.

Nowadays they've moved the start of the race to just beyond the hairpin so that when the drivers set off they have to negotiate Ste Devote first, which is a 90 mph corner, a lot faster than the hairpin, and everyone just has to get into single file.

This particular year something quite unusual happened on the start; Richie Ginther who was somewhere in the middle of the grid, backed off for the hairpin and his throttle stuck wide open. He just went cannoning into everything that was in front of him, and pushed them into everyone else. In one of the photographs which I saw later, my back wheel was missed by only a fraction. It was a very nasty accident and put three or four cars out of action, three immediately. One marshal was killed instantly when he was hit by a flying wheel, but otherwise nobody was hurt. It was a pretty shattering start and knocked out a lot of the field; there are only sixteen cars anyway.

Just after the start, Willy Mairesse in a Ferrari made a bit of a violent manoeuvre coming into the hairpin—he went charging up on the inside of everybody and some people suggested that he was to blame for the accident, but this wasn't the case. He was a bit rough, however, and he bounced off one of my back wheels.

He was actually leading me on the first lap up the hill, but he made a rather slow entry into Ste Devote and I came through there pretty quickly; so I managed to get by him going up the hill, which is normally very difficult to do—it's slightly twisty and most people make a straight line of it so that you are going from one side of the road to the other as you are going up. I was anxious to slip by him because I reckoned he was just a little bit hairy. It was one of the best things I ever did because just exactly what I anticipated happened. At the Station hairpin, Willy spun round broadside across the track. Jack Brabham was just behind him and had no option but to stop with him because Willy was simply blocking the road; so poor old Jack was cornered into the kerb and he couldn't move while all the other cars went streaming by.

I held the lead for quite a while and I had a bit of a battle with Bruce McLaren. I was strongly challenged by Jimmy Clark and Phil Hill in a Ferrari.

At about the halfway mark I noticed that my oil pressure gauge was starting to slip downwards as I went round the right-hand corners, which indicated to me that the oil level was dropping. As I drove round the corners, what oil was left in the tank would swill to one side and the pressure pump would then suck and pump air to the bearings instead of oil. I had to start driving on the oil pressure gauge; if I only accelerated hard when I'd got pressure and just tickled the throttle when the pressure dropped right off in the right-handers and just immediately after them, then I could perhaps hope to complete the course.

The situation got worse—I only accelerated gently when the needle started to come up off the stop and, of course, every time I backed off or put on the brakes the pressure would drop to nothing; the left-hand corners weren't too bad, but on a right-hand circuit there aren't too many left-handers. Somehow I was still losing oil and eventually it was getting very very bad; I still had a 45 second lead on Bruce McLaren so I had a lot in hand. Then, on my 93rd lap—I hadn't completed it, I'd done 92½ with 7½ laps to go so there were only 13 miles still to run—the engine finally gave up the ghost.

One of the bearings on a conrod seized and broke the conrod, which suddenly appeared out of the side of the engine. I coasted to a halt round by the hairpin. I was bitterly disappointed, having led for such a long time and with only another seven slow laps to do, but there was nothing I could do except walk back to the pits.

There were thousands of people all round the track, they're terribly close to the race at Monte Carlo, and they gave me a tremendous reception as I walked back. It becomes very difficult to be disappointed and miserable when you're getting such a tremendous reception. Eventually I was smiling and waving quite gaily. When I arrived back at the pits, they thought I was round the bend, being so bloody happy.

In fact, it was discovered at the post mortem in the garage that I had used over 3½ gallons of oil; the engine was a bit of an oil burner with the low gear ratios that you need at Monte Carlo. We accelerate very fiercely in low gears, using maximum revs, and then back off, creating tremendous depressions in the cylinders which suck all the oil down past the valve guides and up past the piston rings, thus burning the oil. There wasn't any leak—we actually burned over three gallons in this fashion. The mechanics measured what was left; there was just over half a gallon and I'd been circulating with just that amount in the engine. It's amazing that the car continued in that state for so long.

Anyway, that was Monte Carlo for 1962 and Bruce McLaren won the race, which must have been a very nice windfall for him. But we all have our share of luck.

Phil Hill, who had won the Championship in 1961, and myself were now jointly leading the World Championship with 10 points each, so they had the two Hills at the top of the Championship table, which was rather a coincidence. It looked good on paper.

At Spa, the fastest Grand Prix, I managed to get pole position, but mainly because one or two of the other cars had trouble in practice, Jimmy's in particular. But I was plagued throughout the race with a peculiar misfire and one of the exhaust pipes became disconnected, consequently the engine wasn't pulling too well. I got a bit left behind by Willy Mairesse and Trevor Taylor, who were going particularly well, and I gradually lost them as this persistent misfire got worse. Actually, this may have saved me from injury, because these two touched on one of the very fast left-handers coming up the hill and both cars spun off into a bank and rolled over. Mairesse's Ferrari was completely burned out and Trevor Taylor's car had knocked a telegraph pole over on top of him. It was a very nasty scene, but fortunately Taylor was not hurt at all, he was just badly shocked, and Mairesse got away with a few burns and slight facial injuries. I then became second, so I was rather lucky. My second place put me back in the lead again for the World Championship; Phil Hill came third, giving him four points, so he was now runner-up in the Championship.

. . . .

I was invited to drive an experimental Aston Martin, the 212, at Le Mans, with Richie Ginther, my team-mate at BRM, as my co-driver. One of the big problems was getting us both to fit the car; Richie had a special seat made which fitted inside the seat that I used, to get him further forward. He is quite a lot shorter than me—I am six feet and he is only about five feet three inches, minute and very light.

The Aston was a jolly nice car, but the only snag was that going down the straight at Le Mans, I found that the back wheels were coming off the ground over some of the little undulations that you get along there. Richie suggested that we put a spoiler on the rear of the car—he had a lot of experience with Ferrari, test driving—but Astons didn't agree with us. This was a pity, because from my subsequent experiences the reason for the back wheels lifting at high speeds was certainly aerodynamic lift on the car, and this made it pretty unstable on the entry to some of the faster corners because of the lack of weight on the rear wheels. Otherwise the car was very pleasant to drive and very quick through the fast right-hander past the pits, once the car was well settled in the corner. A most enjoyable drive but unfortunately we packed up.

This was one occasion when, I must say, I made a fabulous start. I was miles in front on the first lap. In fact, all I could see in my mirrors was a great big dust cloud coming down the straight way behind me with a couple of red cars in the front jockeying for position. One of them was Michael Parkes in a Ferrari and as I got round Mulsanne corner, which is the very slow right-hander at the end of the straight, and was about to draw away, I could see Mike stuffing it straight into the sand bank on the outside of the corner where he stayed for some hours as he tried to extract himself with a shovel conveniently placed within reach. I must say I felt some relief to see him disappear; that's one of them out, I thought. Not very kind, but rather natural.

It must have been a grand sight to see a green car well towards the pits before the next car, a Ferrari, had emerged from White House; very stirring, especially for those connected with Aston Martin and all who hoped for a British victory.

Unfortunately it came to nought, because we had a piston go and the race was eventually won by those champion long-distance drivers, Phil Hill and Olivier Gendebien in their 4-litre Ferrari.

The French Grand Prix was a disappointment. Jimmy got pole position on the grid, but I was next to him. After five laps, I was leading from Surtees with Jimmy in third spot and losing ground. After twenty laps I had a lead of over twenty seconds and Jimmy then went out with suspension trouble, which had been bothering him for most of the race.

Then, going into the top hairpin, Jackie Lewis's Cooper, which I had just lapped, braked late and shunted me up my backside, spinning me round. I had to call in at the pits, but I got back into the lead again by lap thirty-three. All went well for another nine laps and then my fuel injection failed—and I finally limped home in ninth place. Dan Gurney chalked up Porsche's first Grand Prix win.

The British Grand Prix was to be held at Aintree which from my point of view was a disadvantage because the BRM never really went on these very tight circuits, it didn't go too well round hairpins—it didn't get the power down onto the road as well as the Lotus. And another point to be considered was the fact that we were one hundredweight heavier than the Lotus which was, on a circuit that has five hairpins, something of a disadvantage. The circuit itself is extremely flat—not particularly interesting, with five hairpins, and a couple of fast corners, three fast corners in fact, and I think it's the very nature of the circuit that makes it fairly demanding; although it looks to be fairly boring you have to make a good job of every hairpin every lap, otherwise you lose a lot of time over the whole race.

The race developed into a bit of a one-man demonstration really. Clark more or less had it made from practice onwards and I had a bit of a duel with Jack Brabham and Bruce McLaren, though at about halfway, after about forty laps of the seventy-five-lap race, I noticed in my mirror that my rear tyre, the outside rear tyre, was pretty bald. Now as I had almost half the race to complete I realised that I was going to have to let up a bit, go like hell round the left-handers and ease it up a bit on the right-handers. As it was a right-hand circuit this was a bit of a disadvantage! So anyway I carried on and eventually finished fourth though it was not a very good race for myself or BRM. Clark won, Surtees was second in a Lola which was pretty encouraging for Lola's, and McLaren as I said was third and I was fourth. Jack Brabham in fact drove a Lotus on this occasion which sounds unbelievable now. I don't know whether he ever drove one again or not, but there he was, in a Lotus.

That brought Jimmy Clark very close on points—I then led the Championship with 19 points, Clark had 18, having won the British and the Belgian Grands Prix, and it put BRM and Lotus into a tie for the Championship.

The German Grand Prix at the Nurburgring in 1962 was to be one of the finest races that I'd driven up to that point. The practice itself was marred from my point of view by an accident, a rather peculiar and unpleasant accident that happened when I was rushing down the 'Foxhole', which is a very steep, twisty descent about a third of the way round the circuit. I appeared round a hedge doing something like 120 – 130 mph when I saw a rather large black object in the middle of the road. Now, I was unable to move across the road to avoid it at this stage because of the speed I was travelling and I was having to cut the corners on this sort of zig-zag downhill road; I could only move about six inches off line, so that my wheels didn't hit it—I didn't know what it was as I ran straight over the top of it, and unfortunately it pierced the oil tank which was just behind the radiator.

The oil of course dropped out onto the road and got onto my back wheels and I spun round and went into a ditch on the left of the road, going forwards again, and went down this ditch rather like a giant mole at great speed—tearing off wheels, suspension bits—and eventually I came to a stop half-way up the other side, looking very denuded, lying in the ditch, more or less just a chassis. Luckily I was still in it albeit a bit breathless. I remember thinking: Thank God it didn't turn over. I got out of the car—I was a bit winded—and had just climbed up to the top of the ditch; as I was peeping over the top with my eyes level with the track, I was just in time to see Tony Maggs rushing down the 'Foxhole', hitting my oil, spinning round like a top and bouncing end to end off the hedge—eventually destroying his car but without injuring himself. I then ran down the track waving my arms just in time to save Trintignant from doing the same thing on all the oil I had dropped.

I got the flag marshal to wave his flag and slow everyone down, and I walked back to see what it was that had holed my tank; I found the shattered remains of a television camera with film all over the track.

Apparently what had happened was that Carel de Beaufort had been persuaded to have a television camera mounted on the back of his Porsche and do a lap with the camera going. And of course the mounting had broken and the camera had fallen off; it couldn't have fallen off in a worse spot, and that was what caused the accident. From that moment onwards I don't think the organizers have ever allowed this sort of thing during official practice.

Anyway, both cars were wrecked and of course BRM and Cooper were without the cars. I managed to get back to the pits and we fortunately had another car so I was able to practice the following day, and that was the car I used in the race. I was feeling a bit rough; I'd strained my neck and my chest, arm and shoulder muscles and I was a bit bruised, but I was able to compete in the race.

Now the race itself couldn't have been worse. It was raining cats and dogs—in fact, the race was delayed by about forty-five minutes because some earth bankings had subsided due to all the rain and had collapsed onto the track. So we had to wait awhile while that was cleared.

Now I remember distinctly in this race removing both my front and rear anti-roll bars so that it would give me some advantage in the wet conditions; every car was on the Dunlop D12 wet tyres, so no-one had an advantage from tyres. After practice it was obvious that the opposition was going to come from the two Porsches driven by Dan Gurney and Jo Bonnier, Clark in the Lotus, and Surtees in the Lola.

On the start, Jimmy Clark forgot to switch on his fuel pumps, so when the flag dropped and he accelerated forward, the engine dried up, and he was left behind. I made a reasonably goop start, and on the first lap Gurney was leading, followed by myself, Phil Hill and John Surtees. Phil Hill went off the road or dropped out some time on the second lap, and I managed to get by Dan Gurney coming past the pits and enter the lead which I never lost for the rest of the race. The rain never stopped coming down, the conditions could not have been worse for the tremendous battle between Gurney, Surtees and myself. I don't think five seconds separated us for the whole length of that race—something like two and three-quarter hours of racing under the most appalling conditions.

We finished, with myself first, Surtees second and Gurney third. It was a classic race as far as I was concerned—the pressure was tremendous, the conditions were foul; I'd had a particularly nasty experience in practice which was enough to put anybody off for a whole year and I was delighted to think that it hadn't done so and that I was able to come out on top in another car. Clark had made a big effort early on in the race to get up with the leaders but he had one or two nasty moments and decided to settle for where he was in the race.

The German Grand Prix was probably one of the most tiring races I have ever competed in, and I must say that some of the photographs show it—I look pretty drawn standing on the winners' rostrum, even though I was particularly happy to have won. That evening we flew home; we were racing the following day, Bank Holiday Monday, at Brands Hatch. The German Grand Prix organisers only agreed to the BRSCC running a race at Brands Hatch the day after their Grand Prix on condition that we all turned up for their prizegiving. So there we all were, twiddling our thumbs whilst we waited for the prizegiving; we all like to attend, but it would have helped if we could have had the prizegiving a bit earlier—then we could have got on the plane sooner and enjoyed a little more sleep.

As it was we had to wait for endless people to arrive, and then, with all the traffic trying to leave the circuit and people

getting lost, we eventually didn't take off until about 2 a.m.
By the time we got to Gatwick, had driven home and then
driven to the circuit for early morning practice, we really
didn't get too much sleep.

I think it showed up in the race. The race day was wet and
I was driving a 3.8 Jaguar; going up the hill into the hairpin,
my foot slipped off the brake pedal—a lot of water was getting
into the car, it was a pretty racy sort of 3.8, not your actual
road car. The brake pedal was a rubber one—I should have
had the rubber replaced with an expanded metal pad, like a
cheesegrater, so that it gives a grip on the leather shoe. My foot
slipped off the brake and went straight onto the throttle. Well,
of course, the thing leapt forward and I went headlong into
a bank. And I think being so tired contributed to this happening.

I can remember a similar occasion once at Brands Hatch,
when I spun coming out of one of the hairpins; I knew that
I was losing it and whilst spinning I was definitely conscious of
the fact that I was reacting slowly because I hadn't had enough
sleep. There was another occasion when I went off onto the
grass at Brands Hatch and thumped the bank after the Bottom
Bend in a 3.8 Jaguar (another one of John Coombs' cars!).
Fortunately I had on seat belts—I always wear them racing a
saloon car—and I didn't do myself any damage, although the
car looked a bit short. There's no doubt about it, if you're
tired you do react slower.

.   .   .   .

I drove a Lotus for Rob Walker at Karlskoga in Sweden; it
was the second time I'd driven for Rob Walker that year—
the first was at Mallory Park in a 4-cylinder Lotus, when I
came third behind a couple of V8s—and this time he had
actually got his own V8 Climax engine and we ran that. I had
the throttle stick open during practice, fortunately on the
slowing-down lap, and I went off the track and bent the front
wishbones. It upset Alf Francis quite a bit and I am not sure that
he actually believed me when I said the throttle had stuck open,
but the throttle was still open when I got him back to the car
to have a look at it. We got it going in time for the race, but
I only did one lap and then I had to come in to have the nose
removed; the oil tank was found to be leaking badly so that
was that; it was a long trip for nothing.

The Tourist Trophy race was at Goodwood which is always a delightful circuit to race on and one I have always enjoyed. This year I was driving John Coombs' Ferrari GTO which was a beautiful car to drive, especially at Goodwood with such long, drifting corners—a beautifully controllable car.

Anyway, the race itself was most enjoyable. The main opposition was going to come from Salvadori in an E-type, Clark in an Aston Martin and John Surtees, Innes Ireland and Mike Parkes, all in Ferraris. But early on Surtees and Clark touched going into Woodcote and put themselves out against the bank, so that eliminated a lot of the competition. I managed to finish in front of Parkes and just 3.4 seconds behind Innes Ireland— I was catching him rapidly towards the end of the race and I remember catching sight of him on the last lap and just not quite making it. But of course it was his race, though there was an instance during the race when somebody hit the chicane rather badly and partially blocked it; Innes arrived and, instead of going through the chicane, completely missed it out and shot round on the grass—thereby gaining quite a few seconds on myself as I picked my way through the chicane and set off after him. Bearing in mind the 3.4 seconds by which he won, it looks as though that tactic might have contributed quite a bit to his race. Of course, John Coombs was in a position to protest but neither he nor myself were willing to do that, or to win a race in that fashion, so it was a good win for Innes and an enjoyable race for myself.

We went up to Oulton Park for a Formula 1 race, but I mainly remember this meeting because my brother turned up from Canada and came to watch; it was the first time he'd ever seen me race—he had left England before I had started motor racing. I hadn't seen him for about ten years and, of course, it was very pleasant to have him around; I didn't actually know that he was going to be there and I remember walking out of the pits and suddenly bumping into him.

This was the race in which Roy Salvadori in his 3.8 lost it under braking going down to Cascades, and ended upside down in the lake; there he was hanging upside down in his seat belts with his head under water. Most unlike Roy; he always looks rather smart and dapper and it rather spoilt his image when he walked back to the pits covered in black slime. It was funny afterwards, but it must have been bloody unpleasant at the time. Of course, nowadays there's a barrier there to stop anyone repeating his act.

.   .   .   .

The next Grande Epreuve was Monza which I was fortunate enough to win. After the German Grand Prix I was still leading the Championship with 28 points and my next rival was Jimmy Clark with 21 points; then came Surtees with 19 and Bruce McLaren with 18; Phil Hill had 14—he hadn't scored in the last three Grands Prix.

Monza is a very fast circuit with not too many bends, but what there are require quite a lot of skill. There's one particularly fast one just after the pits with a slight bump just as you turn the wheel to start the corner at 150 mph; it can be taken virtually flat out by $1\frac{1}{2}$-litre cars.

Jimmy and I had about the same lap times and we shared the front row of the grid. The battle for the title was getting closer and getting more and more exciting. In the race poor Jimmy had some trouble and retired after 18 laps. I led for all 86 laps of the race and my team-mate, Richie Ginther, came second: a very good one-two for BRM. I now had 36 points and Bruce McLaren, who had come third, jumped into second place with 22; Jimmy didn't improve at all. So there I was with a good old lead.

The race itself was comfortable—I had never been in such a position before where I had a safe lead and on a circuit which takes a lot out of the engine—you are running flat out for most of the way. The race just seems to go on and on, it is 310 miles long; I led for every lap and, except for the first mile, I was in the lead all the time. It was a pretty satisfying race and a very convincing win.

Roy Salvadori had a lucky escape when the fire extinguisher in his cockpit, which we all carry, burst while he was racing and covered his face with foam. He couldn't see where he was going and spun round, but fortunately without any damage to him or anybody else. This same thing happened once in Spain to Frank Gardner whilst he was driving in a Formula 2 race. The top blew off the fire extinguisher. It was a very hot race and the thing had obviously been sitting out in the sun; it blew up with a tremendous explosion and bent the chassis! When they got the car back to the garage, Jack Brabham was laughing about it and inspecting Frank Gardner's car, when all of a sudden there was another almighty explosion and the same thing happened to Jack's car which wiped the smile off his face. It was something that we hadn't really thought about.

Another incident that happened at Monza that year was that Masten Gregory was arrested by one of the policemen employed by the organisers to help them run the track—someone seems to be arrested every year—and he was escorted to the cooler where he stayed for nearly half an hour during the final practice session. There was some query about a paddock pass and Masten was hauled off to jail. His manager, who speaks fluent Italian, was not allowed into the police precincts to sort it out. We always seem to have a lot of drama at Monza, but I must say they are getting much better.

Next we went to Watkins Glen and I took Bette across with me for the race; she had never been to America before. I really wanted to win the American Grand Prix to clinch the Championship, but it was not to be. I lost to Jimmy Clark by 8 seconds—I held the lead for about five laps but I am afraid he had just sufficient to beat me. That left the Championship wide open until the final round which was to be held in South Africa at the end of the year. I was going to have to dock some of my points because only the best five races out of the total of nine could be counted. The six points I had picked up gave me quite a useful lead but I was not going to be able to count them all because I had already scored in too many events. Jimmy had won the American Grand Prix and so, if he won in South Africa, he would take the Championship.

.   .   .   .

My next venture after that was the London to Brighton veteran car run in November. It was arranged by Reg Parnell whom I had met one evening in the Steering Wheel Club. He asked me if I would like to compete in the London to Brighton Run which is always held in November. He then started to regale me with what a great pleasure the whole thing was and how I ought to do it. He had got just the man for me to do it with, he told me, Philip Fotheringham-Parker. So naturally I took all this in and agreed.

I had to turn up at Philip's mews house in London at 7.30 in the morning. I had had no idea of what to expect, but the moment I clapped eyes on the car, I realised why Reg had substituted me for himself. It was a most extraordinary looking contraption, one of the oldest cars in the race—an 1896 Lutzmann. It had an enormous frame with four wheels and tiller steering; at the back was a most rudimentary engine with one cylinder and a combined carburettor and fuel tank—it was certainly a very haphazard arrangement. Anyway, I turned up to see this thing standing in the middle of the mews, shaking like crazy—everything was miles out of balance. We got on it—I was well wrapped up because there was no protection at all— and off we drove to Hyde Park Corner for the start. The early cars start first and I think that we were number seven. The steering was just a lever attached to links on the front wheels. It wasn't terribly accurate. The brake was a large lever on the driver's side with a leather belt running round a wooden wheel attached to one of the rear wheels; as you can imagine, this proved to be pretty useless.

Off we set, on this weird machine; it went in fits and starts and we had to keep it running by fiddling with the air valve in the fuel tank. We got over Westminster Bridge all right and then I began to realise that this thing wasn't too safe. You get a tremendous reception on the Brighton Run and you get a lot of cars following. Well, of course, all these cars following would overtake and pull up in front of you—they had no idea that you hadn't got any brakes. In fact, we only hit two cars on the way down but why we didn't hit twenty-two I shall never know. We completely wrecked somebody's trailer; we rode right over the top of it and simply crushed it to pieces. We went straight down the side of a Minivan and tore the wing off; straight down the other side of a Ford Zephyr and put a great graunch in that from stem to stern. They just had no idea that you cannot stop in these veteran cars.

We got as far as Pease Pottage by some miracle and there we pulled in at a pub. That's a very good idea, I thought, and I bought a large double whisky, something I've never done in my life before. Unfortunately, Fotheringham-Parker took one too, which rather offset the effects of my double whisky, as far as I was concerned.

Shortly after this pleasant pub there is a terrifying steep descent and we set off over the brow of the hill gathering speed.

The thing had no engine braking and was on free-wheel—Philip was trying to keep the engine running all the time and was fiddling with the air and fuel valves as the speed of the wheels was outrunning the speed of the engine. By then we were going down at a hell of a bloody speed. He started to pull on the old handbrake and all that did was to produce a smell of burning wood. Then we got a speed wobble on the front wheels and they started to flap like crazy. The whole thing was shaking so much that my eyeballs were being shaken about in their sockets.

I had better get ready to abandon ship, I thought. I felt it was high time to get off; I was perched about twelve feet in the air and all we could see in front of us was a dual carriageway jam-packed with cars at the end. This is it, I thought. Here we go, boring straight in to the mass of cars. I put my shoe onto the rear wheel to try and slow it down. Of course that didn't make any difference at all. Time for action, I thought, and Fotheringham-Parker supplied it—he drove straight over the centre strip, straight through some bushes and onto the up lane on the other side of the road. He continued completely undaunted—it handn't made a scrap of difference to our speed—and there we were whistling down to Brighton on the up road to London. You can imagine the horror on the faces of the drivers coming the other way.

It ended up with me jumping off and pushing this thing up the hill. We had our own service wagon following us and while we were driving along, the mechanic was pounding along behind working on the engine to keep it running. Well, you're allowed, I think, about eight hours to make the journey and we in fact made it with about a quarter of an hour to spare. Nothing would induce me to go back on the thing; Fotheringham-Parker drove back on his own. It really was the most terrifying experience I've ever had and I vowed never to be tempted again.

Anyway, that was the first time. The next time I did it was with Edward Montagu in a 1901 Durkopp; it was a very nice machine with brakes and we made the trip in a couple of hours. One of the things with Fotheringham-Parker's effort was of course that when we were still only halfway there, other veterans were already returning to London having been to Brighton. Anyway, he seems to get a kick out of it, but it beats me. Amazing chap!

.   .   .   .

It was a bit of a bore having to wait so long for the outcome of the Championship, and it rather got everybody on edge fairly early on; there we were, sitting in England, fiddling around waiting for the outcome of the race. We really wanted to get it over and done with. There were two races in South Africa during December before the Grand Prix which helped to relieve some of this tension, and of course the Christmas festivities contributed enormously to our relaxation. The hospitality was superb and helped tremendously to alleviate any feeling of homesickness on Christmas Day—although I must say it felt a bit odd eating Christmas lunch on the lawn. The first race of the tour was at Kyalami, which is now the scene of the current World Championship series, and the other at Westmead, in Durban. I had never been to Durban before and I found it particularly hot and muggy, more or less like walking in a wet oven; for the race it wasn't quite so humid, though it was still extremely hot. In the race, I had ignition trouble and packed up. Then we went on to Kyalami, which was the first time we had raced there. I went quite quickly in practice, but again I had ignition trouble; my difficulties in these two races didn't augur too well for my Championship chances in East London the following weekend. It's far better, however, to have these troubles in a minor race with time to cure them for the main effort. The fault was something to do with the new ignition system we were running on the V8 engine and it rather messed us up. We were all keeping our fingers crossed for the Grand Prix at East London.

There was a lot of interest in the race which was very encouraging but added to the tension. Sir Alfred Owen was able to come down to see the race, combining it with some business of Rubery Owen in South Africa. It was going to be covered by NBC and another American television company.

The situation for us was that Jimmy Clark must not win the race. I was exactly nine points in front of him, which meant that if he gained nine points for winning the race, he would then equal my score—providing I didn't make any points. Now if there was a draw, it would mean that they would take the number of races won and he would then have scored four Grands Prix to my three, which would mean that he would come out on top. If, for instance, I came second to Jimmy, I would then pick up six points but I would have to drop a result because we could only score the best five out of nine races; I would have to drop my next lowest score, which was also six points, so really I had to improve my score—I must pick up another first and drop a second to get anywhere. Jimmy, if he won, would pick up all nine points and would then win the Championship.

The first day's practice was on Boxing Day—traditionally a day for sport and hang-overs. The way practice went, it looked very much as if Jimmy was going to win and we just were not going to be able to do anything about it. Barring any accident to his car, we weren't going to win. One can always tell by practice what sort of chance you have. You must be within 0.1 or 0.2 of a second; anything more than that and you begin to feel you're out of the running. In fact, I was something like 0.7 of a second slower than Jimmy in practice, which is quite a lot. I could see that it was going to be very difficult for me to hold on to him at all, and my fears were realised.

The circuit at East London is right on the side of the Indian Ocean and we were getting some terrific winds—it was seriously affecting the cars on some of the faster corners, making them especially twitchy to go through. There are two fast ones just past the pits and the track itself is very exposed; in a high cross-wind, these two particular corners were very dicey—the car might be moving sideways two or three feet and, when you're working to within two or three inches of the side of the track, you just haven't got that sort of room. The wind also affected our gear ratios—one day it would be against you down the straight and you'd go flogging along the straight about 500 revs short—and so you would change the ratio; the next day it would blow the other way and you'd go charging down the straight over-revving about 500 revs. It was all very confusing, but it was a nice circuit—a little bit narrow but quite interesting.

Before the start of the race, both Jimmy and I were being interviewed and one fellow, Chris Economaki, an American commentator with the NBC, interviewed me about the World Championship final. He rather tends to get over-excited and to introduce a lot of drama into a race. Well, of course, just before the start of the race, and particularly a needle match like this, one doesn't want to get too excited. He came bounding up with his crew, bubbling over with excitement, and I remember him asking me: 'Well, Graham, what is it that bothers you on a day like this?'

'Well,' I said, 'it's people like you coming up and asking me questions like that.'

It was a little cruel of me, but on occasions like that the temptation is too much. I remember he did exactly the same thing at Riverside, California, when I was over there for a sports car race. He came up to me and said: 'Now, Graham, what's significant about the straight here?'

'Well,' I said, 'it's significant insofar as it joins one corner with the next'—and of course this went over the loudspeakers to some 80,000 spectators. You really can't help sending them up sometimes.

Before the start we were paraded around the track sitting on the backs of MGs—each driver had his own car and it was quite a good way of presenting the drivers to spectators. The crowd are terribly enthusiastic in South Africa and they climb over the barriers and come over to pat us on the back and shake us by the hand.

Eventually we were driving through an avenue of people. On the far side of the track there was one particular section which was wired off for coloured people and they too poured out over the track. They saw all the white people busy patting us on the back, congratulating us and cheering, so they thought they'd do the same. They don't often get a chance to pat a white man on the back and they went to town on it. In the end we were cowering in the backs of the MGs under a rain of blows from very enthusiastic Africans. I got pretty badly bruised and there was no way of telling them to belt up or lay off so they really had a ball.

Jimmy made a fabulous start in the race and shot out into the lead. I got in just behind him, but I was not able to challenge him, though I was driving as hard as I could.

It was not until I saw Jimmy stop at the pits for two consecutive laps that I realised that I was going to win the race. In fact, I didn't even have to win it—with Jimmy out, it wouldn't matter whether I finished or not. I was still nine points in front of him. I realised that even if I broke down, I would still win the Championship. Then the pressure was right off and I was able to cruise home and win the race and the Championship.

It was very lucky for me that Jimmy broke down in the race,

and of course he was extremely unlucky to have done so, but during the season I too had had a couple of failures whilst in the lead, though not in anything quite as exciting as this last race for the Championship. But I'm not going to knock my good fortune—I was delighted to have won and what made it all the more pleasurable was the fact that I had won in the BRM, a car which at one time had been the laughing-stock of motor racing, although some of the best mechanics in the world had spent years working on it. I was delighted to have been the driver to have helped to contribute towards the success of the BRM and it was a particularly successful moment, too, for Tony Rudd who had become Chief Engineer early in 1962 and had run the team all that year. The beginning of 1962 had been made pretty tough by Sir Alfred Owen more or less saying that we had to win a Grand Prix race that year or else the whole team would be disbanded.

The South Africans poured onto the track again and I had to drive round the circuit very slowly in the car to receive their acclaim. There was only one thing that marred the day. I did not know it at the time, but during my run round I ran over the leg of a small boy and broke it—he got pushed under the back wheel by the crowd and the wheel went over his leg. It was very unfortunate and it upset me quite a bit. I corresponded with him for some time after the accident. The reception we received was tremendous and we were all very pleased. I particularly remember the laurel wreath—it looked rather like a privet hedge round my neck and reached right down to my feet.

Back at home, of course, Bette had heard the news from Reuters and she threw a party. It was only the second Grand Prix that season that she had not been with me.

CHAPTER NINE

1963

New Year's Day, 1963, was rather an unusual experience. I spent it in Karachi jail. There were three of us, Innes Ireland, Peter Bryant—our mechanic—and myself and we were on our way to New Zealand from the South African Grand Prix. Our first stop-over was Nairobi where I spent the night in a Dr. Barnardo's Home with Sir Alfred Owen—he is connected with this wonderful organization. I remember sleeping in a cot surrounded by Teddy bears, dolls and toys and thinking that it was rather an odd situation for the new World Champion. From there we changed airlines to travel on an Air India plane going to Aden, and then on to Karachi, where we were supposed to connect up with a BOAC plane for Sydney. By then it was New Year's Eve. There were all these beautiful Indian hostesses swanning around with bare midriffs and sloshing out champagne. We'd been uprated to first class because the plane was crowded and they wanted to accommodate more passengers. We were having a lovely time and I thought it was too good to last; the moment we landed at Karachi, we discovered that three of us had not got yellow fever certificates—now we didn't know this but we had apparently been in a yellow fever area in Nairobi—and we were promptly slapped into jail in the middle of the desert, to await our BOAC plane. This, unfortunately, was late because it had been snowed up in London.

So there we were on New Year's Day, with me a fresh new World Champion, in bloody jail. As we were ushered in—hardly the word—some Pakistani fellah sprayed each one of us with a sort of flit gun. Naturally I thought this a bit off, and I didn't fancy the look of him either, so I grabbed the spray gun and gave him some of his own treatment. I reckoned that if he was to be our jailer I didn't fancy catching anything off *him*. The jail had bars everywhere and soldiers walking around outside with fixed bayonets. They gave us a couple of slippery eggs and we ordered up a bottle of brandy, which we polished off pretty quickly and then ordered up another one. BOAC said that they had just sent us one and we replied: 'We've drunk that and we'd like another one.' We spent the whole of New Year's Day in this way, but eventually the plane arrived and we got to Darwin. But our troubles were not over, because something went wrong with the tailplane of the Boeing. BOAC had to send another plane from Sydney to collect us. Eventually we arrived in Sydney, but we still had to do the last leg to New Zealand. The plane which was going to take us—this was on Thursday night and the last practice for the race was Friday —couldn't land at Sydney because there was an electrical thunderstorm; the pilot was circling around waiting for the storm to go away and then at the last minute he decided to have a go, rather than turn back. If he hadn't got in, we would never have made the last practice in Auckland and we would not have made the race—after spending four days travelling trying to get there. The whole trip had been a bit fraught.

The Auckland race was the New Zealand Grand Prix and I was to drive the Ferguson 4-wheel drive car; it was the first race in which I competed as World Champion. I was second right up to the last lap in a particularly long race when the gearbox broke within a mile of the finish. It was very disappointing; it had been a very gruelling race and I was particularly hot and quite exhausted. To pack up so near the finish was a bit of a blow.

I flew home immediately after the New Zealand Grand Prix and I went straight into hospital for a tonsillectomy, and then I had to go back out to Australia two weeks later for the continuation of the Tasman Series.

This was the Australian Grand Prix at Warwick Farm, which is a race track just outside Sydney. Unfortunately, what with having my tonsils out and playing the World Champion, answering all the letters and telegrams, giving interviews, television and radio shows, attending functions and luncheons, and going to the Town Hall to be awarded, I had had a very busy time and by the time I reached Australia, after a straight-through flight, I was feeling a bit peaky. The Press all commented that I looked a bit pale, tired and ill.

I was driving the four-wheel drive Ferguson, the same car

that I had driven in the New Zealand Grand Prix and which Innes Ireland had been driving in other races in the meantime; we were sharing the car for this series.

We had a peculiar misfiring with the engine, which we were not able to cure; it was cutting out on all the right-handers, which was a particularly tiresome problem because it meant that I couldn't control the car and lost power when I really needed it. We never discovered what the trouble was. The four-wheel drive was fantastic out of the tight corners, putting down all the power to the four wheels meant that you had terrific grip and it was a most interesting car to drive. Another problem at Warwick Farm was the temperature, which, when I got there, was around 100°. Now the front-engined car is always particularly hot to drive because a lot of heat comes back through the cockpit from the engine compartment and it is very difficult to seal off the cockpit from this surplus heat—unlike the cockpit of a rear-engined car. I finished the race in fifth place, but I wasn't really in it. I was well and truly beaten, though I had managed to get on the second row of the grid for the start.

What really impressed me was the start; I just wound it up and let the clutch out and there I was climbing all over everybody in front of me; on the first lap I was in second place—it really was terribly impressive the way the four-wheel drive got off the line and put the power down.

The car had a little bit of understeer for the tight Warwick Farm circuit whereas it could really have done with some oversteer. Understeer is a problem with four-wheel drive—because you're putting power through the front wheels and you also want to steer with the front wheels—and it's difficult to get a balance so that you don't promote understeer every time you put your foot down. With a normal car, you use the power through the rear wheels to steer the car; when you want to get the back out a bit more and point the car more into the corner, you put down a bit more power and rob some of the road-holding available for cornering and put it down in traction. But when you put your foot down on a four-wheel drive car, of course, you're putting down power to all four wheels, so the car if it's going to break away at all, breaks away evenly front and rear, which of course gives understeer. Because you're not able to steer the car into the corner, it's more difficult to control a four-wheel drive car. What you can do is set the car up perfectly for one particular corner; Indianapolis is a good example of this. Four-wheel drive is a tremendous advantage there because there is only the one type of corner and you can set up the car so that it is perfectly balanced for this one corner. On a very tight, twisty circuit like Warwick Farm, an understeer condition is a real slow way of getting round the circuit so you've got to have oversteer. This is one of the main problems. The torque split between front and rear wheels can be altered, of course, but it still won't give the driver the same directional control in a drift as a rear-wheel drive car. But the Ferguson was a most interesting car to drive and certainly nicely engineered.

The next race was up at Brisbane and this is where the car really came to the fore because it rained during the race. Somehow or other I finished second to Surtees, although I did not make a very good start and I was on dry tyres. I remember being particularly impressed with the driving of a young New Zealander called Chris Amon. He has certainly fulfilled this early promise.

The Ferguson didn't exactly set the tracks alight, but it gave quite a good account of itself and gave the Australasians a glimpse of the future.

I took part in the Sebring, Florida, 12-hour race in March of 1963—and finished without any lights—but I seem to have described all that in the previous chapter. So the next excitement was the Monaco Grand Prix at Monte Carlo.

Richie Ginther and myself went there as the two BRM drivers. Our cars had not been changed since the final Grand Prix of 1962 in South Africa—where we had clinched the Championship—and they were virtually the same cars, so they were already getting just a tiny bit out of date—and we were going to have to use these cars all through that year.

Practice ended up with Clark being the quickest in the Lotus 25, showing extremely good traction and roadholding, especially through the twisty sections. I was alongside him on the front row of the grid, with Surtees and Ginther right behind us. Dan Gurney had shown considerable promise with his Brabham, but Jack himself had had a lot of trouble with his and ended up driving a Lotus 25 in the race—which was rather an unusual sight. His own Brabham was hors de combat; the engine had blown up on the first day of practice and, although he had put it in his plane and flown it back to Coventry Climax for repairs on the second day, he had had more trouble with it on the third day and ended up driving the Lotus.

This year the start of the race was different; instead of the start-line being on the seafront side of the pit area, it was now moved round the hairpin and nearer the town, so that when the starter dropped the flag the cars no longer all rushed into the first hairpin and concertina-ed up, with the chance of a collision that could knock out a few cars as everyone anchored up and tried to get round the hairpin. This year we all accelerated from the grid towards Ste Devote instead. This is a fairly fast corner—something in the order of 90 mph—and the cars don't have to slow up so much; there is less bunching and concertina-ing. The cars have to go through Ste Devote in single file because there is just no way you can get two cars through at once at any speed. This change certainly seemed to eliminate the possibility of collisions at the start—and the race has started from there ever since.

The pattern of the race soon became clear. Both Richie Ginther and myself made excellent starts and went into the lead with Jimmy third and John Surtees fourth. The race went on in this way for a while, until Clark got by Ginther and then began to press on me. We had quite a big battle for a number of laps until he went by me and gradually began to pull out a bit of a lead. It just seemed that I was not able to put down the power quite as well as his Lotus 25 did. I was also very impressed by the Ferrari of John Surtees—he was showing very good form. In fact, he did overtake me at one stage, only to drop back again—I think he suspected oil pressure trouble.

Clark had a bit of bad luck about the 70th lap when, just as he was going into the hairpin, his gearbox selected two gears at once. The gearbox locked up and the car spun round—I arrived on the scene almost immediately afterwards and saw him parked with his nose into the hairpin. I realised at once that he was out of the race and then of course I was in the lead. I was able to come in quite a comfortable winner, with Richie Ginther in second place, giving BRM the old one-two. Surtees started speeding up towards the finish—the Ferrari camp having hung out the go faster signal—and set fastest lap at 1 minute 34.5 seconds on the last lap.

This was the first time I had won the race and it made up for my having narrowly missed winning it the year before, when I had run out of oil with only seven laps to go. Some consolation, and of course it was going to turn out to be the start of a hat-trick for this circuit.

From most people's point of view—except, of course, that of Colin Chapman and Jimmy Clark—1963 was a bit of a disaster, the Lotus and Jimmy were so superior to practically everything on the circuits that year; he won seven Grands Prix—something of a record in one year, and nobody could touch him. Surtees won the German Grand Prix and I was to win one more, but that was it. I finished second in the Championship, but quite a way behind Jimmy with just two wins—Monaco and then the American Grand Prix at Watkins Glen, much later in the year.

. . . . .

The most interesting car that I drove in 1963 was probably the Rover BRM gas-turbine car. BRM converted one of their 1961 Formula 1 cars into a sports car to comply with the regulations for running at Le Mans and they fitted it with the Rover gas-turbine engine. I was asked to go up to Nuneaton, to the MIRA* test track, so that I could try the car out for the first time. I went up there not knowing quite what to expect. I was planted in the seat of this rather weird-looking device and informed on how to start it. You've only got a button for the accelerator, which moves about an eighth of an inch, so that the engine is either on or off; there was also a footbrake, which I had had made nice and large so that I could put both feet on it. When you have got all the fuel pumps and everything switched on, you press a button which starts the engine spinning—and you get a noise like a Boeing 707 starting up at London Airport. It is really a most impressive roar— which frightened the life out of me the first time I started it up.

You're sitting in this thing that you might call a motor car and the next minute it sounds as if you've got a 707 just behind you, about to suck you up and devour you like an enormous monster. It just got louder and louder and I thought the whole thing was going to blow apart. Of course, this was my first experience of it and eventually I got used to it.

You have to hold the thing on the brake, because there's a residual power output even when it is running slowly—and

* Motor Industry Research Association.

slow is 30,000 rpm; some tickover! To apply the power you put your foot on the little button which opens something or other and then you get full power. At the same time you have to keep your foot on the brake as the thing is permanently in gear; if it wasn't, it would just rev up till it burst at some astronomical rpm. It drives through the torque converter, and you put your foot on the button and up go the revs so you get this peculiar turbine-like whine. By then the engine is turning at over 72,000 rpm. You have to keep your eye on the exhaust gas temperature, which must not exceed 900°F, which is pretty hot. If you exceed that you start damaging the engine. All this time the car is trying to edge forward but you manage to hold it at full power on the brakes and then you just lift your foot off the brake and away she goes.

It accelerates rather slowly at first, but once it starts to get into its stride, boy, it really does move. It's quite impressive and the first thing you notice is the complete lack of noise. When you start her up and sit there revving the engine, everyone is deafened and there's a huge heat vapour coming out of the exhaust. The moment you let your foot off the brake all you hear is the rush of wind and the racket completely dies away; there you are whistling along in comparative quiet. If you are watching the car come by, all you hear is the noise of the wheels; they make the most peculiar noise, little thumps as they run over ridges in the road, and a sort of whoosh; that's it, there is no other noise and, to my mind, no spectacle.

Off I went round the MIRA test track. It's a little bit difficult because to start with there is no throttle response. When you back off with a normal, conventional piston-engine you get a braking effect due to the engine trying to suck in air when the throttle is shut and thus creating a vacuum. In a gas-turbine, when you back off all that happens is that the engine just slowly dies away, but you are still producing power; when you back off for the first time you think that the throttle is stuck wide open because the car doesn't slow down at all—it's still accelerating because it's still got power. Then you panic and jump with both feet on the brake and the damn thing stands on its nose. But even then it doesn't stop all that quickly because the engine is still driving. All you succeed in doing is to lock up the front wheels, which aren't being driven. And to lock up the back wheels you've got to stop the turbine—and that takes some doing, it's still spinning around at a few thousand rpm. You wouldn't want a brake failure on a machine like this— you'd never stop it!

I gradually got the hang of it at MIRA and then we took it over to Le Mans for further testing. Owing to the peculiar regulations at Le Mans that year we were not able actually to compete in the race. We were going to be allowed to start after the field had gone and we had a special number—double zero. We were not really supposed to be figuring in the main race, but we were in the running for a prize for the first gas-turbined car to average over 100 mph.

I shared the driving with my BRM co-driver mate, Richie Ginther, who is a very small chap. We had to make up a special seat for him to sit in, but he managed all right. The particular skills we had to develop to drive this car were rather interesting. Because of the lack of throttle control, when you backed off it took two or three seconds to slow down to tickover, and for all that time it was driving. In the same way, when you accelerated it took about two seconds for the turbine to get up to maximum power. The normal business of throttle control—which is the art of motor racing—went completely by the board. In fact, to start the thing moving took me about eleven seconds, which is a hell of a time, and of that it took some eight seconds just to get up to a tickover.

We developed a technique whereby, for example, at the end of the Mulsanne Straight, we would start to brake about 300 yards short of the corner—and you had to brake pretty hard. The brakes took quite a caning because the engine was still driving when you backed off. With left-foot braking we were able to get onto the brakes pretty smartly—the moment you lifted your right foot off the throttle you'd be on the brakes with your left foot. Then, just before we reached the corner— so as to anticipate the amount of power we would need for the corner—we would put our right foot back on the throttle, say a hundred yards before we actually reached the corner. The power would start to build up whilst we were still braking, then when we'd got to the point just before the corner started, where we wanted the power to come in, we took our left foot off the brake. We'd have our right foot right down on the boards and would just hope that we'd estimated the correct amount of power to come in at the right time. Quite often we found that we'd put our foot on the throttle too early and the power would come in just a bit too much just a bit too soon; we would start to accelerate too early. Our immediate reaction, of course, was to brake harder—and the moment we did that, of course, we would lock up the front wheels, lose our steering and the car would fly straight off the road into the sand banks.

If, in fact, we pressed the throttle too late, when we arrived at the corner we didn't have the power, so there we were, freewheeling through the corner and waiting for the power to come in—terribly frustrating. You have to get into a rhythm at Le Mans—it's a good place for this and you've got twelve hours each to manage it. We kept going pretty well and the car handled magnificently. I think I was going through White House quicker in that car than in any car I have ever driven at Le Mans. It really was amazing, because we hardly had to back off at all, it really whistled through at a hell of a speed. And you have to remember that we didn't have much horsepower, only about 140.

It was a fascinating experience and we won the prize for the first gas-turbine car that's ever been raced. A feather in the cap for both Rover and BRM.

It's very rewarding to contribute towards making a little bit of history and both Richie and myself were grateful for the opportunity to play our part.

.   .   .   .   .

The American Grand Prix at Watkins Glen was, as I have said, the only other Grand Prix which I was to win this year. In practice, Jimmy and I were round about fastest with Surtees in the Ferrari very much a contender. At the beginning of the race, Jimmy's starter wouldn't work—the battery must have been flat or something—and after a new battery had been fitted he got away one and a half laps behind the field; after catching back a lot of time, his engine started to give trouble and he did well to finish in third spot.

The race developed into a battle between Surtees and myself. Surtees got by me and I was only about a second behind him until about the halfway mark when my rear anti-roll bar linkage broke and I was left with a very badly understeering car. With a bit of a struggle, I still managed to hold onto Surtees, but was just beginning to drop slowly behind him, when he went out with a collapsed piston. And that left me very comfortably in front with my team-mate, Richie Ginther, some 40 seconds behind me and running second. So we finished again with the BRMs in the one-two formation, which was very gratifying.

And that was the last successful event on the Grand Prix scene for me in 1963, which was a year of almost complete victory for Jimmy Clark and Lotus.

CHAPTER TEN

1964

My first race of 1964 was at Warwick Farm in Australia. I drove a Brabham for David Mackay, who was a racing driver and is now a journalist; the Brabham was actually Jack Brabham's car of the previous year, the first model of the Grand Prix cars—and the first Brabham I had ever driven. I had the car for the whole Tasman Series. I did in fact win a race at Longford in Tasmania, one of the very few road circuits left in the world, with some very fast straights. It's a peculiar circuit insofar as it runs across a couple of wooden bridges and it also crosses a railway level crossing. The race and practice sometimes had to be held up to allow a train to pass; it's rather quaint. Just recently, in 1968, when I was over there some youths set fire to the bridge in the middle of the night, and by the morning it was burning away merrily; the fire engines came out and the racing was delayed a couple of hours. Then, just before the start of the main race, it all burst into flames again, even though it was raining cats and dogs, so the race was delayed once more. We nearly didn't have a race at all as part of the roadway across the bridge was burned away—very hazardous. But not so dangerous as the race itself, which was run in the rain. On the longest straight we were reaching speeds of 170 mph and the cars felt like those flat stones we used to throw as children, skimming across the water of a pond. This race was won brilliantly by Piers Courage with some ultra-narrow Dunlop tyres which cut through the water and reduced the risk of aquaplaning.

For 1964 Ian Walker and myself teamed up to do the Monte Carlo Rally. In an effort to be competitive we set aside ten days to reconnoitre all the special stages on the course. I was also competing in the New Zealand Grand Prix and the Tasman races in Australia—it is always very difficult to fit everything into the programme of an active racing driver, so we scheduled the recce for December of the year before. We were entered to drive a Ford Falcon for the works, which was a big car for the Rally, but it had quite a lot of power and was fun to drive.

For the recce we took along a works staff Falcon and planned to run over all the course and make our own pace notes. We worked quite hard at it, getting up at six every morning, rushing out and spending all day running over the special sections —we were quite pooped by the evening. We really went to town on the recce and, nowadays, you have to if you want to win. You must go out to practice and make your own notes. The snag is that when the rally actually takes place, the weather is usually different. It's no use marking down a fast left-hander when it's all nice and dry, only to arrive during the rally and find it covered in snow and ice; it completely fouls the notes up. If the team is an efficient one, the team manager will have had the notes checked and corrected by a crew immediately prior to the rally and will also check on the weather forecasts.

One innovation we used this year was to have an intercom system; we had to wear helmets over the special stages so we fixed a headphone in our helmets so that the navigator could talk to me without actually shouting, which gave us a tremendous advantage. He was able to talk in a natural voice and I was able to pick him up all the time so it was a useful modification. I don't think all the other teams used this method, but I must say I was rather impressed with it.

Before the Rally, I remember going down to Lincoln Cars on the Great West Road at Brentford to pick up my rally car. 'Just drive up the road and see what it's like,' they said. I drove it gently as far as London Airport when there was an enormous clatter indicating that the big ends had melted.

I wasn't very pleased about that. The mechanics had to change the engine overnight and we set off on the rally. The first thing that happened was that one of the bolts holding the leaf spring on the rear axle broke and the car went all over the road. It happened once again and we robbed the service van —unfortunately this one was too small and the whole spring and axle were leaping and banging about; there was obviously something out of line that was causing the bolt to break.

A further catastrophe occurred whilst we were going up one

of the special sections—the throttle stuck wide open and I ran into a mountain. The whole front of the car was stove in. We put a rope round the front end and tied it to a tree; then we put the car into reverse and tried to drive off. This drastic manoeuvre pulled the front of the car off the wheels and we were able to continue, looking very second-hand—most embarrassing. Not a very successful Monte.

.   .   .   .   .

Before the Grand Prix season really got into its stride, there was a curtain-raiser at Snetterton, which ended rather suddenly for me when I had a monumental shunt with the brand-new monocoque BRM. I was in the lead and was being pressed hard by Pèter Arundell in a Lotus; it was very wet and going down the short straight from the hairpin down to the Esses we got onto some water; the car just did a sharp left and went straight into a bank. I rode up this bank, knocked a wheel straight off which shot miles into the air, ran along the top of the bank and came back down onto the track the right way up. I was extremely lucky.

By a most extraordinary coincidence Michael Cooper, a motor racing photographer, happened to be on the other side of the track at the time and he took a very startling picture of the accident; at the same time there was a *Daily Mirror* photographer standing just beside the bank which I hit—and he took some photographs before he fell over. The photographs, of course, appeared in the *Mirror* and they won him the award of the year for action photographs.

I could not understand what the hell he was doing there anyway, because I would never have expected any action there. It was rather a strange place for him to be, because nothing has ever happened there before. But anyway, he was there and got some fantastic pictures. The acid test, I suppose.

It was rather a nasty old shunt, which didn't do the car much good, and of course I had to walk back to the pits.

At the May meeting at Silverstone I had a big tussle with Jack Brabham. At one stage Jack was about 20 seconds ahead, but I'd managed to catch and pass him, but I could not shake him off; he hung on to my tail and there was just no way I could get rid of him.

Coming up through Abbey for the last time he made a tremendous effort and came into my slipstream beautifully, pulled out and passed me and just pipped me to the post— it was almost an exact copy of the way that I'd done Jim Clark in 1962. It was a bit of a blow, losing in that fashion, though I must say it was a splendid effort on Jack's part.

.   .   .   .   .

Monte Carlo was again the first Grand Prix of the season and once again I was fortunate enough to win. I had a big dice with Clark, Brabham and Gurney—Clark and Brabham were slightly quicker in practice with Surtees and myself on the second row of the grid. I remember making a very good start and trying to squeeze through between Brabham and Clark; they both closed up and my two front wheels were trapped in between their rear wheels—there was smoke pouring off both my front tyres at once. Brabham's rear tyre was rubbing one front wheel, and Clark's rear tyre was rubbing the other, so I was being pinched. I had to back off and let them go. But I managed to win the race for the second year running, which was immensely satisfying. It's a pretty gruelling race— two hours and forty-one minutes this particular one lasted. That is a long time to go racing, especially on such a tight circuit as Monte Carlo, which keeps you extremely busy and requires a tremendous amount of effort, stamina and patience. Richie Ginther came second and that completed the old BRM one-two at Monte Carlo—a tremendous technical achievement because very few cars finish the course. To have only entered two cars and to get them into first and second spot says a lot for the designer, mechanics and engineers and for the car itself.

We were all delighted to see Richie come in second after a particularly sticky start to the year: he had a very nasty accident at Aintree when his car went on at the end of the straight, hit a ditch sideways and turned upside down, sliding along the grass with Richie inside it. Fortunately, the anti-roll hoop at the back of the cockpit helped to save him and also to save the car. The car was of such a low design that although it was upside down it was still running on all its four wheels. The hoop, of course, was digging into the turf and dug a great furrow, but it saved Richie; he was very fortunate in being such a tiny fellow. He was a bit dazed and shaken up—it was a rather nasty old experience for him, and it was very encouraging and confidence-inspiring for him to finish second at Monte Carlo after such an unpleasant incident.

.   .   .   .   .

I was entered for the Formula 2 race at Crystal Palace in John Coombs' new Formula 2 Cooper. In practice we had a problem with our shock absorbers. The leverage ratio was too high and was overworking the shocks. The practice was on Saturday and the race on Whit Monday. We stripped the shock absorbers down on the Sunday and we poured in a very thick castor oil. All this did was to delay the oncoming uselessness of the shock absorbers. It was not actually a cure. In the race it worked for three or four laps, but then they stopped functioning altogether and the wheels just flapped up and down over the bumpy sections as if they were not attached to the car at all. But the worst was yet to come. During the race the rear anti-roll bar, which helps to stop the car from rolling too much —there is one at the front as well—came adrift when a bracket broke. Well, this meant that the rear wheels then had tremendous grip and completely upset the balance of the car; all of a sudden the car developed a colossal understeer characteristic.

From then on I had to throw the car about in a most alarming fashion; I had literally to throw the car into corners to get the tail out or I wouldn't have got round the corners at all. Of course, this used up a lot of road. Jochen Rindt got by me while I was trying to cope with this malady, but poor Alan Rees didn't quite make it. He finished half a second behind me in the race. I think he was a bit cheesed to find me blocking his road on every corner with the car literally sideways on. It was obviously a very hairy exhibition of driving and, of course, he was not aware that my roll-bar had broken and he thought that perhaps I was just deliberately baulking him. It was a tremendous success for Jochen Rindt and it really showed that he had arrived in motor racing. He got a tremendous Press from it, and very deservedly too.

I was able to watch him driving—he was someone I had never seen before—and he drove extremely well and never put a foot wrong. I finished one and a half seconds behind him and there was absolutely nothing I could do about it. It was a most exciting race and it was also my very first Formula 2 race.

The crash at Snetterton was to have a bit of a delaying effect on our Championship hopes, because we had written off the very first new monocoque car which we were to use for that season's Championship series. Anyway, at Zandvoort for the Dutch Grand Prix, I had another car, a new one; it was very good-looking—it had beautiful lines, very clean, and looked sleek and workmanlike. It was also a very nice car to drive, but I had trouble in the race.

Jimmy shot off at the beginning of the race and I was lying in second place when the electric pump which supplied fuel to the fuel injection unit started to overheat; it warmed the fuel and the next thing was that instead of supplying fuel it supplied fuel vapour. The pump wouldn't pump the vapour so the engine ran dry of fuel—and there was a good deal of banging going on. We had had some experience of this before and when I rushed into the pits Tony Rudd was pretty quick to spot the problem. He threw cold water over the pump and I was soon back in the race, eventually to finish fourth.

.   .   .   .   .

I drove a Ferrari in the 1,000-kilometre race at Nurburgring for Colonel Ronnie Hoare with Innes Ireland as my co-driver. It is always a lot of fun driving for Ronnie Hoare—you know that you've got the chance of doing a David and Goliath act against the works and it gives me a lot of pleasure to tweak the tail of the works team. To do it with someone who is as pleasant to drive for as Ronnie Hoare gives me an added fillip. He is a good organiser and very efficient and you know that you are driving for someone who really enjoys motor racing. He is in the same class as that other great amateur, Rob Walker. The team is run on sound military lines which is very useful for long-distance racing and the pits are always first class. I had one or two good years driving for him and this offset one or two rather bad years in the Grand Prix events. He is not as active in racing now as he was, but we remain good friends and I am still able to shoot with him occasionally.

After twenty-nine laps—the race was run for forty-four laps —Innes was in the lead battling with two other Ferraris. One was being driven by Vaccarella from Sicily and the other by

Bandini from Rome. In fact, the heat had been so great that
the Ferrari team manager turned up in our pits and suggested
to Ronnie Hoare that he should slow down his car so that
there should not be any internal scrapping between the three
Ferraris. The Colonel, of course, suggested to Dragoni, who
happened to be the team manager, that he should slow down
the two factory cars instead. In the event, of course, there was
no solution and the three-cornered battle continued unabated.
Innes Ireland was thoroughly enjoying it, but Surtees—Bandini's co-driver—was not too pleased about the thing at
all. He had been in the lead before he handed over to
Bandini.

Then, on lap twenty-nine, Innes disappeared from the scrap.
At last, we saw him running over the brow of the hill towards
the pits and he arrived in a state of complete collapse, having
run all the way from his car, which he'd parked along the
straight. He had tried to push the car back to the pits but it
was uphill and he had not got very far. He was absolutely
bushed and as soon as he arrived he just collapsed on the pit
floor and shouted, 'Fuel! Fuel!' At least, that was all that we
could make out. I collared a five-gallon drum of fuel and I
set off back to the car at the gallop. I asked an official and he
said that it would be all right, so I rushed off with it.

If you've ever tried to run carrying a five-gallon drum of
fuel, you will know that it's pretty difficult. But with 50,000
people in the stands watching you you've got to make a bit of
an effort; I didn't like to slow down too much, though I felt
like it, and it wasn't until I had disappeared from view over
the hill that I slowed to a walk—my lungs were bursting and
I was absolutely whacked.

I poured the stuff in and I managed to start the car and
bring it back to the pits. Then we filled her up again and I set
off in pursuit, but some way behind due to the time that we
had lost.

But it wasn't to last and I was given the black flag and disqualified by the organisers. In fact, the fuel tank had split,
which was why the fuel had leaked out, and so we would probably not have finished anyway and it would have been fairly
dangerous with a lot of fuel aboard, driving round and spilling
it out all over the tyres. It was a shame, because the car was
going extremely well and we stood a chance of winning the

race, which for a private owner like Ronnie Hoare would have
been quite an achievement in the face of the works cars.

.   .   .   .   .

And so to Spa for the Belgian Grand Prix and one of the
fastest road racing circuits in the world. It's a beautiful setting,
but not the sort of place where you want to take to the country.
We did reasonably well: I was on the front row at the start as
we shot off. The race more or less divided itself into several
groups, as it always does on a high-speed circuit where you get
a lot of slipstreaming going on. Dan Gurney showed up his
potential and ran true to form; he left everyone, as he had done
in practice. Then there came a trio, McLaren, Clark and
myself and we were having a rare ding-dong, battling for second
place.

Eventually I managed to shake these two off, which is unusual on a circuit like Spa, and I was then out on my own,
some thirty seconds behind Gurney and drawing away from
McLaren and Clark. All of a sudden Clark had to call into
the pits, apparently for water because he was overheating; so
that dropped him back behind McLaren and he was then in
fourth place. Now, with three laps to go Dan suddenly found
himself running out of fuel. He rushed into the pits and shouted:
'Fuel, everybody!' and then rushed on out again—he didn't
stop for it. Apparently, he didn't think that the Brabham pits
had any fuel, so I guess he must have thought he would prepare
them for fuel and then come back for it on the next lap. Unfortunately, he never made it. He stopped right down at the
bottom end of the circuit . . . and that was him, out of the
race.

When Gurney called into the pits and shouted 'Fuel' at his
staff of mechanics, I went by and I didn't see him in the pits;
I didn't know that I was now in the lead. Gurney then set off
again in third place behind McLaren and myself. Dan, of
course, never made it back to the pits to collect his fuel. I continued for two laps and was given the signal that I was running
first. Then, on the very last lap, as I was climbing the hill back
to the pits—with the car going beautifully—it just coughed
and ran out of fuel.

I just couldn't believe it. As I slowed down, I kept turning
the starter and putting it into gear, but there was absolutely

nothing. The car just stopped. By the time I'd come to a stand-still, Bruce McLaren came by with his engine sounding terrible. I could see his eyes getting bigger and bigger as he saw me standing beside the road; they got as large as saucers and as he went by me with the engine coughing and spluttering, he got up in the seat, turned round and looked at me. Even then he wasn't sure that he was seeing the right thing, and then he realised that he was in the lead with an engine which was coughing and spluttering.

Well, eventually he did get back up to the hairpin, with a steep slope down to the finish. He was only doing about five or ten mph as he staggered round the hairpin and then more or less freewheeled down to the start. And then Jimmy Clark appeared, having made his pit stop for water, and going like a bat out of hell. He flashed past McLaren just before McLaren staggered over the line, and he beat him by about a car's length.

Of course, Jimmy didn't realise that he had won the race, because all he saw himself doing was passing McLaren; he was not aware of what had happened to Gurney, and I doubt very much whether he'd seen me—he might have done, but I don't think it dawned on him. Anyway, he continued on round on the slowing-down lap, having received the chequered flag.

By then they had been giving the chequered flag to every-body. First of all they had expected me and I didn't turn up. Then they gave it to the car which they thought was me, but in fact it was my team-mate, Richie Ginther. The next bloke round was Arundell and they thought that might have been Clark, so they gave him the chequered flag. They'd already given the chequered flag to two people before Clark and McLaren arrived and by then everyone was getting it and nobody knew who was the winner.

Poor Bruce McLaren, of course, knew all right, but Clark didn't and he went off on the cooling-down lap and then, believe it or not, he ran out of fuel on the far side of the circuit. He stopped down with Dan Gurney and started to commiserate with him, saying what bad luck it was that he had lost the race. Then, over the loudspeakers came the fact that Jimmy had won the race—he didn't know and had difficulty in believing it— what a lovely surprise. It was pretty hard on McLaren and I felt pretty dejected myself.

What had happened to my car was this: We had a spare fuel tank on the car with six gallons in it which wasn't connected to the two main tanks; about halfway through the race I was given a fuel signal from the pits which told me: 'Fuel pump on.' All I had to do was flip a switch down and this set an electric pump going which would then transfer the fuel at a rate of about a gallon a minute. There were six gallons in the tank so the pump only had to work for about six minutes and it would have pumped all of the fuel over. But it only worked for two minutes and then stopped. If it had only worked for one more minute it would have pumped another gallon over and I would have made the finish. So, although I had the fuel in the car, I was unable to get at it and it lost me the race. Jimmy won what must have been the luckiest race he'd ever won—to be fourth and then win on the last lap is almost unbelievable.

A racing car, of course, is built down to a very fine limit and nobody wants to carry about more weight of fuel than is necessary; it would be a great penalty. Every designer tries to make his car as light as possible within the bounds of safety. In fact, the racing driver is really sitting inside a very fast fuel tank; our cars were of monocoque construction, a single shell construction like an eggshell divided into three compartments with fuel on either side and the driver in the middle. We sit in our little compartment surrounded with fuel, at the back of our seat and sometimes over our legs. It is a mobile fuel tank. Nobody wants to build a car that carries more fuel than is needed so the designer looks at the races that have to be tackled and decides which is going to consume the most amount of fuel —this gives him a top limit for the amount of fuel he is going to need. In those days, for that Formula, this was about thirty-five gallons and he designs his car around this figure, to keep the weight and also the frontal area down.

A designer will spend a fortune on lightweight materials to cut the weight of his car. We worked to a very close margin, and obviously occasionally people will miscalculate and this can cost them a race. In our case we were relying on an electric fuel pump lasting for six minutes, when it only lasted for two. If it had only lasted a few more seconds, I would have won the Championship in 1964, but that is what motor racing is about; it is an extremely exciting sport, but, boy, it can be shattering and extremely disappointing.

It really takes a lot of courage to go quickly at Spa and everybody is very, very relieved when the race is over—the spectators, the technicians, everyone who is connected with it. It's a fairly dangerous circuit, for if something goes wrong or if you go off the track, you are going so quickly that you don't stand much of a chance.

. . . . .

Richie Ginther and myself were supposed to drive a modified gas-turbine Rover at Le Mans again in 1964, but Rover's had trouble with the heat exchanger, I believe, and the car was not ready. I contracted to drive for Colonel Ronnie Hoare, sharing a 4-litre Ferrari P3 with Jo Bonnier. It was pleasant getting back in a car with a chance to win the race again. A Ferrari is a useful piece of machinery for a race lasting twenty-four hours—there's a lot of experience behind you and you can always reckon that if you've got a Ferrari you should be in at the finish. Well, as it happened, we didn't actually win—but we were second.

The car did not prove quite as reliable as I had hoped. We had a spate of curious little maladies which delayed us on several laps during the course of the race. In fact, we were fortunate to finish in second place. We had to change the condenser twice, we over-heated and we had a broken throttle cable—stupid little things that could well have put us out of the running. We finished some five laps behind the leading Ferrari. Nevertheless it was the best performance that I've ever put in at Le Mans, and probably the best that I ever will, because I don't seem to be racing there these days.

Jo Bonnier and myself teamed up again to drive the same car in the twelve-hour race at Reims. It starts at midnight on the Saturday night and runs through to lunchtime on Sunday. It is the only race I know that starts in the dark and is quite the most electrifying start I think I've ever taken part in, or even seen. It's a Le Mans-type start on the very narrow pit road.

The Reims circuit itself is roughly the shape of a triangle and is about five miles long and extremely fast. There are a couple of tight hairpins and a very, very fast swerve just over the top of a hill past the pits—you go over the brow of the hill and there's this very fast 150 mph right-hander, followed by another fast right, then a short straight, and then a fast left-hander before arriving at a slow hairpin. Then there's just a straight old blind up hill and down the straight to another hairpin.

All the cars were lined up in echelon in front of the pits for the start of this race and the pit area was floodlit for the occasion. It was a very colourful scene. All the town had come out, late as it was, to see the start of the race and all round the pit area was brilliantly lit, but the rest of the track was in pitch darkness.

We stood there waiting for the seconds to tick away and then the flag dropped and off we went. The start was tremendous. I managed to get to the car fairly quickly, leapt in, started it up —you have to remember to put on the lights as well—and away we rushed into the inky blackness. I couldn't see a damn thing. I went straight out of the pits sideways, across the road with a great deal of opposite lock, drifting into the direction I wanted to go and shot off in the lead, closely followed by Richie Ginther in the new 4.2-litre Ford.

The Ford was going to give us a lot of trouble, but behind that came John Surtees in another Ferrari.

Having stood about in the very bright light of the pit area, it is most frightening to find yourself rushing out at full bat into the blackness with lamps that seem quite useless. It takes a while for your eyes to get accustomed to the darkness. My first thought was: Where the hell am I going? Because all you can see is bright lights reflected in your rear-view mirror; they shine straight into your eyes, which doesn't help matters at all. Anyway, I had made a pretty good start and I was able to pick my way among the cornfields fairly well.

Going down towards the hairpin and just before we turned sharp right and came back to the pit area, I suddenly had a rather nasty feeling that somebody was gaining on me at a fantastic rate. I kept well to the right and, lo and behold, John Surtees went by me like an express train, straight up the road towards Reims: he missed the corner completely. Well, I thought, that's handy! I've got rid of him for a while.

I was driving a Ferrari and so was he—but he was driving for the works and I was driving for Ronnie Hoare, so we wanted to win just as much as he did. And, of course, we were all going to have to contend with Richie Ginther in his 4.2-litre Ford. Dan Gurney was also in the race driving a Cobra, but his car just wasn't as quick as ours.

Well, of course, Surtees didn't waste any time getting turned around and rejoining the race. In fact, he only lost a few seconds, but Ginther and I started having a ding-dong. Surtees caught us up and then we had an almighty thrash in the dark with speeds of up to 180 mph—on this very narrow road. One moment we would be bursting into the brightly lit pit area and then rushing out again into the darkness. Unfortunately, just after the pit area, which was of course extremely bright, we went over the brow of a hill and the road turned right into the very fast right bend—almost flat out in the dark. We were just lifting a fraction and the car was getting into a great hairy old drift. With all this slipstreaming going on as well, you had to be careful that the draught from the other cars didn't unsettle your car. We were having a tremendous race. It was really an exciting fight and motor racing par excellence. It was also pretty hair-raising.

We managed to hold our lead and drew out a little bit, leaving the other two to scrap away behind us. I came in and handed over to Jo. The race went on all through the night but eventually the Ford packed up with some sort of trouble and this put it out of the race.

The tremendous duel went on between Jo Bonnier and myself in Ronnie Hoare's car and the works car of Bandini and Surtees. There were just no holds barred.

The pit stops were going to be decisive, because obviously it is no use driving round and knocking fifths or sixths of a second off if they are all going to be thrown away during the pit stops. If a pit stop lasted a second longer than it should, it was going to be difficult to make that up on the road.

With just two hours to go, with myself in our car and Surtees in the other, I had a lead of about 40 seconds, and I had to come in for one more pit stop; Surtees had to make one more as well, but I wasn't quite sure how long it was going to have to be. With $1\frac{1}{2}$ hours to go, at 10.30, I brought the car into the pits and refuelled it in 66 seconds. This of course immediately cancelled out our lead and turned it into a deficit of 22 seconds, with Surtees in the lead. Bonnier took over from me and went out and the gap got to about 40 seconds—because obviously when you leave the pits you lose time joining the circuit and getting up the speed again; with a heavy load of fuel, he was not able to lap at the same speed as Surtees was lapping with a lighter fuel load.

About ten minutes later Surtees called into his pits and they had to change their brake pads. So they not only had to refuel and change their tyres, but they had to fit new pads as well—they had been completely worn out. This set them back quite a while; it's a long job changing pads and it completely messed up their race strategy.

With Surtees stuck in the pits. Bonnier was able to go into the lead. By the time Surtees rejoined, Bonnier had a $1\frac{3}{4}$ minute lead over him. But Surtees then started to whittle down the time on Bonnier. Bonnier could ease up a bit—realising that he had about 100 seconds in hand over Surtees—and he naturally wanted to be sure of finishing the race. Surtees was going like a dingbat trying to whittle this lead down. He was clocking about 3 or 4 seconds a lap off Bonnier, which meant that at the end of the race he ought to be just about level with him.

The whole thing was getting pretty exciting, but then, all of a sudden, Surtees was overdue. Finally he came limping back towards the pits with a flat tyre. In one of his do or die efforts to make up time he had locked up a front wheel under braking at one of the hairpins and worn straight through the tyre and burst it. He had to come in and have it changed, which put him right out of the running. We were able to coast home and win the race. It was a most exciting race and one of those unforgettable experiences.

Long distance races don't normally figure too largely in a Grand Prix driver's season—normally we are too busy with Formula 1 or 2. It's rare to see a Formula 1 driver in these long-distance events but when you do you generally see some fireworks. The race was run from start to finish like a two hour Grand Prix and each time a driver got into the driving seat for his stint he ran just as fast as he could. The Ford did expire out on the circuit, but the two Ferraris were going just as strongly at the end as they had at the beginning, having done the equivalent of six Grands Prix on a high-speed circuit where the engine is really going for full bore for a longer period than on any circuit anywhere except Le Mans. The Ferraris had beautiful engines and they came through with flying colours. In the dark we were reaching speeds of about 180 mph down the straight and averaging 130 mph per lap including two 40 mph hairpin corners, which gives you some idea of the high speeds involved.

.   .   .   .   .

The British Grand Prix this year moved from its traditional post-war home at Silverstone to Brands Hatch and the *Daily Mirror* were to sponsor it for the first time. It was obvious after practice that it was going to be a battle between five of us, Clark, Brabham, Gurney, Surtees and myself. When the flag dropped, Jimmy Clark took the lead and I was in third position with Gurney in front of me and Surtees and Brabham following behind. Gurney didn't last too long and he went out with transistor trouble in the ignition. That left Jimmy and myself drawing away from the rest of the field.

There was a good deal of oil about on the track and I was able to close up on Jimmy and started to press him really hard. I rather got the feeling that I was getting through the corners quicker in my car on the oil than he was—this was probably a direct result of the car's handling. But as the oil dried out so he began to draw away. My next hope was that somebody would drop some more oil and/or that it would rain.

As the race progressed I noticed a large dark cloud drifting towards the circuit and I thought that, if only it would rain, the chances were I might be able to make up on him. I was certain that my car was handling better under slippery conditions and I would be able to go a little bit quicker than he. Unfortunately, it didn't rain, so I wasn't able to test my theory. He never got further away from me than $7\frac{1}{2}$ seconds and towards the end of the race I'd reduced that to about 2.8. After two and a quarter hours to be only 2.8 seconds apart shows a pretty hard race, but that's all one needs to win.

Brands Hatch is a pretty gruelling course and with six speeds in our gearbox we were kept very busy. There is hardly any respite, even down the main straight itself; there is a kink about a third of the way along and then there is a sharp drop with a very bad dip at the bottom—and then you have to start braking for the next corner. The corners are all different from each other and the course is quite hilly. It is a most enjoyable track to drive on and the crowd is always very enthusiastic. They get particularly good viewing at Brands Hatch; the area of the pits and the main grandstand is a natural amphitheatre in a valley in the Kentish hills. The hills provide a perfect viewpoint for people to see any part of the track they wish and they can see a lot of it sitting in their own cars. It has always been a great favourite with the motor racing enthusiasts in Great Britain and there is always a friendly atmosphere and a very partisan crowd.

The day after the Grand Prix, most of the drivers attended a charity cricket match at Farningham cricket ground, just a mile away from Brands Hatch. We played as the Grand Prix drivers versus the combined Farningham and Hartley Country Club Eleven—the proceeds were destined for OXFAM. It was organised by Les Leston and practically all the drivers turned up. It was worth going along just to see people like Jo Bonnier playing cricket for the first time—he handled his bat like a baseball club. We had a great day and made £200 for OXFAM. After the match, we went on to Kingston, to a restaurant called 'The Contented Plate', to celebrate Chris Amon's 21st birthday. We had a tremendous party which ended up with some rather lewd singing—a memorable evening. It was difficult to believe that, with all his racing experience, Chris was still only 21.

The next Grand Prix was in Germany and this Surtees was to win. He always goes extremely well at Nurburgring. I came second with an engine that misfired all through the last half of the race.

In between the German and Austrian Grands Prix, we went testing at Snetterton. We were experimenting with shock absorber settings and were adjusting them softer and softer, until I came round Coram Curve and the car suddenly took a big dive into the bank on the inside of the corner. The bank is about three feet high and normally you hold the car in as close to the bank as you can. But on this lap, due to the soft damper settings, I think the back end must have bottomed out on the shock absorbers and the car took a sudden dive. The front wheel rode up the bank, the car spun round and went along the top of the bank, back onto the track and went straight across backwards into a bank on the other side of the road, coming to an abrupt halt.

When something like this happens you just hang onto the steering wheel like mad and lean forward; on contact, my head snapped back and I got a very severe dose of whiplash—in fact, it knocked me out for the moment and I was unconscious, although my head hadn't hit anything. My mechanics, who had seen it all from the pits, came and got me out of the car. I was in quite a bit of pain and they drove me very carefully to Norwich Hospital, where I was X-rayed. Apparently there was a little bone chipped in my neck. It was extremely painful to ride in any car, even as a passenger.

I bought an inflatable rubber collar to support my neck, which I wore for about six months while racing—I looked a bit like the Michelin Man. The worst difficulty was sleeping at night—I couldn't rest my head on a pillow and I was getting very little sleep.

The very next race was the Austrian Grand Prix at Zeltweg about a week later, which was unfortunately on a military aerodrome and the most bumpy circuit we'd ever raced on. The airfield had been laid down during the war, obviously, and was pretty old; consequently the surface had a bad ripple.

Well of course it couldn't have been worse from my point of view; I only did about two laps' practice and then I found that I couldn't bear the pain—so I came in and took some codeine tablets. I waited a quarter of an hour for the codeine to work and then went out again—it was enough to dull the pain, but when I got to a corner I had to support my head with one hand, so as to take the not inconsiderable load of my head away from my neck. So that's how I practised, with one hand holding my head and the other holding the steering wheel.

Funnily enough, I got the fastest lap in practice with this new technique and stuffed full of pain-killers, which gave me something to ponder on. I had to take codeine for the race and that was the first and last time I've ever taken any drugs for a race, though I suppose codeine cannot really be considered a drug. You can imagine my qualms about using it. Normally I wouldn't dream of taking anything anywhere near a race or practice session. But I couldn't have driven otherwise, the pain was too excruciating and I just couldn't concentrate.

On the other hand I have finished races in the past to discover third degree burns on my feet, caused by hot air from the radiator heating the pedals through an unsealed front bulkhead. The fact that I hadn't felt the pain during the race gives you some idea of the concentration required to drive a racing car at racing speeds. It also gives an illustration of mind over matter, and perhaps this is the secret of those chaps who walk across hot coals or lie on beds of nails.

In the race, the car broke, as most of them did; the transmissions and steerings were failing because of the bad hammering the cars were getting over this very rippled surface.

Jimmy Clark also retired so I was still leading the Championship with 32 points to Jimmy's 30.

.　　　.　　　.　　　.　　　.

For the Italian Grand Prix at Monza, of course, things were really hotting up in the Championship stakes. It was the last race of the European season before we went across the Atlantic to the New World for the final two races, the American and Mexican Grands Prix. The Championship had been warming up steadily through the season and it now looked as if we were going to get a third contender for the title. Jim and I had a reasonable lead, but Surtees on Ferrari's home ground at Monza was bound to be a tremendous threat.

The Italians love to see Ferrari win in Italy and of course Ferrari rises to the occasion splendidly. They are tremendous engineers at Ferrari and they build beautiful engines; their cars always go terribly well at Monza.

Surtees got the fastest lap in practice, followed by Gurney in a Brabham and then myself; Bruce McLaren and Jimmy Clark were on the second row of the grid. We were all set for a searing pace and a closely fought duel. Monza is a very fast track—so of course slip-streaming plays a very important part and it is vital that your engine is reliable as well as powerful; the fact that they are at full bore for such long periods means that they are very highly stressed.

At the 30 second signal I depressed my clutch, engaged first gear and watched the starter like a hawk. You never know, especially in the Continental races, when the starter will drop his flag, so you want to be well prepared.

With about 5 seconds to go, the starter raised his flag and the drivers raised their revs to near maximum. The noise and tension were terrific. With a flourish, the starter dropped his flag; I let the clutch out and absolutely nothing happened. I didn't move one inch.

The field rushed off into the distance and there I was all alone. The gearbox had obviously not broken as there had been no load, so I was a little perplexed. All I knew was that the clutch pedal was flopping about and there was no way I could get the clutch to engage. Apart from that there was nothing wrong. So I just switched off.

By this time the officials were going berserk. There was I

still sitting in the middle of the track with not another car in sight, and within another minute and a half there would be all hell let loose as the whole field swept round to engulf me. The officials all started shouting and leaping up and down; then the mechanics reached me and there was nothing to do but to push the car back into the pits and try to find out what had happened.

The race continued and I just had to sit and watch my two rivals sort the race out between them.

I was very lucky that I had not been clobbered on the line with such a long field. Fortunately Monza has a very wide starting area and everyone managed to miss me, but it was a particularly uncomfortable moment—all I could do was just sit there holding my arm up in the air, hoping that the other drivers would see it. Everyone whirled round me in a cacophony of noise, dust and smoke and disappeared into the distance. I was left there in front of heaven knows how many people absolutely motionless, never having crossed the line.

Jimmy had bad luck; his car blew up and Surtees went on to win, which of course put him very much in the reckoning. It gave him 9 points and brought him up much closer to Jimmy and myself. He now had 28 points; Jimmy had 30; and I had 32. At the same time it put Ferrari into the lead in the Con-structors' Championship, so they must have been delighted. Naturally the crowd loved it.

After the Italian Grand Prix, I took the family off to a very nice hotel at Formentor, at the top of the island of Majorca. We had a very pleasant time. My family stayed there for about three weeks and I was able to get a few days there and relax in the sunshine. It was a great treat to be with the family and spend the time lazing around doing nothing, swimming and generally relaxing.

Before we went to America BRM announced that they had signed up Jackie Stewart to be my team mate for the following year—a bit of a surprise because Jackie had not yet run in a Formula 1 race but he had been very successful in Formula 3. At the same time as BRM were signing on Stewart, there was a rumour afoot that Richie Ginther was going to sign for Honda and their Grand Prix team which was quite exciting news. In fact he did eventually sign for Honda and drove for them.

Richie was an extremely good team mate and I had thoroughly enjoyed having him in the team and driving with him. He was a very small man—as I may have mentioned before—and it must have made Honda-designer Nakamura's eyes light up when he heard the weight of the new driver who had been signed on. A saving of 56 pounds is just what a designer dreams about—and to do it by simply changing the driver seemed almost too easy! It would probably be impossible to save that amount on the weight of a car and would certainly cost a fortune. But really I don't know how much difference it makes in practice. For a Grand Prix driver I am on the heavy side—over thirteen stone. Richie weighed about 125 pounds to my 185: it's a tremendous difference.

Anyway, he was a first-class team mate and although he never had a win, we did the one-two act on several occasions.

And so we all moved to America where we were to race at Watkins Glen. I had been lucky enough to win the year before and was second the year before that. At the end of practice I found myself on the second row of the grid with Clark and Surtees on the front row and Dan Gurney popped up from nowhere at the last minute and was tucked in beside me. The race really centred around us four. We had a tremendous scrap, but Jimmy packed up whilst in the lead—his engine started spluttering and banging and naturally we closed right up on him and about this time I went into the lead. Then Surtees and Gurney and myself had a tremendous scrap.

Just before the halfway mark, someone started spewing oil around and the track got very slippery indeed; Surtees flew off the circuit at one particular point on the oil and Dan and myself were all set to fight it out. Then Dan went out with engine trouble and there I was all on my own, leading the race by some seventeen seconds in front of Surtees. The race came to a finish with me in front, Surtees second and Jimmy nowhere.

That left the Championship still open. Counting my six best performances I had 39 points; Surtees had 34; and Jimmy had 30. So it left a very interesting situation. Now obviously with 39 points I stood the best chance. But anything can happen in motor racing and really I had to win the last race—the Mexican Grand Prix—to make sure.

Anyway, my win at the American Grand Prix was a good

one and my second on the trot. The prize-giving there is always pleasant. They manage to select a beautiful girl to come up and plant a great big kiss on your lips which is really one of the nicest things to have happen after $2\frac{1}{2}$ hours or so of hot, sweaty tension, high speeds and dust. The contrast is enormous. Motor racing is a very hard, aggressive sport with all sorts of dangers and tensions; but when it's all over and you have won, there is someone to remind you of the more gentle ways of life and refresh your memory with a kiss.

On my return I went to Paris; I was going to co-drive with Jo Bonnier in Ronnie Hoare's Ferrari, the same one that I had used in the Tourist Trophy at Brands Hatch. Paris is always a pleasant place to visit and we had a rather pleasant result in the race. We won. All in all we had had a successful season with Ronnie Hoare that year driving his Ferrari and I don't think I have ever had that sort of success in long-distance events before or since; it was a most enjoyable season racing for a privateer in a very well-prepared and competitive car. We ended up the season with three wins, a second and a third. I was very grateful to him for the chance to drive such a wonderful car.

Jo drove exceptionally well; it seems as though he does better in sports cars than he did in his Formula 1 cars and on his day he can be extremely quick, as we witnessed when he gave Denny Hulme a run for his money at Silverstone in 1968.

Perhaps he takes on too much; he runs a business and he is kept extremely busy as president of the GPDA*—he puts in a lot of time, work and energy as president which I am sure no-one else would be prepared to do—and then, of course, he tries to run his own Formula 1 and sports car team. Well, that is an awful lot for one man!

. . . . .

The final Championship race in Mexico coincided with an invitation from the Mexican Government to the Duke of Edinburgh; he was there for an eight-day State Visit as the guest of the Mexican Government. The Duke's advisers and the Foreign Office in London had ideas for his Sunday engagements including an afternoon spent on a ranch somewhere. However, representations were made on behalf of the British

* Grand Prix Drivers' Association

racing drivers back in Paris and at the Foreign Office and it was pointed out that his absence from the race would cause great disappointment in British motor racing circles and his presence would be of great value to the prestige of Britain at a time when her drivers led the world. Cables were sent off to the Duke who was then sailing towards Mexico in the *Britannia* and to the British Embassy in Mexico, asking him to change his programme—and so he did, cutting short his afternoon visit to the ranch and arriving at the Grand Prix circuit just before the race ended. Prince Philip is, in fact, the President and Chief of the British Racing Drivers Club.

There was a lot of pressure on this race; three of us could win under various combinations and permutations; one of us was going to end up Champion on that day. The whole year's racing depended on this last round—it was a fine way to finish the season. It caused a lot of excitement and drama with three drivers and three different makes of car contending for the final. I think this was the first time it had ever happened, so you can imagine the sort of tension that was building up amongst the Press and the public, the teams, the mechanics and the drivers.

Mexico is a very funny circuit. It is designed in a park and I would describe it as a Mickey Mouse circuit. It is terribly tight and twisty with lots of funny little bends in the middle. There is a fairly long straight and one bend goes through almost 180° with a slight banking, so the circuit as a whole presents peculiar problems. It requires a car to be set up specially and also the engine must be tuned a bit differently, because the altitude is over 7,000 feet above sea level—so there just isn't the air about to get sucked into the engine. Roughly, you end up with the engine twenty-five per cent down on power, about 100 hp. This affects every car the same way, or is supposed to, but we normally find that the multi-cylinder cars—the 12-cylinder cars, for instance—are slightly better off than the 8-cylinder cars. They just have four more pots to suck in air at every stroke and they somehow or other seem to be a little bit more efficient at that altitude than the V8 engines. So it looked as though the V12 Ferrari was going to have a slight advantage due to the fact that its breathing was probably a little bit better.

For the race, I was on the third row of the grid—quite a way back for somebody who had to try and beat the field. Jimmy Clark was quite a bit faster than myself and in fact by practice times I was well out of the running. We had a lot of trouble getting the cars to go round Mexico quickly and I was 2½ seconds a lap slower than Jimmy and 1 second a lap slower than John Surtees, so things looked pretty grim from my point of view.

On the start line something happened that might have affected the whole outcome of the race. Just as I pulled my goggles down before the start of the race, the elastic gave way and my goggles fell down over my face. So there I was sitting on the start line for the final round of the World Championship, in which I had to finish third or higher to win irrespective of what anyone else did, with my goggles in my lap and no means of getting them to stay on.

I started fiddling with the elastic, but as I had my gloves on it was a bit difficult to work the tiny adjustment catch. Anyhow, I managed it and put the goggles on. While I was doing all this, the starter dropped the flag. I dropped four places after the start and at the end of the first lap I was tenth, so I had a lot of ground to make up.

Anyway, I got up to third place which was the position in which I had to finish to secure the World Championship; as long as I did that, Jimmy or Surtees could win the race, but they couldn't win the Championship. I just had to get those four points for a third place, and I was safe.

Jimmy and Dan were in front of me; immediately behind me was Lorenzo Bandini in a Ferrari and Surtees was behind him, so I looked in a fairly strong position at that point. In other words, lying in third place, I was in fact leading the World Championship. If I remained in third place, that was enough to ensure that I won.

Well, of course, I was having a go at coming first or even second, but I was being left behind by Jimmy at that particular stage. My car wasn't getting round the circuit all that quickly, although I had had quite a good scrap to get up in third place.

Then Bandini started to challenge me and made one or two wild attempts to pass me going into the hairpin. On one lap he dived straight in underneath me and I had to move out to give him room—it was a bit of a desperate effort—but as I was coming out of the hairpin, his front wheel hit my back wheel and spun me round into the guard rail.

I managed to get my car going—I was still in third place—but it sounded most peculiar. What had happened was that I had gone backwards into one of the guard rails and it had closed up the exhaust pipe. My engine was working properly, but had no means of getting the exhaust out; it was making rather a flat noise. And so it was stifled and couldn't produce the power. I had to call into the pits and the mechanics broke off the end of the pipe which was closed up. I was on my way again, but I lost so much time in the pits that I finished well down in the race. This automatically robbed me of any chance of winning the Championship unless the other two packed up or didn't finish high enough.

At that point Jimmy was in the lead, Dan Gurney had dropped out, Bandini lay second, and Surtees was third. The position looked fairly straightforward. Jimmy was having a quite uneventful race on his own way out in front and it looked as though he had the race sewn up, but one or two laps from the end he ran out of oil. The engine seized—and he was finished.

Suddenly, the Ferrari pit realised what had happened. The moment that Jimmy dropped out, I became once again the World Champion because Surtees was still lying in third spot—and the four points for third spot would leave him short of one point to beat me; he had to get into second spot and gain those six points so as to edge one point in front of me. If he finished in third spot, with the four points from that, he would then have got 38 points to my 39; in second spot, with six points, he would have 40 points to be one point in front of me.

Well, of course, the Italians realised this and immediately they all rushed out in front of the pits and stood in the road frantically waving to Bandini to slow down and let Surtees go by. Fortunately for them, and unfortunately for me, Bandini understood what they were getting at—it was pretty obvious what they were asking him to do because they were all standing in the middle of the track—and he slowed up and let Surtees take the second spot behind Gurney and therefore the Championship.

I didn't know anything of all this, of course; all I had seen was Jimmy packing up and then I tried to work out whether I was in the lead or not. I don't know what position I was in at that time, but I was well down in the field because by now I had lost a lot of time in the pits.

When I arrived back at the pits after the slowing-down lap I looked at all the faces to see whether or not I was the Champion and I could tell from their expressions that I hadn't won. It was a pretty disappointing moment for me.

Bandini certainly earned his money for Ferrari that day, apart from the rather desperate effort at the hairpin. A lot of people suggested at the time that it was deliberate, but I certainly didn't think so. I wouldn't believe that of Bandini; it was obvious to me that he was making a desperate manoeuvre to get by and he just overcooked it. Well, that was that, and my tough luck. He then went on to let Surtees through so he played a very valuable part in the Championship, unintentionally in one case and, of course, with the aid of the team manager in the second. But it was a very good Championship season and a very exciting finish, real Hollywood style.

CHAPTER ELEVEN

1965

Bette came with me to the *Daily Express* Trophy meeting at Silverstone, although she was expecting our third child any minute, and she was also pretty determined to get to Monte Carlo if she could by hook or by crook; fortunately, the baby was born between Silverstone and Monte Carlo. It was a little girl whom we subsequently called Samantha, although originally we thought her name was going to be Charlotte. In fact, she was registered as Charlotte, but I remember looking at her one day and thinking, 'She doesn't look like a Charlotte to me,' so we changed her name to Samantha and that is what she was baptised. A lot of people were very surprised to see Bette at Silverstone looking frightfully prosperous and then seeing her in Monte Carlo two weeks later looking considerably lighter, but the holiday did her good.

The 1965 Monte Carlo was a race which I have always considered to be one of the best races I have ever run or ever won. I did reasonably well in practice—I put up the fastest time and therefore, as I had won the race the two previous years, I was considered the favourite for the race that year. Now that is something I never really like to be—because everyone expects an awful lot of the favourite and it certainly raises the tension.

Monte Carlo is always a tricky race, one of the trickiest circuits in the world because it is so easy to be just a little bit untidy at any one particular corner, clobber a kerb with the wheel and break the suspension or break a wheel or cause yourself to spin off. And, of course, there is just nowhere to spin at Monte Carlo; you bounce off hotels, night clubs, brick walls, telegraph poles, street lamps. Everything around is absolutely solid, although we have managed to get a few Armco barriers set up at one or two spots which might prevent us from coming to a stop rather smartly.

It's a proper road circuit and one of the few remaining in the world. You can look at pictures of the first race track— I think it was 1929, the year I was born—and the track looks exactly the same. The only difference is the cars; they are a bit antique-looking. The circuit hasn't altered its shape at all, although the chicane has been moved in the last year to make it just a little bit safer. In fact, if the chicane had been in the right place—in the place where it is now—I wouldn't have been forced to go up an escape road taking avoiding action during the race in 1965.

The race had been on for about twenty-five laps and I was in the lead when I came over the brow of a hill towards the chicane. I was doing about 120 at that particular point and was just getting on the brakes as I started to go down the hill. As I straightened up and the chicane came into view, I saw Bob Anderson in his Brabham literally creeping down towards the chicane—apparently the car was stuck in first gear. I had seen no flag and no signals or anything. All I could see as I blasted over the hill—in that fleeting second that you get to make a decision—was that he was going to be occupying the chicane at about the time that I wanted to flash through it doing about 95 mph.

There was only one thing to do: I just stood on the brakes as hard as I could, locking them up. I made as if to go through the chicane and I left things until the point of no return, and then I saw that there was just no way I could get through without clobbering him. I came off the brakes for a second so that I could steer and changed direction down the escape road. Then I stood on them again and I left some rare old skid marks. I came to a grinding halt well up the escape road. I had to get out of the car, push it backwards onto the track, climb in and then start the engine. Well, of course, all this took time and by then the leaders had gone through. I had lost I don't know how many seconds: about thirty-five. And I had had quite a comfortable lead. Anyway, I lost over half a minute in this operation which dropped me right back to fifth place. I was pretty narked about this—it had more or less knocked me out of the fight for the lead. So I jumped into the car and set off in hot pursuit.

The race was a hundred laps and I had done twenty-five so I still had three-quarters of the race to make up the time. I was a bit cheesed off over the whole business—if I had come by a second later I would have been able to squeeze through, but as it was I just couldn't get down to a sufficiently slow pace to follow Anderson through the chicane at his speed. It was bad luck that he just happened to be in that position. There was nothing he could have done about it—he was stuck in first gear. There should really have been a warning—the yellow flag should have been hung out warning the drivers that there was a car proceeding at a slow pace ahead. I would have lifted off a bit earlier and approached the brow of the hill a bit slower; then I would have been able to stop.

Things have been tightened up since then and I don't think the same thing could happen again. In any case the chicane has now been moved 100 yards further on down the quayside which means there is more room to brake and a car could in fact get stopped before the chicane. If there was a pile-up and the chicane got blocked now, anyone coming round the brow of the hill would have time to stop. This place had of course been the scene of a famous crash in 1957 involving Moss, Hawthorn and Collins; Fangio managed to slip through the debris. Nobody wants a race to get messed up because of something stupid like that.

Anyway I set off after the leaders and gradually whittled the time down.

First, I caught up my team-mate Stewart, who had moved into first place when I went down the escape road, but Stewart had spun at Ste Devote and lost the lead on lap 30. I caught him up and passed him; I set off to catch up Surtees and Bandini who were both driving for Ferrari. They were having a tremendous ding-dong among themselves. Brabham had been after them and had taken the lead on lap 34, but on lap 43 he ran out of oil and had to coast into the pits to retire. I was having a terrific scrap and broke the lap record a number of times—I was motoring faster and faster as the fuel load got lighter. Gradually I got to see this tussle going on and then of course the Ferrari team saw that I was closing up. They made frantic efforts to signal to their drivers to stop dicing for the lead and go faster. As soon as Bandini and Surtees got the message that I was catching them up from their pit signals, they started to pull the stops out. By the time I actually caught them up, Bandini had got a bit clear. On lap 53 I got by Surtees and set off after Bandini. I had quite a few goes at passing him.

Monte Carlo is an extremely difficult place to overtake anybody and you've really got to work at it. You start building up to pass somebody more or less a lap in advance. If you decide that the best place to take him is at the Gasworks Corner, you've got to start the manoeuvre more or less from the Gasworks on the preceding lap so that you arrive at the Tobacconist's Corner—the one before the Gasworks—in just the right position to make a 100 per cent job of taking the corner on the limit, and that little bit quicker, to draw alongside him going down the straight—and hoping to pass him under braking for the Gasworks Corner.

It takes a lot of planning, a lot of strategy to actually pass somebody; it just doesn't occur in a flash if the bloke's going at roughly the same speed as yourself. You don't simply say to yourself, Right, I'll pass him now; you must build up for it. You probe and you feel; all the time that you are racing against him you are working out where you are going to pass him, where is going to be the best place to pass, where he is a little bit quicker than you and where you are a little bit quicker than he. All these things have to be weighed up and you've just got to time it right. It takes a lot of working out—unless the fellow makes a mistake; then of course you want to be in the right spot when he makes the mistake. If you pressure somebody hard enough he might make a mistake, but then you have still got to be on his tail and in control to take advantage of it. And this is not always possible.

You haven't just got to make up a car's length; if you're right up on his tail—nose to exhaust pipe—you have to make up three cars' lengths to get ahead and allow yourself room to cut in again—which is a lot when it is a tight circuit. You have to follow the leader round the Gasworks Turn and round the Station hairpin, so there are very few places to pass. One of the best places for overtaking is after the Gasworks and it's the safest, but it requires making a much quicker exit and being sufficiently closed up to be able to pass under acceleration before Ste Devote.

In the end I got Bandini at the same place as I got Surtees— on the short straight going down the hill towards Mirabeau after leaving the Casino Square. It's a very short sharp downhill stretch and I managed to come round Casino Square just that little bit better, holding a tighter line, and I got down the inside of both of them under braking.

Bandini gave me quite a hard time but eventually I got by him; he didn't give in, though, and we had a rare old ding-dong. Then Surtees got by Bandini and put the pressure on me for a while around the 80th lap and I know I put in some very fast laps at about this time. It was a tremendous race and I think that this with the 1962 German Grand Prix were probably my best races ever. They both had some extraordinary circumstances. (I had had a collision with a cine-camera in practice at Nurburgring.) To have actually won the race at Monte Carlo after having had to push it back onto the track and then push-start it was quite something. The added pleasure that really put the icing on the cake was the fact it was my hat-trick; it gave me three wins in three consecutive years, which made it even more satisfying and memorable for me.

Surtees was really very unlucky—after an extremely good fight, he had the disappointment of running out of fuel on the last lap and, though he was classified as a finisher in fourth place but one lap behind, it was tragic that he was not able to take second place. Nothing is more galling than to run out of fuel on the last lap; it does make you think that the whole 99 previous laps have been a complete waste of time. When you have really been fighting tooth and nail, to have that sort of thing happen is a very bitter pill indeed. Two hours, 37 minutes, 39.6 seconds is a long time to be motoring flat out on a circuit like Monte Carlo.

My car had run perfectly; I had absolutely no trouble with it—my hat-trick was a great credit to BRM and a tremendous technical achievement, because Monte Carlo is undoubtedly one of the toughest circuits on a car.

The prizegiving itself is a very proper and pukka affair at the Hotel de Paris, which is one of the swankiest hotels in the world, and a very swept-up do. I always somehow managed to forget to take my dinner jacket and arrived wearing a lounge suit; for three years I have arrived in an ordinary suit and everyone else was wearing a dinner jacket. The trouble is I have noticed since that when I have taken my dinner jacket, I haven't won the race, so I don't like to anticipate the victory banquet in this way. Immediately after the race Prince

Rainier and Princess Grace received me up on the dais and of course they were getting quite used to seeing me; there were a few 'Not again!' sort of remarks. They always attend the race and present the awards, and show a lot of interest in the event.

The night of the race we went to the Tip-Top, a little bar which doesn't seem to have much to recommend it except that it sells drink, but it is a popular meeting place for all the British contingent—we always go there. I look in every year and every year the owner treats me to a drink—this time it was champagne. After the official prizegiving I had my drink with the owner of the Tip-Top and a plate of spaghetti. By this time it was three or four o'clock in the morning and I was starving again: after 100 laps around Monte Carlo it was not very surprising.

I remember the next day Bette and I spent on the beach at Cap Ferrat and I really felt completely relaxed, though that's hardly the word. I knew that I had taken a lot out of myself mentally and physically, but the victory had really put a glow in me. I don't think I have ever felt quite like it before. A tremendous feeling of peace, serenity and fulfilment. I just felt entirely relaxed and every muscle in my body felt as if it was completely rested.

.   .   .   .   .

The next Grand Prix that year was the Belgian on the very fast Spa circuit. In practice I managed to lap it in 3 minutes 45.4 seconds which is an average of 139.9 mph—just a fraction off making it a 140 mph lap—and it was two seconds quicker than my next competitor which surprised me enormously. It was immensely satisfying to be that much faster than anybody else and I was quite optimistic for the race. Unfortunately it rained on race day; I had set the car up pretty hard with fairly stiff springs and rollbars and it just didn't handle at all in the wet—it was just like driving on ice and at high speed it's ten times worse.

Jimmy Clark won the race—his fourth Belgian Grand Prix in succession, which is a pretty tremendous achievement—and Jackie Stewart my team-mate came in second, which must have been very satisfying for him and showed his potential. There were therefore two Scotsmen in first and second spot, so the Glasgow and Edinburgh papers had a ball on the following Monday. It was pretty miserable going all the way through and conditions were atrocious. Dick Attwood had a very nasty shunt—he clobbered a telegraph pole—but got away with it. The car just aquaplaned and spun down the road for about half a mile. Fortunately he was okay. I came in fifth, but I had to work quite hard even to do that.

All this altered the picture of the championship because it put Clark in the lead with 18 points, myself second with 15 points and Jackie Stewart was catapulted up into third place with 11 points, which was a pretty good debut into Formula 1 racing.

The French Grand Prix this year was held at Clermont-Ferrand in the Massif Central—it's a very twisty, pretty circuit high above the town. Unfortunately in practice I had the throttle stick open when a stone got lodged in the slides of the fuel injection system. I probably picked it up in the paddock and in any case it nicked the slides and they stuck open as I was going round one of the corners. It was on a tight series of bends—left—right—left—right—second gear corners really; you give a good hard squirt of power in between the corners and if the throttle sticks wide open you go straight forward into the mountain as quick as lightning. There is no question of braking or getting time to flip your switch off. It is just a very quick on-off, on-off. Anyway, on one corner the throttle just didn't come off and I went straight into the rock-face and gave myself a bit of a thump. I strained all my neck muscles, my shoulders, arms and legs, but otherwise I was all right. The car was stove in at the front and a wheel was ripped off. It all happened unbelievably quickly. All in all, I was not feeling in my best form for the race.

Jimmy Clark was on great form, fresh from his Indianapolis victory. He managed to win quite easily, with Stewart second. I limped in to a fifth place with the spare car and was quite thankful to get that.

We all met up again for the British Grand Prix at Silverstone in July—a race I have never won though I have come near it on one or two occasions. Jimmy Clark was fastest in practice; I was second fastest but I just couldn't catch Jimmy. He relentlessly pulled away from me during the race and we finished in the same order as we had completed practice— Jimmy first and myself second, though neither of us had had a clear run. Jimmy was running short of oil and had to watch his oil pressure gauge; he could only accelerate when he had got sufficient pressure, so that towards the end of the race he was really slowing up hard so as to make sure of finishing. On the third lap, I put my foot through the floor on the brake pedal which meant that I had to pump the brake pedal for the whole of the race; I couldn't get my left foot across and so I was pumping it up with my right foot, which meant backing off early and really pumping like crazy to get the pedal up before I could get any brakes. So we were both in some sort of trouble.

Jimmy had drawn out quite a lead but, of course, he then began to lose ground when he had trouble with his engine. He timed it pretty well, however, and though I had got his scent and set up a new lap record for Silverstone on the last lap, I was to lose the race by 3.2 seconds. I had lost the same race to Jimmy Clark the previous year by 2.8 seconds, so it seems as though the British Grand Prix is always just a few seconds out of my reach. It was a damn good race and I must say I enjoyed it. It was very nice to get the fastest lap, especially on the last lap, though it is a small consolation for not winning.

We were both in the Formula 2 at Rouen the next day and, just to rub it in, Jimmy beat me again and I came in second to him in John Coombs' Brabham-BRM. So that was two races in two days that I wasn't able to do anything about Jimmy, though I managed to set up the fastest lap on both days.

Jimmy won the Dutch Grand Prix at Zandvoort the next weekend—it was run later than usual that year—and I couldn't do better than the fourth place. My car had a broken rev counter, but even so I didn't do at all well and I was a bit disappointed. The win at Zandvoort cemented Jimmy's championship; in theory I could still win, but only if I won the four remaining championship races and Jimmy did not score any points at all.

The big drama at the Dutch Grand Prix in 1965 occurred when Colin Chapman was arrested by some irate policeman. Just before the start he had tried to get back to the pits to fetch something for Jimmy, I think it was a pair of goggles. He had his official armband attached round his waist and a policeman didn't see it and tried to stop him. The race was just about to start and Colin was in a hurry; he was running back to the pits and this policeman gave him a shove and sent him flying over a straw bale backwards. He got up, brushed the policeman off and ran to get the goggles. When the race was over the police arrested him.

The whole thing got pretty nasty and he was kept in jail overnight to face charges of assaulting the police. It was quite ridiculous because he was going about his legitimate business just prior to the race and a policeman had tried to stop him. I don't altogether approve of policemen on the startline of a road race. The race officials are quite strong enough and powerful enough for that sort of thing. It was rather an ugly incident which I am sure the Dutch regretted as much as we did. Nothing was to come of it, fortunately, and the whole matter was settled amicably. But it was a bit distressing at the time, especially as Colin had his wife and children there; I remember taking Hazel and the children back with us on the plane, leaving poor Colin in jail.

With the Dutch Grand Prix having been postponed, it was followed a fortnight later by the German Grand Prix at Nurburgring. Jimmy Clark stormed home to win, setting up a new record on lap one, from a standing start. I came in second, and that was that. Jimmy had clinched the Championship—nobody could touch him. He had 54 points and I was runner-up with 36—but I had run out of races. In an ordinary year 36 points might have been enough to win, but Jimmy's performance had been fantastic.

Most of us were racing at Brands Hatch on the Monday— it was the Bank Holiday—in the Guards Trophy. On the Sunday we had the second of our charity cricket matches arranged by Les Leston. This time it was at Mersham in Kent near where Les has a cottage and, in fact, I now have a cottage near there myself. It was a great success. Nearly all the drivers turned up and we played the Mersham and District Eleven. The proceeds went to the boys' club at Clacton of which I am now the President. We are always wanting money for this club and we managed to raise quite a useful sum— we had had some rather shabby old premises and we needed to raise £25,000 for the new building which we had put up on borrowed money—we still owe quite a lot for it.

The Italian Grand Prix in September turned into the usual sort of slipstreaming effort that we get at Monza every year, with the pack breaking up into various groups, all slipstreaming each other, with no car quite able to shake off the rest. It started off with Clark, Stewart and myself fighting for the lead. But Clark's fuel pump went on lap sixty-four and the race was just left between Stewart and myself, both in BRMs, which must have been a very nice sight for the BRM team.

Coming down into the last corner before the pits straight before the finish on the penultimate lap, Stewart came up on the inside and I moved across to give him room; we had the race in the bag so there wasn't any sense in chopping up my own team-mate but I wouldn't have moved if it had been anyone else. We had a nice little system going of passing and re-passing and as far as I was concerned I was going to win that race. Anyway, I moved over to give him room and I got onto the marbles—all the loose grit that always collects on the outside of a corner. The constant cornering of the racing cars tears up the surface and throws all the dust and grit to the outside of the course. As I moved over, I got onto this and the car went sideways off the track and hit the sand; I caught it again, regained control and set off, fuming. By then Stewart had got himself quite a nice lead and we completed the lap in that order, with Stewart winning the Italian Grand Prix. Naturally I was pretty disappointed but there it was; I had been a bit over-polite and thrown away my chances of winning. Nevertheless, it was a great win for Jackie and it was his first Grand Prix win. BRM came in first and second so it was a great victory for the team as well.

.   .   .   .   .

We had a very homely little scene that autumn at our local church where we christened Samantha. John Coombs, much against my better judgment, was the godfather and to compensate for this rather odd choice, we had Gregor Grant's wife, Eba and Les Leston's wife, Doreen as the godmothers. It was a very happy event with lots of motor racing people, a lovely sunny day and a bit of a party afterwards with the champagne flowing like water. We had the trampoline out in the garden and we managed to get all the racing contingent to perform on it at one time or another. Altogether a hilarious, drunken, athletic afternoon. It ended up with Coombs and Leston performing a trouserless duet rather like Peter Cook and Dudley

Moore as dancing nuns. It was a tremendous party and we were very grateful to Samantha for providing the excuse.

.   .   .   .   .

In October we went to the States for the American Grand Prix. I had won it the previous two years so naturally I had the same feeling that I had had at Monte Carlo—that I'd like to complete the hat-trick. It looked like a real needle match between Jimmy and myself; I collared the pole position on the grid with a time that was only a tenth of a second quicker than Jimmy but he went out on lap 11 with engine trouble. It was a gusty autumn day for the race—in fact, the crosswind was blowing the cars all over the track; then it started to rain on and off and sometimes it was raining on one part of the circuit and not on the other; all in all, I was quite glad to see Jimmy go.

On lap thirty-eight I came around onto the fast right-hander before the pits hairpin, about half a mile from the pits, and I went straight off into the field. I did a long sort of detour over the grass, bounding along like a mountain goat, and eventually regained the track and, of course, this gave Gurney and Brabham, both in Brabhams, a chance to catch me up—I was in the lead. They had been picking up quite a bit of time on me every time it rained—they were running on Goodyear tyres which were showing up extremely well on the wet track. I remember Jack Brabham going past me on the back straight, going like a dingbat, and as we came to the hairpin just before the pits he went straight on—never made the corner at all and went bounding all over the grass and disappeared from sight in a cloud of spray, stones and grass. So for one brief moment he actually led the United States Grand Prix, though it was never shown in the results because he only led for half a lap and he never actually crossed the finishing line. Naturally, I was very pleased to see him go bounding off the circuit; I realised that he couldn't come to any harm just there.

As it dried out, I began to draw away again and managed to win by 12½ seconds from Dan Gurney, but what with the rain and the wind the speed of the race was quite slow—in fact the race lasted two hours and twenty minutes.

The prizegiving was quite fun with loads of champagne. They always have a Grand Prix Queen to present the prize and I managed to steal what I consider to be a well-earned kiss.

For the trip back to New York from Elmira, which is the local airport for Watkins Glen, we were taken aboard a Lear jet—the Lear Company was a great supporter of motor racing and they had placed the jet at our disposal. We flew to the Piper factory at Lockhaven, to have a look around, and then continued on from there to New York. The Lear is a beautiful little executive plane, capable of over 500 mph, and it can climb at a rate of 7,000 feet a minute. Of course, the pilot put it into a maximum rate of climb as we took off and it really was the most exhilarating feeling; he let us all have a go at the controls—it was a fascinating trip and I was able to put 'it down in my logbook as 'Pilot No 2' for a Lear jet which impressed all the pilots at Elstree airfield no end—I had taken up flying in a big way this year and spent a lot of time there. I was able to recount the whole experience round the bar and I think they were more impressed by this than with my having done the hat-trick in the US Grand Prix.

The Mexican Grand Prix which followed at the end of the month provided a tremendous shock to the establishment when Richie Ginther led from start to finish on the Honda and gave Japan their first Grand Prix victory, and Richie also. It was a pleasant surprise to see the Honda and Richie win a race.

The BRMs never went well at Mexico—I think it was the nature of the circuit—it's a bit Mickey Mouse and our cars never got round those little corners terribly quickly—and something to do with the altitude at Mexico City. This year, actually, we weren't all that much down in practice, we were a lot better than the year before; I was only 0.9 of a second slower than the pole position man, but of course that's a tremendous amount for a Grand Prix race. With a deficit of 0.9 a lap you're in a different race; you've got to be within 0.1 or 0.2 to be in the hunt. In the event, my car played up and I didn't finish the race. That concluded the year's racing, as far as the Championship was concerned. Jimmy Clark had had a tremendous season, winning at Indianapolis and also winning seven Grands Prix, a record in one season—it was undoubtedly his year. I finished second in the Championship for the third time; I had won two Grands Prix and I had scored 40 points to Jimmy Clark's 54.

On the way back from Mexico I went to Riverside to drive a McLaren sports car for John Coombs; the car was a new one that year. I was doing quite well in the race until the rear wheel fell off—McLaren tells me that this has never happened before, but I was very lucky and only just missed striking a wall as the wheel disappeared off into the distance. It was a pity, really, because I enjoyed driving the car, although we were a bit under-powered for that circuit. Going through the twisty sections between Turns 1 and 6, apparently, mine was the quickest car—so that was something. We put a lot of work in on the car and it was sad that it didn't finish.

.   .   .   .   .

The Mexican Grand Prix was the last race before the new 3-litre Formula came in. The end of the 1½-litre Formula was an event that nobody really minded too much. I don't know why it was brought in in the first place, and now the bigger sports cars were lapping a circuit quicker than the Formula 1 cars. In my opinion, Formula 1 has to be the highest form of the art and therefore they should be the cars that get round the circuit in the shortest possible time. This is exactly what the 1½-litre cars were ceasing to do.

Anyway that was that, and it meant that all the current Formula 1 cars were done for—immediately the last race had finished a lot of constructors were going to be left with equipment which was of no real use. That's what always happens when a Formula changes and that's why there is always resistance to change.

CHAPTER TWELVE

1966

The year 1966 started off well with a win in my first race, the New Zealand Grand Prix. Except for that, the Australian Grand Prix and the Indianapolis '500', that was my lot for 1966. My name was conspicuous by its absence on the results lists. From a Formula 1 point of view it was a lousy year altogether, mainly attributable to the fact that there had been the change in the Formula, and BRM were just not ready for it.

We had to start off using last year's $1\frac{1}{2}$-litre car with the engine bored out to 2 litres, whilst BRM frantically tried to get the new 3-litre H16 sorted out.

Anyway, Jackie Stewart won the Tasman Championship and the Monaco Grand Prix, so that was something for BRM, but, together with my two wins in the Tasman series, that was about it.

I went out to New Zealand for the weekend—the whole trip took a week, but I spent just a couple of days there for the race and flew straight back home again: a round the world trip for the weekend. I returned later for the Australian part of the Tasman series and spent over a month there for the four races. This time I took Bette, Jackie Stewart brought his wife Helen and Jimmy Clark brought his girlfriend Sally, so the three girls had an enjoyable month in Australia.

The Tasman series is the best time of the year to be out of England. On top of the two wins, I had a second at Warwick Farm, Sydney, a third at Sandown Park, Melbourne, and a second at Longford, Tasmania, making it two firsts, two seconds and a third in all. But of course missing the New Zealand races meant that this wasn't enough to win the Tasman Championship. Jackie, who did the lot, managed to clean up. The main reason I wasn't there for the whole season was that

I had arranged to go back to test the new H16 engine, but in fact I found it wasn't ready.

The development of the BRM H16 engine is itself an interesting story. The original thinking behind the design of the 3-litre engine was basically that it would be a good idea to utilise all the development work, expertise, knowledge and all the data which had been accumulated on the 1½-litre—if all this could be drawn on, we would start with perhaps half the development work already done.

The only way that Tony Rudd could see to achieve this was by using the H16 configuration and more or less superimpose two flat-8's, one on top of the other. In this way, all the previous work on cylinder head, piston and valve design could go slap bang into the new engine and we would end up with a 16-cylinder engine which would be of a reasonable size—the new one would be the same length as the old 1½-litre, but deeper and of course considerably heavier. We also had to have two crankshafts, and they had to be connected by means of a gear train—and in this lay the main problem.

Tony Rudd had learned something about the H16 layout from the aircraft industry—which had employed this type in the past. The trouble is that with an engine of this particular configuration you get peculiar harmonic vibrations passing between the two crankshafts and these can lead to broken valve springs and cause damage to the valves themselves, the gears and even the crankshafts. You get all sorts of problems. The firing order makes a great deal of difference—this needs different crankshafts and so we had to experiment with the various types. The other difficulty was that the engine itself was rather heavy and quite a lump. It developed the power all right, but we couldn't always keep all the power inside the engine.

. . . . . .

The first World Championship race to be run under the new 3-litre Formula 1 was at Monte Carlo. We used the 2-litre Tasman cars; I had a slipping clutch for the whole race and only managed to finish third, whilst Jackie won and gave BRM their fourth consecutive win at Monaco. We had the first H16 car out there for practice, but I decided not to use it in the race because we were not too sure of its reliability and we were still having some oil feed problems.

One of the big things about Monaco in 1966 was the way that Hollywood took over and disrupted the whole life of Monte Carlo and its environs. It made things difficult for the racing teams, too, because John Frankenheimer, who was filming *Grand Prix* for MGM, was closing the circuit at odd times and you couldn't move about the town unless you circumnavigated the whole of the road course, and that meant that all the traffic passing through Monte Carlo had to use the same road. It caused tremendous congestion. From that point of view it was a bit of a bore, but I must say that the result made it all seem worth while.

Obviously MGM wanted to make it a success, so a lot of money was going to be spent on motor racing and we were going to get a lot more people interested in the sport. From my point of view, I thought everyone carping about the hardships of having Hollywood filming a Grand Prix was either very shortsighted or a bit bitter and twisted. I was delighted to see someone taking so much interest and such pains to portray Grand Prix racing; obviously you had to grant them a certain amount of licence to provide something of box office material, but the background racing was real enough nevertheless. If the story seemed a little far-fetched from the point of view of the ordinary motoring enthusiast, we were given the opportunity to see a film in Cinerama which had some fantastic racing scenes which will probably never be repeated again. MGM spent eight million dollars on the film itself and they would not start recouping their money until they had taken 20 million dollars at the box office—they work on a percentage basis of publicity and distribution at 2.4 times the cost.

I had backed John Frankenheimer from the beginning, although for a while another film company had appeared on the scene to make a motor racing picture starring Steve McQueen—it was eventually abandoned because of McQueen's ill health. Injunctions were fairly flying around as different organisers and circuit owners became involved in signing film contracts with the two film companies. The racing drivers were divided into two camps—Stirling Moss, Jimmy Clark, Jackie Stewart, John Surtees and Sir John Whitmore elected to go with the Steve McQueen and John Sturgess team; whilst Jo Bonnier, Mike Spence, Phil Hill, Richie Ginther and myself joined John Frankenheimer.

This of course was my first appearance, and probably my last, as a film star. Naturally I only had a small part as Bob Turner, having initially balked at being called Billy Turner —I never saw myself as Billy. Frankenheimer later told me that I had just missed receiving the award for the best supporting actor. But I'm sure that the people who voted for me did it for a laugh. At the Premieres I attended in New York and London, I could never understand why, whenever I appeared, people roared with laughter.

MGM came up with mock Formula 1 cars which were, in fact, Formula 3 cars with special bodies and dummy exhausts and so on, built by Jim Russell of the Jim Russell Racing Drivers' School in Norfolk. He did a remarkably good job and from just a short distance away the cars looked very realistic. MGM's problem was that they didn't know who was going to use what cars and, whereas we weren't racing any H16 3-litre cars ourselves, here was the film company turning up with the replicas of them. When we left Monte Carlo after the race the film crew stayed on for another two weeks, thoroughly disrupting the locals.

Next came Indianapolis. I had first been asked to drive there three years before in 1963 by Mickey Thompson—he's a strange man, full of ideas, full of enthusiasm and energy—he had once come very near to beating the land speed record and in fact did beat it in one direction, but his car blew up on the return run. For Indianapolis he had a very revolutionary car, a streamlined, saucer-shaped thing with a very flat elliptical section and bodywork which enclosed the wheels; the wheels themselves were tiny with great big fat tyres—which were a new idea then. Small wheels have to turn faster, involving more stress, and Firestone were worried about the increased centrifugal force; they therefore used a pretty hard old tread compound which meant that there wasn't too much grip. When I drove it, I thought the car was diabolical—a wheel came off in practice and I clobbered the wall—so I reckoned I was wasting my time and went home without attempting to qualify.

In 1966 I was back again, driving for the wealthy young American, John Mecom Junior. Jackie Stewart was also in the team and we were to drive Lolas prepared by George Bignotti and his team of mechanics. Bignotti had been in motor racing for years and at one time worked for A. J. Foyt, a great Indianapolis exponent. My entry was a late one because it only came about after Mecom's original driver, the American Walt Hansgen, met with a serious accident practising at Le Mans and died soon afterwards. I was down to race in Europe in May and I didn't agree to do Indianapolis until the 4th of May, which was four days after the track had been opened for practice—normally everybody is there on the first day testing and practising like crazy. I couldn't go there immediately because I had to do a Formula 2 race at Zolder. The result was that I didn't arrive at Indianapolis until the Monday before the first qualification date.

The Indianapolis 500 miles race is tremendously promoted, but it's a longwinded affair and goes on and on for more or less the whole month of May. After two weeks of testing, and during the second and third weekends, they have the qualification trials. The race itself is always on May 30th, Memorial Day. They have a slightly funny way of qualifying: all the cars which qualify on the first day fill up the first rows of the starting grid; the cars which qualify on the second day might be faster than those which qualified on the first, but they don't get to go in front of them on the grid, as is customary in European racing, they just start filling up the next row of the grid. If you are the fastest on Sunday you will still be behind the slowest on Saturday, even if you are miles quicker. We had a lot to do before the first qualifying day—I had to make the car fit me, take my 'rookie' test and sort the car out for we were having all sorts of niggling little troubles. I had to qualify during the first weekend of qualification in any case, as I was racing at Monte Carlo the following weekend.

The qualification itself is quite a rigmarole and each car is allowed three attempts. You have to do four consecutive laps, declaring your attempt before you cross the start line by a hand signal; if you or your team manager isn't satisfied with the speed, either of you can abort the qualification run—as long as this is declared before you finish the four laps—but the third attempt has to be it. Once you have set up your qualification run, your place on the grid is fixed at the end of that day's qualifications and you can't improve on it in that car. But you could in another car—it's the car's qualification, not the driver's.

I had a bit of a moment during my qualification run. I was

hurtling into Turn 3 when I suddenly noticed a little black object in the road. That's funny, I thought; that wasn't there last lap. And I wondered if something had fallen off my car. It turned out to be a little sparrow sitting in the middle of the track. This distracted me slightly and I am quite sure that I was not as quick through that corner as I should have been.

Fortunately it worked out all right and I qualified fifteenth which put me on the fifth row of the grid—the grid at Indianapolis is arranged in rows of three cars.

I started the race on the outside of the fifth row—there were 33 cars in the race—and we had to complete two warming-up laps, behind the official pace car. After the third lap, the pace car pulled off into the pits, the starter waved the flag like it was alive and he was trying to shake it off, and the race was on. But somehow or other two cars touched and all hell was let loose within the closely-packed bunch of 33 cars accelerating like mad into the first corner. It set a whole holocaust going and immediately I was having to take avoiding action, weaving in and out among the flying wheels, castings, radius rods and other debris while cars were spinning like tops and crashing and banging into each other like dodgem cars.

I managed to get through this whirling mass of destruction before the gate finally closed—I and another chap who followed on my tail were the last cars to get clear of that shunt. My immediate thought was, Lord, where are the others? And so I put my foot on the throttle and went hurtling after the leaders who had got well away. They, of course, were quite unaware of what had happened, but the track was completely blocked and so the red light went on immediately and everyone slowed and came back to the pits while the mess was cleaned up. Fortunately nobody got hurt, although A. J. Foyt cut his hand on the wire fence as he clambered up into safety. It was tragic to see eleven cars knocked out within three seconds of the start.

After about an hour and a half of clearing up the wreckage and cleaning the track we re-started the race—this time I started thirteenth because the two cars alongside me had been eliminated in the accident. We had to circulate at a slow speed in Indian file under the yellow cautionary light for a while to clear all the cement dust which had been put down on the oil. Eventually this cleared and the green light gave the signal to start racing again. As I went into the first turn the car in front of me spun, and I thought: Oh God, not again. But fortunately I was able to miss him and so did everyone else. After a few laps I discovered that my Lola wasn't handling too well and I soon realised that the rollbar was too stiff. We had only managed five laps' testing after the qualification, which was enough to scrub the tyres but not enough to sort out the handling.

The track got terribly slippery that year, because so much oil was dropped. We weren't lapping at much more than 140 mph at some stages of the race. I found that my car went quicker when it had a full fuel load so that was another handling problem. Anyway, I pressed on and what with various cars dropping out, and Jimmy Clark spinning twice, I found myself winning the race. Poor Jackie Stewart had terribly bad luck when he was well in the lead and his engine broke with just a few laps to go. Lloyd Ruby, too, had the race well sewn up in the earlier stages and then he too had the bad luck to pack up. So I was very fortunate to win. It was only the second time that anyone has won Indy at the first attempt. The first time a rookie won was in 1926. Mark you, it is only fair to say that there were 'extenuating' circumstances—like a third of the field being knocked out on the first lap! But I am sure that no-one has completed so few laps of practice and won the race—you've got to have some luck sometime.

.   .   .   .   .

After Indianapolis we went back to Spa for the fastest road race in the world. We practised the H16 at Spa, but again we used the Tasman V8 in the race. I must have made a poor start, because I can remember Phil Hill in the MGM camera car—a McLaren loaded with cameras and so on—come flashing past me going down towards the first corner. After about a mile and a half comes Burnenville, a very fast 140 to 150 mph right-hander which passes between two farmhouses, and just as we got there it started to rain. One second it was dry and the next there was a wall of rain and the track was soaking. Nobody could see anything and cars spun in all directions. I remember picking my way amongst these spinning cars and getting through somehow to carry on until I got to the kink in the main Masta Straight, which is usually taken in the dry at about 150 mph. Somehow it didn't look right and I was partly expecting trouble; the next thing I knew I was spinning round like a top and going down the road backwards at a fantastic speed, trying to steer clear of everything. Eventually I came to a halt at the side of the road, with my back wheel against a straw bale and with the engine stopped. I was trying to get it started and to sort out a gear, when I looked down and saw Jackie Stewart's BRM in the ditch beside me but on the other side of some railings. Jackie was still in the car and obviously in some sort of pain; he looked terribly helpless. I leapt out of my car and rushed to see what I could do for him. The side of the car had been pushed in and had trapped Jackie. He was in quite a lot of pain because the fuel tank had split and he was soaked in petrol. The first thing I did was to turn off the switches to stop the fuel pump pumping petrol everywhere and also to make sure there were no sparks flying around. The fuel was burning Jackie, it is very strong stuff and it can take all your skin off just by chemical action.

I tried to lift Jackie out; he was pretty dazed and complained of pain in his shoulder and I then realised that I would have to take the steering wheel off before I could get him out, as it was jammed up hard against his leg. By this time Bob Bondurant, an American who was driving a privately entered BRM, had turned up—looking decidedly secondhand. 'What the blazes has happened to you?' I asked.

He said he had been upside down as well—on the other side of the road. So that made all three 2-litre BRMs out at the same place! Bob had climbed out of his car and he had come across to see what was happening.

I ran off to ask a marshal to find a toolbox—he brought one back and we undid Jackie's steering wheel, took it off and got him out. Our immediate fear of the BRM going up like a torch was now over and we took him to a small farm building nearby. I took all his clothes off because they were all smothered in the fuel.

No assistance had arrived, so I ran to the marshal's post again and telephoned from there for an ambulance; when I got back it was just arriving. The first thing the nurses did when they saw Jackie was to cover him up again with his petrol-soaked overalls, so I had a big battle with them. They seemed more concerned about their embarrassment than about Jackie's pain. They couldn't understand what I wanted and I couldn't understand what they were trying to say, but they carted him off and I leapt back into my BRM and drove back to the pits.

By then I had lost a lot of time and, as anyone who doesn't finish 90 per cent of the race distance is automatically excluded, there was no point in my continuing.

Our main concern, of course, was that Jackie was all right. He was taken to hospital and flown back to England very quickly, thanks to Louis Stanley. He was very badly bruised and the fuel had burned his skin quite a lot, the main area affected seemed to be his private parts, which was causing him some consternation. I gather they later recovered fully and are just like new! When we went to see him in hospital he had recovered from the shock—it must have been terrifying to have been sitting trapped in your motorcar, drenched in fuel, knowing that it only needed just one little spark and that would be it. There was just no way of getting him out quickly. As a result, from that day on, every BRM has a spanner attached to the steering wheel, taped on, so that if ever anyone needs to take the wheel off quickly he can.

John Surtees won the race in brilliant style and Jochen Rindt put up a tremendous performance—he spun at the same place as we did, but another 100 yards beyond the kink, and he recovered to go on and take the lead. He was only overtaken by Surtees in the closing stages of the race when the track began to dry out.

.   .   .   .

With Jackie Stewart in hospital it meant that I had lost my partner for Le Mans the next weekend, where we were to have shared a 7-litre Alan Mann Ford. The American, Dick Thompson, stood in for Jackie, but then there was a drama as he was disqualified by the organisers after an alleged incident during practice. He was reported by a marshal for dangerous driving at White House Corner; he had bumped into the rear of a Ford GT 40 driven by Bob Holquist, another American, and it spun off and overturned. No one was hurt. After a lot of drama the Ford racing chief, Leo Beebe, arranged for the Australian Brian Muir to be flown over at the eleventh hour to drive with me.

I must say that the 7-litre Ford GT Mark II was the one car I have driven at Le Mans which really gave me the feeling it was going to go on for ever. It had a fantastic engine, very understressed, which thumped along down the straight and just didn't seem to be revving. We were doing over 200 mph and I think Richie Ginther got 220 mph with a tow—I am sure that I was up to 215 mph on one or two occasions when I got a tow from some of the other cars. It just galloped along. This was the first time I felt sure I had a car which was going to finish. Little did I know!

We were quite well placed after a few hours of racing; it was now dark and I was doing about 100 mph coming out of Arnage when all of a sudden there was an almighty bang and the Ford veered all over the road. I had a good old wrestle with it and brought it to rest on the grass. I tried to drive it slowly forward, but it seemed the left-hand front wheel casting had broken and the whole front suspension had dropped onto the road, spring and all. I abandoned the car, walked back to a marshal's post and accepted the offer of a lift back to the pits.

They promptly took me to an ambulance which looked as if it had been resurrected from the 1914–18 war. I got onto the bed affair in the back and I had a most hair-raising drive back to the pits. It went across country down the back lanes and the ride was so rough that I was thankful that I had had nothing wrong with me.

The race was won by the Ford of Bruce McLaren and Chris Amon. Actually, the car of Denny Hulme and Ken Miles would have won but it tried to stage a dead-heat, and the organisers disallowed this. As the McLaren-Amon Ford had been slower in practice and had therefore started behind the Hulme-Miles car in the line-up, it had covered a few yards more distance in the twenty-four hours and so was declared the winner. So it didn't pay to be fastest in practice and philanthropic at the finish.

It was the eleventh time I had been to Le Mans, although I hadn't raced there for the first two years, 1956 and 1957. I raced a Lotus in 1958 and 1959, Porsche in 1960, Ferrari in 1961, Aston Martin in 1962, Rover-BRM in 1963, Ferrari again in 1964 (when I came second), Rover-BRM again in 1965 and the Ford in 1966. This was, in fact, the last time I raced at Le Mans—although I wasn't to know it at the time.

At Le Mans John Surtees walked out of the Ferrari team after a row with the team manager, Eugenio Dragoni. It was a bit of a shock to everyone to see him go. It looked as though he was in line for winning the World Championship for Ferrari that year. He signed up to drive for Cooper-Maserati in the French Grand Prix, but there were some problems over contracts. Surtees was signed up with Shell and the Cooper team was on BP; Shell actually released him to drive the car which was very considerate of them—they didn't want to stop him getting into a Formula 1 team, so they very kindly agreed to release him from his Formula 1 contract so long as he used Shell in his sports cars.

It was back to the 3-litres again for the French Grand Prix at Reims. Jackie was still not fit. We had the BRM H16 out and, boy, was that impressive! The thing came down the straight past the pits at a fantastic speed—I've never been so fast at Reims before. The car was so obviously faster than anything else in a straight line that everybody standing in the pits could see that I was visibly faster and it really was a superb feeling. But we weren't sure of its reliability and the handling wasn't fully sorted, although I could almost take that corner after the pits flat out.

We didn't race the H16, so I drove a 2-litre. This really was going like a bomb in the race and I got a fantastic tow from Mike Parkes, who was having his first Grand Prix drive. I only had a 2-litre and he had a 3-litre Ferrari, but we were having a bit of a dice for third place—ahead Bandini was way out in front with Brabham up with him. I was getting a terrific tow down the straight and the engine was over-revving by about 600 rpm—it should only go to 10,000 but it was going to 10,600 in top gear. I thought that while I was there I might as well have a go and I tucked myself up his exhaust pipes, but eventually the inevitable happened and the camshaft broke. Up front Bandini went out with a broken throttle cable and Jack went on to win with Parkes second. It was Jack's first win since 1960 so he had been a long time out in the wilderness; it was a great win for him.

Coinciding with the Formula 1 race at Reims that year was the Formula 2 event, which was to be held on Saturday, the day before the French Grand Prix. I was racing a Matra-BRM for John Coombs, but it just didn't seem to have the power of the Cosworth engine that most people were using, and I wasn't featuring too well. During practice I was coming down the straight to Thillois, the corner before the pits, when all of a sudden there was an almighty explosion and the engine blew up. I started to brake and pull off to the side of the road and at this moment there was a searing pain around the cheeks of my bottom. I leapt into the air as best I could—we are pretty well encased in those cars—and, of course, I couldn't get away from the seat too much because the steering wheel was in the way. Apparently when the engine burst, all the oil had come out (it was extremely hot, well over the boiling point of water) and as I braked so the oil had run forward on the undertray and encircled my backside—I was sitting on the undertray as there wasn't room for me and the seat.

I eventually managed to get the car stopped and I leapt out of it and started dancing round on the grass at Thillois trying to pull my pants and overalls away from my bottom, which presented a most amusing spectacle for the crowd. They couldn't possibly imagine what had happened to cause a driver to suddenly pull up in the middle of the green, leap out and start dancing round like a dervish clutching his backside. I suffered some rather nasty burns and I bear the scars today. Unfortunately, the wound got worse because the very next week we went to Rouen for another Formula 2 race and when I arrived I went up to my hotel room and had a bath. The wound was well and truly open by then and I must have picked up an infection from the water, because during dinner that night I got the most terrible itching on my backside— most embarrassing! The wound had become infected and this delayed the healing for some time.

I had a similar experience with another open cut and a bath in Spain—I picked up another infection which turned into a fever and I became very ill with blood poisoning. In this case it was even more stupid because the reason for the cut was my attendance at Cliff Davis's annual staff party. Cliff is an ex-racing driver and he more or less retired from racing at around the time I was just starting and he's now in the motor business. Well, as his staff consists of about four people and about four hundred turn up for the staff party, you can see it's a bit of a joke. It's always a stag do and I think probably the most riotous stag function that I ever get to attend, but it's always very amusing and something to which everybody looks forward. In fact, I did myself more damage at this particular staff party at the Connaught Rooms than I'd ever done in motor racing until 1969.

Cliff, by popular request, had invited a stripper and I decided to join her during her act. As I was sitting at the top table and she was at the far end of the room, it meant running along the table to reach her. Well, unfortunately, as I was tripping daintily between the glasses—the dinner was over, of course—one of the tables collapsed and I went with it. I fell onto one of the wine glasses, the tulip broke off and the stem went straight into my leg, just below the knee. Fortunately, I was in my underpants at the time or else I would have ruined my trousers.

When I stood up amidst all the broken glass and crockery I noticed that there was a wine glass bottom which seemed to be stuck to the top of my shinbone, so I went to pick it off, thinking it was just stuck there, and of course it was rock solid. So I gave it a bit of a tug and pulled out two inches of wine glass stem from my leg; the moment I did that, blood spurted out all over the place so we got a table napkin to staunch the flow. By then there was a hell of a commotion and people were shouting out for doctors, then the manager turned up and everyone was telling him to go away, or words to that effect. Then I decided I'd better go to the hospital and get it stitched up as I seemed to be ruining the party. So I walked out with my trousers over my arm and hailed a taxi to take me to the Charing Cross Hospital.

It was very difficult to explain in fact how I'd come to be in this state and when two nurses asked me how I had done it I said: 'Well, there was this girl, see!'—and I tried to explain the story to them and of course they didn't believe me. 'No, sir,' they said, 'not at the Connaught Rooms,'—and they just wouldn't believe the story at all.

Unfortunately, somebody tipped the Press off—this is normally an occasion when one is able to whoop it up with one's friends without getting reported to the Press: now some rotten blighter at the function had got on to the Press, told them what had happened and that I was now at the Charing Cross Hospital. We had no sooner arrived than they were clamouring around outside the hospital, so Colin Chapman and a few of the lads who'd come along with me got one of the chaps—John Coombs I think it was—and they put a coat over his head, made him limp and took him out of the hospital saying: 'Okay Graham, this way to the car.'

Immediately all the photographers were taking a photográph of Coombs with a coat over his head as he was rushed away in the car followed hotly by the Press. They then proceeded on a wild goose chase all over London. But the reporters twigged it eventually and they returned to the hospital. When I came out, there they were waiting and I made one great big bound into the car with my good leg, with flashlights flashing and cries of 'Hold it!' Fortunately I had an automatic Zephyr at the time, which somebody had brought round to the hospital for me, so I was able to drive home with my good right leg. Lo and behold, when I got home, there was another pressman with a camera waiting in the driveway; he'd been pestering my wife and he wouldn't let me get out of the car without taking a picture. I tried waiting in the car and asking him to go away, but he was very determined and eventually took a picture of my foot as I leapt into the shelter of my own house. On the front page of the *Daily Express* the next day was a photograph of my foot entitled 'The Foot' and a rather lurid story which sounded dreadful in the cold light of day.

As regards the race at Rouen, the only thing I remember was having a big bust-up with John Coombs, my entrant, in the pits. I said that I wanted an adjustment made to the car and he disagreed strongly; then, all of a sudden, his heart started to go at about 200 revs per minute and he came all over queer and was literally jumping up and down. I took him over to the First Aid tent, which consisted of an old army tent with a stretcher and a couple of pretty nurses. You could see his heart leaping about inside his chest as he lay on the stretcher and his whole body was dancing up and down.

Practice had just started, so I left John in the care of these people and apparently the doctor gave him an injection, but nobody seemed to know quite what to do. About an hour later the spasm stopped as quickly as it had started. When he got back to England, he consulted one of the experts who said: 'Oh yes, the old mechanism must have tripped,' and went on to tell him that it was probably due to the fact that he had got a bit irate with me. So I told John to watch his step in future and treat me with a bit of respect; to try not to get annoyed, because otherwise his old ticker was going to play up.

.   .   .   .   .

The British Grand Prix was at Brands Hatch again and it certainly looked as though it was going to be Jack Brabham's year—he was already leading on points when he arrived. He furthered his stake to the claim on the title with an untroubled win in the race itself. Jimmy Clark and myself were at a disadvantage in that we had 2-litre engines, Clark in a Lotus Climax and myself in the 2-litre BRM.

We had a rare old ding-dong for about half the race, until Clark had to stop at the pits to top up a brake cylinder and I finished third behind Denny Hulme.

A week later Brabham cleaned up at Zandvoort, too, although he was pressed very hard by Jimmy. Clark did in fact overtake him and drew out a small lead, but then he had to call in to the pits for water and eventually came third. I finished a lonely second and Jackie Stewart came fourth, so BRM managed to get second and fourth places. Jack was 40 at this time and some wag had sent him a long beard and a walking stick, so he walked to the start line dressed in this gear, much to everyone's amusement. It is out of character for Jack to be flamboyant and I was pleasantly surprised.

The German Grand Prix at Nurburgring was another wet race and it's miserable when it's wet there. The surface changes are so numerous—they have been patching it up since it was first made in 1927—and it now has such a variety of surfaces that you need to have a computer brain to remember which bits are slippery and which bits are not quite so slippery in the wet. Jack won it and had a tussle with Surtees, who really pushed him. Surtees always goes well at the Ring and had a good drive in an uncompetitive car—the Cooper-Maserati seemed to go better in the wet; it might have been something to do with their weight, they were rather heavy cars. I finished fourth after a dice with Clark, Gurney, Hulme and Stewart. That win clinched the title for Jack—he became World Champion for the third time, this year in a car of his own manufacture, which was a tremendous achievement.

.   .   .   .   .

A rather sad occasion in August was the announcement that Goodwood would never again be used as a race track. It was a lovely circuit; I think the Easter Monday meeting was always one of the best, with a great atmosphere and in such a beautiful setting. I had some good scraps there and, with its long drifting corners, it has given me a lot of pleasure over the years. Goodwood is still open for testing but there is no more motor racing. The closure was something to do with taking down a lot of advertising which could be seen from the road and the owner, the Duke of Richmond and Gordon, was worried after reading alarming reports that the new 3-litre cars would be taking off at high speeds on every straight.

We went to Monza for the Italian Grand Prix with a bit of a problem, for Tony Rudd had been instructed not to take the 2-litre BRM. We had to run the 3-litre H16 and I wasn't too happy about this as I didn't think they were too reliable. Mine had a new eight-throw crankshaft giving a different firing order which was intended to reduce the torsional vibration problems inherent in the original flat-crank unit. Although the first engine actually felt smoother, they used to set up vibrations which went right through the gearchange and broke the camshaft and crankshaft. We also had different clutches.

I had trouble with my H16 on the first day of practice so we went along to the motor museum at Monza and managed to extract a conveniently placed race-prepared 2-litre BRM which just happened to be there. As we had had instructions to run the 3-litres, it was a tremendous coincidence that this fully-equipped 2-litre BRM happened to be in the museum just at the time we needed it. . . . So we whipped it out and went practising, but then this gave trouble so I was forced to run with the 3-litre anyway! And when the race started the engine blew up at the first corner in the most spectacular fashion, in the middle of the pack, causing everyone a lot of concern.

We went to the Gold Cup at Oulton Park with the 3-litre cars, but we weren't expecting to make much of a showing as they were considered to be too heavy for that circuit—we were expecting Jack Brabham and Denny Hulme to walk away with it. At the beginning of the race there was a tremendous battle with Hulme, Brabham, Stewart and myself. I was leading the race in front of Jack when the engine blew up—it dissolved into a cloud of smoke and steam and that was that. We had not expected the BRM to go quite as well as it did and so it was quite encouraging, but it was no use if it was going to blow up.

We went off to the American Grand Prix with not too much hope, but a most peculiar thing happened there—Jimmy Clark

actually won the race with his Lotus using one of our BRM
3-litre engines. In fact, it was our spare, as Jimmy's had blown
up in practice; BRM were delighted to see an engine of theirs
winning, whilst Stewart and I weren't too happy about the
fact that it could win in another car but not in ours! In the
race I had engine problems and gearbox trouble, whilst in
practice I'd had a lot of ignition problems so we were never
really much of a threat.

In between the American and Mexican Grands Prix there
was a race for USAC Formula* cars in Japan at Mount Fuji.
This is a fabulous circuit about 90 miles outside Tokyo and
below Mount Fuji, which is to my mind one of the most wonderful sights in the world. I've never seen such a perfect-looking
mountain in my life and it makes a fabulous background for
the racetrack. They had shipped over 20 cars from America
and Jackie Stewart and I were driving for John Mecom again
in the same cars that we used at Indy. We were met by a chap
from Rolls-Royce who had laid on a chauffeur-driven car, so
we arrived everywhere in style, but something went wrong with
our booking arrangements and we kept finding ourselves in
different hotels. The Japanese have this peculiar custom of
never actually saying 'No' to anyone; they feel it's impolite
and they always say 'Yes' regardless—and then work like crazy
to fulfil their promises. We kept being moved from one hotel
to another all over the countryside—we stayed in the most
peculiar places, way out of town, and often it seemed we were
the only Westerners the locals had ever seen.

Although I travel a lot and go to many foreign countries,
there's nothing like the East to give you the impression that
you're in a foreign country— everyone looks so different that
you know that you are the foreigner, whereas in Europe everyone looks roughly the same and you think that they are the
foreigners. There's all the business of taking off your shoes and
padding about in little slippers and, as for eating utensils,
you're never given anything but chopsticks, which are most
awkward initially, but we soon got the hang of them.

One of the most enlightening experiences, which struck me
as being very civilised and a lot of fun, was the public bathing
habit. I was looked after by a beautiful little Japanese girl
dressed in bra and panties—rather like a swimming costume

*United States Automobile Club Formula for Indianapolis cars.

but it looked like underwear to me—who, completely un-
abashed, undressed me and proceeded to give me a lovely
bath, massaged me, dried me, folded and unfolded my clothes
and then dressed me again. I must say that I thoroughly enjoyed being fussed over. Well, of course, we couldn't keep out
of the damn baths; I've never been so clean in my life!

The race itself was quite good as I nearly won it; Stewart
actually won but I'd been having a battle with him and then
retired suffering from engine trouble with five out of the eighty
laps to go.

Mexico produced a surprise win for John Surtees in his
Cooper-Maserati—this race often produces odd results, witness
Richie Ginther's win for Honda the previous year, having had
a very poor season up until Mexico. I was plagued with all
sorts of electrical misfirings during practice and in the race
I had problems with the engine. I decided to retire before I
blew it up in a big way so all in all it was a disappointing Formula
1 season.

It never occurred to me to move from BRM until Henry
Taylor, the Ford Competitions Manager, came and asked me
whether I would ever think of returning to Lotus. That was
towards the end of 1966 and so it all happened in a bit of a rush.
Apparently he'd spoken to Colin Chapman, and Colin had
said: 'Oh no, Graham will never leave BRM. . . .'

Obviously Ford wanted to safeguard their £10,000 invest-
ment in a Ford engine so they had to have two drivers. If
Jimmy Clark caught a cold, or something stupid like that, or
had an accident, or if the cars kept breaking down, the Championship could be lost. So they wanted a second string to their
bow. Also, if they had two top-rank drivers, obviously no other
team could have them and this would reduce their opposition—
so it had a two-fold benefit.

I started to talk to BRM and I told them that I'd had an
alternative offer and that I must consider it, but that I wouldn't
dream of moving if things were going to improve. I then suggested that there were a number of changes that should be
made to make BRM a winning proposition again and, obviously, if they could give me concrete assurances that these
would be carried out then I would not leave. I remember at
the time we were getting far too interested in trying to make
BRM pay by taking on a lot of commercial work. Now, that's

all very well, but in trying to make it pay, BRM was not winning races and was therefore losing a lot of support, financial support. Their policy was working in reverse. The effort to get the commercial side going detracted from the racing effort. It might make a few bob initially but it would cost a lot of money in the long run by their not having a successful racing team—and if you want to go in for motor racing you've got to go in for success; you've got to be single-minded and have one purpose.

Well, I wanted to cut out the commercial side and just go motor racing to win. Anyway, I didn't get these assurances and eventually there came a deadline when I would have to give Colin a decision. On that day I had breakfast with Sir Alfred Owen at his club in London and I told him that by the end of the day I would give him and Chapman my decision.

By the end of the day I had decided to join Colin. At the time I thought it was a hell of a gamble; I was stepping out of a number one position with a team which I had been with for several years straight into what had been the enemy camp, where they already had an established number one, who'd been there for several years and who, quite rightly, would expect to be given preferential treatment. Anyway, it was agreed that I would be a joint number one driver with Jimmy and in fact it worked out very well. We went on to have a wonderful year and there were never any problems at all as far as I was concerned. I was treated very fairly and although it always seemed to be my car that was breaking down, there was nothing to suggest that Jimmy was getting better treatment than myself. I had no complaints at all and we got on famously; I feel, obviously, that the move has paid off, but at the time a lot of people thought I'd gone out of my tiny mind.

There was another reason, less obvious, for leaving BRM; I had been with them for seven years and I felt that I was becoming part of the scenery. People were far too used to me and I was becoming less effective—they were becoming immune to my constant proddings. But that was bound to happen.

Everyone at BRM understood my problem; no-one was bitter, we parted on the best of terms and they wished me luck for the future. Naturally, I did feel rotten about leaving and that's what made it a very hard decision.

CHAPTER THIRTEEN

1967

Having joined Jimmy Clark in Team Lotus, my first race was the South African Grand Prix on January 2nd, 1967, at Kyalami. It was rather ironic that for my first race in the Lotus it was powered by a BRM engine—my old friend the H16. It was about the only engine we had at that time, as the new Ford for which we were hoping had not arrived. So we were back to using the same BRM engine that Jimmy had used in the car to win the American Grand Prix; in fact, I had that actual chassis in the race and he had a later one.

I'm afraid it wasn't to be much of a race for either of us. During practice we were beset with all sorts of silly little problems like leaking fuel tanks, a diaphragm in the injection unit breaking, and the throttle sticking open. Altogether we didn't get too much practice: in two days I managed eight laps one day and five the next, and on the first day I didn't get any practice at all; so during the whole three days I only did thirteen laps. In the race I wasn't doing too badly—naturally, I was well down on the grid—until I put a wheel up on one of the sloping kerbs marking the corners and bent the front wishbone. This caused the car to become a bit lower in the front and sink down a bit on one side. Consequently, when I put the brakes on, the oil pipe which passed under the car touched the ground and eventually it wore a hole in the pipe. The oil came pouring out onto the back wheels, and I spun off at one of the corners, on my own oil, into a bit of a dip and disappeared from view. I selected first gear and climbed back onto the road again rather like a trials car and drove slowly back to the pits, feeling slightly ridiculous. We could see what had happened to the wishbone and the oil pipe only too clearly, so I had to retire from the race. A rather disappointing start to my first race with Lotus.

Pedro Rodriguez eventually won the race in a Cooper-Maserati—the second win in a row for Coopers (they had won the Mexican Grand Prix at the end of 1966) after several lean years. The Cooper team didn't know whether they were standing on their heads or their heels—things were turning out rosy for them after a rather disappointing few years.

Johnny Love was very unlucky not to win this race. He is a Rhodesian and so naturally he was very popular with the local crowd in South Africa, as he was a sort of David among the Goliaths. He was leading the race right up until the very end when he had to come in for fuel—his car just didn't carry enough for the race and so the poor fellow was soldiering round in the lead knowing that he was going to have to make a pit stop. It must have been the most terrible feeling knowing that he was going to have to give up the lead. He lost the South African Prix for the sake of a couple of gallons in the tank. It was tragic.

My next race for Team Lotus was to be in Australia; I persuaded Colin Chapman to let me go out there with a Formula 2 car just for the one race. I felt fairly strongly about sitting back at home twiddling my thumbs during January and February while all the other drivers were racing in the Tasman Series. We got pretty good starting money and I was able to go out for Warwick Farm with a new Lotus Cosworth 1.6-litre FVA Formula 2 car. It put up quite a creditable performance behind Jackie Stewart and Jimmy Clark—Stewart had a 2.2-litre BRM and Jimmy had a 2-litre Climax. I had a good race until it eventually broke down: unfortunately the crown wheel and pinion failed whilst I was in third place. It was the first time the engine had ever run in a race so it was a pretty auspicious debut, a pretty good indication of the car's potential. But it was a pity that we were not able to finish. I wasn't going to do any more races out there, so that was that, as far as I was concerned, and I came back home to test the new Formula 1 car—we hoped that this was going to be ready, but unfortunately it wasn't.

I was entered to race on Good Friday at Snetterton in our Formula 2 car and then I was due to race the same car in the Wills Trophy at Silverstone on Easter Monday, which meant that we had to practise at Silverstone on the Saturday. We all raced at Snetterton on Good Friday and then rushed to

Silverstone to practise on the following day. I had a fantastic
race at Snetterton, fought between Jochen Rindt and myself
—he eventually won by inches.

I remember the race particularly well because it was only
the second time out with the Formula 2 car—the first, of course,
had been Warwick Farm—and this time we were up against a
whole field of Formula 2 cars. The car still needed a bit of
sorting out; we were not exactly sure how to run it and we were
still trying to find suitable tyres. We ended up with some rather
large Firestones which were in fact a little bit too large because
they rather slowed the car down on the straights. In the heat
I had finished fifth after being in the lead; then I made just
one small adjustment to the rear rollbar for the final and it
certainly paid off. For the first three laps I was in seventh place,
and then I began to carve my way through the field. Rindt
seemed to be quite a long way out in front and I had quite a
few people to pass—Bruce McLaren, Alan Rees, and I then
passed Jack Brabham—he is always a difficult customer. That
put me into third place, closing on Denny Hulme whom I
passed on the tenth lap. I was now behind Rindt and we
began to have a tremendous battle for the rest of the twenty-
five laps.

On the twenty-seventh lap I managed to squeeze through and
pulled out a couple of lengths. On lap 34 I lost it again to
Rindt, who was quite a bit quicker down the straight—I just
couldn't hold on to him. Our rather large tyres gave me good
roadholding and the car was first class on corners, but I just
could not hold him down the straight. If I came out of the
corner in front, he was able to use my tow and slip by me;
but if he came out in front, I wasn't able to pass him—even
though I might have got out of the corners just a little bit
quicker. My car was certainly handling better than his and
it was a tremendous race.

I tried to work out how I was going to win. It was vital that
somehow or other I must get into the Esses first—between the
hairpin and the Esses Rindt could pass me but I couldn't pass
him. There was just no way unless Rindt made a mistake. But
naturally, being an optimist, I was hoping that somehow or
other I might be able to manage it. It wasn't to be. With two
laps to go I was three cars' lengths in front; with one lap to
go it was two lengths; and on the last lap Rindt came up

beside me under braking with two wheels on the dirt going into the Esses and that was it. I could not beat him from there to the finish because it was almost follow-my-leader.

It was a fabulous race and one that I thoroughly enjoyed; we both had a lovely time. And so did the crowd. We had equalled Jackie Stewart's lap time in the first heat—an average of 128.2 mph—so all three of us held a new lap record for the circuit.

The Easter Monday race at Silverstone was run in two heats and in the first heat both my inner rear lower wishbone pick-up points on the chassis broke loose—leaving the whole rear suspension of the car swinging in the breeze. All this promoted a very peculiar oversteering effect on the corners and eventually I came into the pits. On inspecting the damage, the mechanics put the car away in the transporter, but I felt we ought to have a go at repairing it for the second heat.

The mechanics all set to and with a bit of hacking and slashing, tons of heat and welding rod, they managed to get the car on the line again for the second heat. It was a bit of a lash-up, but I felt that we ought to make a show, even if we couldn't be placed. We could easily have retired the car but it was one of those occasions when everybody feels that they want to make a bit of an effort and get into the second heat if they can. The mechanics certainly knuckled down to it and joined in with gusto. And they managed it just in time, which was a fantastic effort on their part.

It certainly paid off, because although I had to start on the back of the grid I managed to work my way up into second place; I had a tremendous scrap. I managed to climb up to fourth place and ahead of me I could see Rees and Surtees having a bit of a go—Rees in a Brabham and Surtees in a Lola. I got up to them and I managed to pass both of them under braking for Stowe. It was a delightful experience to take two cars in one fell swoop. That meant I was up in second spot behind Rindt, but Surtees wasn't going to let me get away with it and we had a fantastic dice for second place.

Rindt was too far in front and I was unable to catch him. I wasn't helped by the fact that Surtees hung on to me and I wasn't able to lose him. It looked very much as though he might even get by me into second place. But I managed to pip him by a point of a second.

Everyone was delighted; the mechanics and Colin particularly. Rindt and myself had set up joint fastest lap which was a new lap record of 1 minute 29.2 seconds, which is 118.13 mph —quite quick for a 1600 cc car.

Snetterton and Silverstone were both great races—speaking for myself of course! Little did we know that this was going to be the last year that we would see a reasonable number of Formula 2 races staged in this country. It seems that the organisers somehow haven't taken to Formula 2. One rather suspects it might have been the expense of putting the races on—because staging a Formula 2 race is an expensive business. All the stars are there, the teams are well supported and the starting money is quite substantial. However, there is no doubt that—as was shown at the Easter meeting at Thruxton in 1969—this is where the real racing is. Formula 2 does provide a very good spectacle and it is the mainstay of motor racing on the Continent.

We all missed Jimmy Clark in these races, but he was at this time setting up residence abroad and he was not competing in any English races. It was a bit of a loss to Lotus and also to the public, but he joined up with me for the Continental races.

I like these sort of pipe-openers in England before the Championship Series and of course they do give all the enthusiasts in this country a very good indication of Formula 1 racing before the season starts; they really do whet the appetite. I feel very strongly that they should continue to be held and that they should not have the dates pinched by other races somewhere else in the world. The problem is that the racing calendar is overcrowded and some organisers cannot get dates for their races; with more circuits being built, the situation is worsening.

We would very often take the children with us to the British races, especially to Silverstone, because the girls always had the Doghouse Club caravan there. This club is properly known as the Women's Motor Racing Associates' Club and is for the wives, girl-friends, etc. of anyone connected with motor racing. They do a lot of charity work and run a splendid hospitality service at most of the larger meetings in England. The circuit owners have cooperated and very generously provided club houses at their circuits. I remember on one occasion Bette sent Brigitte—she was then about four—off to the race office to collect some result sheets and lap charts; off she toddled, arrived eventually at the race office and put in a request for these documents. The officials, of course, wanted to know who they were for and who she might be: 'They're for my daddy,' she told them and was then asked who he was. 'Well, they call him Graham Hill,' she replied.

It must be a bit strange for a child to hear people constantly talking about her father as 'Graham Hill' and I don't think they really know what it's all about. But Brigitte, in particular, if I am signing autographs will come and stand very close to me, more or less staking her claim. You can almost see their tiny minds working it out. After one signing session, Damon turned round to Bette and asked, 'Mummy, who can I ask for an autograph?'—he wanted someone else's; Daddy's was a bit too commonplace.

It has always been our greatest concern that the adulation and publicity does not spoil the children so that they get cocky about it and I don't think I have ever seen any signs of this. I gather that Damon hardly ever mentions me at school! But it isn't always easy. I remember coming home once and I had a silver cup in the back of the car, so Damon asked me what it was for. 'I managed to win a race at the week-end,' I told him. You should have seen the delight on his face and it really gave me a lot of pleasure. He got the cup out and showed it to the children with whom he'd been playing and he was obviously extremely proud.

.   .   .   .   .

For the Monaco Grand Prix it was still the 2-litre BRM-engined car that I had used at Silverstone. I broke second gear in practice on the rather small Hewland gearbox that we had attached to the back of the BRM engine and we didn't have too many spares. The one gear we wanted was not amongst them. Anyway, Colin Chapman and I went rushing round the town looking for Bob Anderson who had a private motor with the same sort of gearbox. We managed to borrow some bits from him to put in our gearbox, but the box was obviously going to be in some sort of strife because Monte Carlo is very tough on the transmission. I had to drive with this in mind.

The car wasn't quite competitive enough and I was in the fourth row of the grid—probably the furthest back I had ever been since the first time I ever drove there—or rather, since the second time as well, when I'd driven for Lotus at Monte Carlo in 1958 and 1959.

As normally happens at Monte Carlo, a lot of people dropped out and then the race was marred by the fatal accident to Lorenzo Bandini. He has always done well at Monte Carlo and the crash was one of the most terrible sights I think I have ever witnessed on a racing circuit. I could see the car burning and I couldn't tell whether the driver was out of it or not. It was horrible and we had to drive on through all the smoke and foam that was gathering on the circuit. Really I think it was one of the most sickening sights I have ever seen in my life.

As I had feared, my car was indeed in all sorts of strife: the clutch was slipping and the chassis was broken. I managed to drag it home to the finish, but by then the suspension was hanging off on one side and it was a very, very tired motor car. I was extremely satisfied to have brought it home in second place, and so was Colin; he was delighted to have his car finish, as Lotus had never really had much luck at Monte Carlo. We took the car home in a very sorry state, but it had done a lot of work and seen a lot of races. One could forgive it for beginning to give up the ghost on this very tough circuit.

I went back to test the new Formula 1 car and though we weren't able to get in a lot of testing, we were at least able to give it a run at Snetterton. It was the first time that the Formula 1 Ford-Cosworth engine had actually run in a car. It was the most magnificent looking engine—beautifully designed; it really looked like a piece of modern sculpture. I was the first person to drive it so I was tickled pink to be sitting in front of this very modern Grand Prix engine—a V8 developing 400 hp. And that was exactly what it felt like; it really had some squirt, compared to the Formula 1 cars that I had been driving. Very impressive.

We weren't able to do many laps as there was quite a bit of sorting out to be done on the car before it went to Zandvoort, and of course we were busy building a second car—we wanted two cars for the Dutch Grand Prix. Jimmy couldn't drive his car as he could not come across to England before practice started for the Dutch Grand Prix. The first time his car actually moved under its own steam was at Zandvoort.

In practice for the Dutch Grand Prix I managed to get pole

position with a time that was 4.2 seconds faster than the lap record, which really gave an indication of the potential of this car. Dan Gurney was next in an Eagle-Weslake with Jackie Stewart a second slower; Jack Brabham was one second slower in his Repco-Brabham. The two Cooper-Maseratis, driven by Rodriguez and Rindt, surprisingly enough were on the second row of the grid.

Zandvoort is always interesting because you can see so much of the circuit at the back of the pits and also because it's the sort of circuit where times are always very close. It is extremely difficult to draw out much of a lead on anyone else.

I had a tremendous battle during practice to get pole position and for the spectators and crews alike practice is sometimes as good as the race. On this occasion Dan went out and set up a quicker time and then I would go out and beat it. Then Dan would go out again and so on. Eventually, Dan settled for a time of 1 minute 25.1 seconds which he felt would put Team Lotus in their place. I got back in my car and went straight out and equalled this, doing two or three laps at about the same speed; on my last lap, which was also the last lap of practice, I did a 1 minute 24.6 seconds—which set everybody talking. It was a real bit of gamesmanship of course and also a very exciting finish to an exciting practice session.

I shot into the lead from the drop of the flag and led for the first ten laps of the race. And then the engine just suddenly quit coming into the straight; I was just able to coast into the pits. Apparently what had happened was that one of the gears in the gear train to the camshaft had broken and the engine came to a rather expensive stop. Naturally it was disappointing, but from the team's point of view it didn't really matter because Jimmy managed to come through the field beautifully and won the race—the first time out with a new car and a new engine, repeating his own and Colin's earlier success at Zandvoort with the Mark 33, the first monocoque car. Keith Duckworth deserved tremendous praise for producing an engine that could vanquish the opposition so masterfully and for designing such a beautiful-looking engine. It really was a sight for sore eyes— a joy to behold: so simple, which is the essence of good design. And Colin had been equally successful in coupling the engine to his new car. All in all it was a very successful debut. Ford of course merit the highest praise for backing this, their project to the hilt. Grand Prix motor-racing owes a lot to the initiative and enterprise of the English Ford motor company.

When I broke down, I could remember switching the engine off very very quickly as soon as I felt something go; I free-wheeled into the pits and climbed out of the car. Then some-body started talking to me about an electronic cut-out and I suddenly had the most horrifying thought—perhaps the cut-out had cut in at the rev limit, which was 9,000, and I had been a bit too hasty in getting the engine switched off. I had this horrible sinking feeling that I had stopped for no reason at all other than because I had reached the ignition cut-out.

However, fortunately or unfortunately, that wasn't the case and my fears were dispelled when they discovered that the camshaft wasn't turning round.

.   .   .   .   .

The 1967 Indy was an absolute disaster; we had the most fantastic drama. We were hoping that year to have BRM H16 engines running on alcohol and yielding over 600 hp, but they did not materialise, so we modified the cars to accept the Ford engine—the stock Ford engine that had been used the year before. I had won the race in 1966 with that same engine, but this was a bit of a cobbled effort and we never got the car fully sorted. We were in all sorts of strife.

Jimmy eventually qualified on the first week-end, but I had a real cliff-hanging drama trying to qualify on the last week-end. Here was the previous year's winner struggling to qualify for this year's race. The mechanics were working day and night on the car. On the Saturday morning of final qualification we were allowed half an hour's practice and I was just gently running the car round when the engine blew up, so that was that. I wasn't able to qualify on the Saturday.

We worked over night to get another engine into the car —one that we had borrowed from A. J. Foyt—and I remember sitting in line on the Sunday morning waiting to qualify—and, when my turn came, water suddenly spurted out of the radiator. So we had to loose our place, mend the radiator and go to the end of the queue. After all the strife and drama I managed to qualify towards the end of the afternoon at 163.317 mph which, although it wasn't the slowest in the field, meant that I was number 31 out of a field of 33. Jochen Rindt and myself occupied the last row of the grid.

There is such a lot of ballyhoo at Indianapolis before the start of the race—they get cracking early in the morning. The race starts at 11 o'clock and from eight on we had been having bands, and massed bands, and majorettes, and drumettes, and usherettes with scarcely anything on, marching all round the track twirling their batons, and millions of balloons being released, and personalities, film stars, race-men and rocket-men, all being introduced. It really is a tremendous promotion.

I kept well out of sight on race morning; I got up pretty late, about nine, and I borrowed a motor cycle to ride to the track from the motel. At that time everybody is inside. The quarter of a million people who are going to the track are already there and so I had quite a nice free run in and quietly made my way to our garage—which of course was empty as the cars had been out on the track since crack of dawn. I sat down and had a little think before the start of the race. Then I though I'd better go to the lavatory, so by the time I was walking down the pit road everyone was in their cars and John Hulman, the owner of Indianapolis, had already said the time-honoured words: 'Gentlemen, start your motors.'

Eventually, I reached the end of the line, a long way down the pit road, got into my car and the field started to move off— so I was really a bit late. The thing that properly spoilt it was that the starter shaft broke—all the engines have to be started on an external starter and you just push it into the back of the gear box—it spins the engine round and starts it. It is worked off a couple of batteries in a portable carrier.

Well, the shaft broke, so thirty-two cars set off on the two opening laps, the parade lap and the genuine warming-up lap, and one car was left at the end of the line all on its own— mine. Naturally, with everyone trying to find another starter, there was a certain amount of confusion. Then an official suddenly spotted that there was still one car on the track and another thirty-two cars and a pace car were about to descend on him very shortly from the other side of the track to start the warming-up lap.

There was fantastic excitement as my car was pushed back into the pit road and, what with mechanics trying to start it and officials trying to push it, there was rather a confused scene.

Anyway, we got it going just as the field came roaring past behind the pace car, so I set off down the pit road as they were coming past. As the main phalanx of cars came thundering down the track to the applause of a quarter of a million people, there was one lone car going down the pit road. As I left the pits, I managed to fall into line, but as the pace quickened, I thought: That's funny, I can't keep up.

There was something wrong with the engine and it just wouldn't go. It wasn't long before I was lapped. The whole thing was frightfully embarrassing, tooling along there on my own with thirty-two cars disappearing into the distance in a swirl of dust and leaves. Fortunately for me, it started to rain; the race was stopped immediately and we all pulled into the pits. But you are not allowed to work on the cars and we were dead worried as we wanted to sort the engine out.

Eventually it became obvious that the rain had set in for the day and the cars were pushed away; everybody was given a rain check and told to come back the next day. The cars were all impounded and we were not allowed to do any work on them, so there I was with a duff motor trying to work out what was the matter and not being able to touch it.

When we started the next day I was well to the front of the field because I had been lapped and we started in the same running order. I then proceeded to drop further and further back down the field again, and eventually the engine blew up.

We never discovered what the trouble was, but it really was a disastrous motor race, for Jimmy, too, had trouble; we left Indianapolis that year with our tails between our legs.

A. J. Foyt won the race, but Parnelli-Jones came very close to winning in the first turbine-powered car to compete—the STP Oil Treatment Special. He was very very unlucky to have the gear-box shaft break with just a few laps to go.

.   .   .   .   .

It was with some relief that we returned to Grand Prix racing. Both Jimmy and I were on the front row of the grid at Spa for the Belgian Grand Prix, sandwiching Dan Gurney's Eagle which was to win—a very popular victory for Dan.

I made a disastrous start when the starter wouldn't operate at all—it turned the motor briefly and then just stopped. The car was pushed to the pits, a new battery was fitted, and it started on the button. I suspect that the terminals were not done up, because the battery was certainly not flat. I joined the race when everyone was half-way round the course. But my race didn't last long because on lap 2 I had to go into the pits with something wrong with the clutch. On lap 3 I retired with the gearbox banging and crashing. Then Jimmy packed up with a most unusual malady these days—sparking plugs breaking. Rather extraordinary. Sparking plugs used to be the bane of all motorists' lives at one time, but now nobody ever thinks of them.

And so it turned out an Eagle win—very satisfactory because the year before Dan had run out of fuel on the last lap when comfortably in the lead.

The French Grand Prix this year was at the new Le Mans circuit, called the Bugatti Circuit, which uses the pits and the Dunlop Bridge corner of the Le Mans 24-hour circuit and then branches off into the parking area, where they had made a real Mickey Mouse type of circuit going backwards and forwards with 180-degree corners and then joining the main circuit again just at the beginning of the pits. It wasn't a particularly imaginative sort of circuit, but we had to make the best of it. It was rather a shame, because the Grand Prix cars don't show up too well on this sort of thing—they were coming past the pits accelerating away from a second gear corner whereas everyone was used to seeing the cars coming out of White House Corner at 120 mph and getting up to about 160 by the time they reached the pits. The Grand Prix cars tended to look slower and rather lost on this large circuit. All in all, it didn't do motor racing too much good.

We had a bit of a 'get stuffed' session with the Customs getting our cars through, and Team Lotus missed practice for the first day. The second day I was on pole position, but Jimmy was having trouble with the fuel injection system which was causing the engine to misfire. He had to run the car down the main road during the night to try and sort out this misfire. Well, you can imagine what a Grand Prix car developing 400 bhp sounds like in the dead of night: very antisocial.

Jimmy and I pulled out a lead on the rest of the field and we had a fair old race. I got into first spot, with Jimmy just behind, when the crown wheel and pinion packed up; and very shortly afterwards Jimmy too packed up with the same problem. The power and the torque from this engine was such that the sides of the crown wheel and pinion housing just weren't strong enough and they were flexing sufficiently to allow the pinion to come out of mesh with the crown wheel; then, of course, you get improper loading on the teeth and they wore away. We ended up with a completely stripped crown wheel and pinion on both our cars. From that race onwards we had some steel side plate castings made for the housing, with through bolts running right across; this meant that it was a very strong box section and it didn't give us any more trouble.

The ZF firm in Stuttgart, whose gearboxes we were using at that time, did us the modifications there and then—a very co-operative firm who turn out fine work and have helped us enormously. What impressed me very much was that they said that delivery would be on 20th April and, boy, on 20th April the stuff turned up.

The British Grand Prix this year was at Silverstone—it alternated between Brands Hatch and Silverstone. During practice I was coming back into the pits, I must have been doing about 60 or 70 mph coming down the pit approach road on the inside of Woodcote Corner, when the car suddenly turned sharp right and crashed into the retaining wall. Bits of Lotus flew all over the place and my car slithered to a stop in a cloud of steam and smoke, looking very sorry for itself. I just stepped out and recovered a wheel that was rolling nonchalantly across the road to remove it from the path of the oncoming cars and then I helped the marshals to drag the car off the road. We discovered that the bracket securing the bottom left rear radius rod had come adrift from the monocoque section—the weld hadn't taken because not enough heat had been used. When I put on the brakes to come into the pit road, it had just detached itself; the back wheel had flown out at an angle and steered the back of the car round rather like one of those things at a fairground.

There we were the night before the race without a car for me to drive. Colin Chapman made one of his rapid decisions and flew all the mechanics back to the works. We had one chassis there. All the broken bits of my car were loaded into a trans-porter and I flew back to the works as well. Everybody who wasn't working on Jimmy's car, and all the people at the works who were available, were pressganged to work on the new car. And that night they built a brand new car from scratch.

The chassis was sitting in the shop—it had been piped and wired by Girling Brakes and Lucas—and we collected up all the parts, and what parts we didn't have, we made, and we built a brand new car for the race the next day and it arrived at the circuit just before the start.

I had been at the works the night before, and again in the morning, getting myself fitted in and getting all the pedals right. Then I flew back to the circuit. We were still working on the car five minutes before the start, but we got the car on the grid—and we were still working on it there. It was a fantastic effort to get that car built overnight; a most remarkable achievement. A tremendous credit and tribute to all the mechanics and everyone who took part in building it and also to Colin Chapman for making the decision to have a go at such a task. I was delighted to have a car to race; Jimmy and I were both on the front row of the grid—and me sitting in a brand new car that had never rolled a wheel.

For the first few laps I was sorting out the car, getting the feel of it and having a bit of a scrap with the two Brabhams of Jack Brabham and Denny Hulme. Jimmy in the meanwhile had taken the lead. I always make notes of what I do during practice and I was able to set the car up on exactly the same lines as I had set up the other; in fact, the car wasn't handling too badly. I managed to get into the lead on lap 26.

Thirty or so laps later, on lap 55, I was going into Beckett's Corner when suddenly the car went all over the road. I had a colossal moment and a bit of a fight to regain control. I slowed right down and had a good look round—and I saw the left rear wheel was leaning in at the most drunken angle. I managed to get slowly back to the pits where it was discovered that in the rush to build the car one of the bolts that was holding the rear suspension on hadn't been tightened up sufficiently and it was missing. The rear suspension had fallen in at the top and the rear wheel had fallen in with it. It really was a sad moment. Not only for myself being in the lead in the British Grand Prix and having the car fail, but for everybody who had worked on that car and made such a magnificent effort to get it there.

You couldn't have any recriminations—you couldn't blame anybody. The fact that the car had got there was a miracle, and to have a bolt fall out—well, it was just one of those things. It was fortunate that we didn't write off another car. I didn't think I was going to get a drive at all so having led the race I couldn't be disappointed.

The mechanics found another bolt, stuffed it in and off I charged, determined to try and salvage something. But it wasn't to be; the engine blew up and finally I had to retire. The race turned out well, because Jimmy won it from Denny Hulme. It had been an eventful weekend for Team Lotus: they had won the race; built a new car overnight; and put Jimmy in the running for the World Championship.

．　　　．　　　．　　　．　　　．

For the German Grand Prix at Nurburgring there were all sorts of problems again in practice and it certainly wasn't going to be one of our races. The gearbox seized up on my car after I had done half a lap because there wasn't any oil in it; one of those inexplicable things. Anyway, I then went out in one of the other cars—the spare car—and I hadn't done too many laps when I came down one of the twisty sections, the downhill run before Adenau. I was having some trouble with the brakes —they didn't feel quite right; Jimmy too was experiencing trouble. Anyway, I got to a point where I just didn't get slowed down enough—I went up one of the banks and did a great big wall of death act.

Stewart, who was following me, said he saw me come right out of my seat—we weren't wearing seat belts in those days. The car came back down on the road again going backwards and I was able to step out of the car a trifle breathless.

Jackie Stewart stopped his car and came back to see if I was all right—he looked more shaken than I felt; he was quite white. He had witnessed the whole horrifying incident; he had seen my car go right up the bank backwards with me almost standing up in the cockpit. Of course it made a bit of a mess of the car and so we had to go and get the other one for the next day.

Then we hit a snag. I got back to the pits and it was discovered that I had only done four of the five qualifying laps required. Jimmy was prevailed upon to let me have his car so that I could go out and do one more lap. You can imagine his thoughts as he saw me get into his car and disappear into the distance. Anyway, I completed the one lap very carefully and brought Jimmy's precious car back to him. I must say I would have felt exactly the same way if I'd been in his shoes and everyone breathed a sigh of relief to see me come back.

After all this, I didn't get much of a lap time so I was well down on the grid. At the start there's a fairly wide area for the starting apron but, unfortunately, the first corner is rather a bottle-neck and everybody is channelled into a fairly small opening which is rather a dangerous procedure. I always feel slightly crowded and then somebody bumped into my wheels under braking and pushed me onto the grass. The car spun like a top right in the middle of the pack. I had an almost unbelievable escape, with everybody going all ways at once and executing phenomenal avoidances. There was a tremendous amount of smoke from all the tyres that were locked up—and how anybody could see anything I shall never know. However, when all the smoke cleared away, there was only me left, so I set off in hot pursuit. I hadn't done too many laps when I was going round a very fast left-hander and I found the car's steering a bit indecisive; when I had eventually negotiated the corner with my heart in my mouth, I discovered that the right front wheel was about to fall off—it was actually wobbling. I made it very slowly back to the pits and found that a nut had come slack on this very bumpy circuit. Anyway the mechanics did the nut up again and off I went.

By then I was well down the field and I hadn't done many more laps when the back suspension broke and I came in with the back wheel leaning inwards. So that was that—a very eventful Grand Prix practice and race. I must admit I was rather thankful that the whole thing was over and behind me!

Denny Hulme had a fairly easy old win and it set him well on the way to the Championship. I felt that I had had enough incidents that week-end to last me for a whole season.

.   .   .   .   .

The Formula 2 programme took us to race in Karlskoga, some distance from Stockholm, on a Sunday; then we rushed over to Helsinki for a race there on the Tuesday; and then we had another race in Finland for the following week-end. Jochen Rindt was driving for Winkelmann Racing and we stayed just outside Helsinki with his in-laws; his wife Nina, a beautiful Finnish girl, is the daughter of Kurt Lincoln, a very famous Finnish driver who has been racing for many years. Jimmy Clark and I stayed in their home as house-guests; we had a very amusing time, but one of their customs rather upset me. They were very keen that we should go and have a sauna bath and so, as Jimmy and I were game for anything, we jumped into a motor boat one evening and rushed out into the middle of the sea where we found a small island, on which there was a sauna bath in a timber hut. There were about twelve chaps and we all sat in this sauna bath. Boy, was it hot: it was about 110 degrees centigrade—about ten degrees over the boiling point of water! (Of course, it is a very dry heat.) The idea, apparently, is that you go into the sauna bath, sit there for a few minutes and then rush out and jump into the icy waters; then you go back in again and repeat all this a few times. Well, I did it once, twice, three times and you dive in all steaming hot. It is very difficult to breathe in the sauna because, as you breathe in, the heat burns your nostrils, although, as it is dry heat it is bearable. It certainly gets the old ticker working, thumping away.

After doing it three times, I was about the last one left; while I was sitting there, Jochen came in and threw some liquid on top of the stones. He's just fooling about, I thought, because it gave off a lot of steam and made everything seem a lot hotter. Not to be outdone, I sat there a bit longer and then rushed out and jumped in the sea. By the time I came out, everyone was drying themselves off and tucking into the beer, schnapps and crayfish.

I noticed that I was beginning to feel a bit dizzy and was swaying about; I began to think that the sauna bath had affected me. I happened to mention this and enquired how everyone else felt. I was greeted with peals of laughter; apparently unbeknown to me Jochen had poured some alcohol on the stones, which had immediately evaporated, and I had breathed it into my lungs—the quickest way of getting alcohol into the bloodstream and the quickest way of getting me drunk. I was as high as a kite and everyone was highly delighted by my reactions.

That night we went out and I began to feel a bit queer. We went to another island where we ate crayfish, mounds and mounds of them, washed down with aquavite, which is a very

popular Scandinavian custom. We had a most enjoyable evening, but I became terribly ill after it all and woke up during
the night with a high fever; I wasn't at all well for two or
three days. I never discovered whether I had been poisoned
by the crayfish, ruined by Jochen's trick or given a fantastically severe chill in the stomach by the contrast of the hot sauna
and the icy sea. I am a little suspicious now of either crayfish
or saunas.

Overall the trip was an entertaining one and we were able
to fit in three races in eight days, which is something I have
never done before.

.   .   .   .   .

At the Canadian Grand Prix it was raining and really quite
miserable. Jimmy went out with water on the electrics, took
over a third car that we had entered for a Canadian driver and
went out again with the same trouble. Somehow the water
didn't get into my electrics and my engine didn't stop, but I
managed to spin the car. I had to get out and push the car to
start it which, as it was on the flat, was very difficult. I had to
push it, jump in whilst it was still rolling, disengage the clutch,
slip it into gear with the ignition on, let the clutch out and hope
it would fire. Fortunately it managed to catch—you can't get
up much of a speed pushing on your own so I was very lucky
to get it going and to finish in fourth spot.

It was the first ever Canadian Grand Prix and there was a
big crowd, but the Canadians were unlucky to have had such
lousy weather. At the practice it looked as if Jimmy and myself
were going to have a fairly easy race as we were the only two
drivers to get under 1 minute 23 seconds a lap and we had
a reasonable lead on the rest of the field. But the rain really
messed us up; it was so bad, with water running across the
track, that one or two drivers spun out on the warming-up lap.
Everyone regarded it as a most uncomfortable race. It rained,
then stopped, the track would begin to dry and then it would
rain again; conditions were never the same one lap to the next.
It turned out to be quite a tiring race.

Next came the big slipstreaming act at Monza—and the
electronic timer went haywire during practice and started to
give out some fantastically fast times; they were obviously up
the spout and had to be cancelled. The end result wasn't very

satisfactory and somehow I ended up on the third row of the
grid. There was the usual confusion at the start, because there
hadn't been a drivers' meeting. There was supposed to have
been a dummy grid and we all lined up on this; the starter
raised his flag and dropped it to take everyone up to the grid
proper. Unfortunately, it looked like the real thing and I took
off with everyone else. We were all expecting to roll forward
onto the grid proper, but the way the starter gave the signal
left no doubt in my mind that he was starting the race—
anyway, I wasn't chancing it, so I took off with the rest. I
wasn't going to hang around waiting for anybody as it certainly looked as if the start of the race had been signalled. One
or two of us made a superb start and, from the third row of
the grid, I managed to be second into the Curva Grande—
quite an extraordinary place to be.

The race soon split up into its groups and there were Dan
Gurney, the two Brabhams of Jack and Denny Hulme, Clark
and myself in the leading group. Gurney soon dropped out and
that left the four of us, two Brabhams and two Lotuses.

Suddenly I noticed that Jimmy's tyre was starting to get
bigger and bigger and I realized that he had a puncture. Jack,
who was just behind him, dived into the inside of him going
into the South Curve in a very dicey manoeuvre and started
to wave frantically at the tyre, which gave Jimmy the clue. I
thought this was a particularly courageous effort on Jack's part
because it was quite a dangerous manoeuvre for him.

At high speed the weight of the tyre and the centrifugal force
hold the tyre up, but once you come to a corner there is no
lateral support and you are in trouble. It was the right-hand
tyre and Jimmy must have had one or two moments coming
round the Ascari Curve.

Jimmy went into the pits and that left the two Brabhams and
myself quite comfortably in the lead from the rest of the field.
We had quite a good little set-to. I had the legs of them with
my Ford engine and I was more or less seeing what the situation
was: how fast they were going and how fast I would have to
go to beat them. Jimmy rejoined the race just behind us, so
we were the original four again, though Jimmy was a lap
behind us.

We gradually drew out from the two Brabhams. Jack had the
throttle stick open and the revs go sky high when he changed

gear once, so he had taken the edge off his motor; Denny Hulme had something wrong with his engine, it was over-heating, and he retired; so that just left Jimmy and myself. Jimmy, of course, was anxious to make up time and get some-where near the front again. So Jimmy and I were just towing each other round the track—Jimmy was making up his time and I was pulling away from the second place man who happened to be Jack Brabham at that time.

By lap 57, I was about a lap in front of everyone else with over a minute's lead on the second man, when my engine blew up going down the main straight. There was an almighty bang and I managed to coast around the corner and into the pits; the crankshaft had broken. On inspection we found that the crankshaft had been made of the dirtiest piece of steel that anyone had ever seen.

So that lost me the Italian Grand Prix when I had had the race sewn up and in my pocket.

Jimmy went to catch up the second and third place men, Brabham and Surtees, who were now scrapping for first place. He got into the lead, which was a tremendous effort, and then on the last lap of the race ran out of fuel, coughing and splutter-ing his way round. Surtees and Brabham were able to retake him and have a fantastic dice to the finish. Jack tried to outdo Surtees on the last corner but got onto the oil that I had spilt when my engine blew up. The two of them had a dicey moment at the South Curve just before the finish. Surtees eventually came out the leader, with Jack right on his tail.

The whole of this episode had been witnessed on European Television; it made a tremendous spectacle and was very good motor racing. Jack only just failed to win and John Surtees came out a very good winner; Jimmy coasted across the line with a dead engine in third place after a magnificent drive.

After practice for the United States Grand Prix, we had quite an interesting situation: Jimmy and I were both on the front row of the grid and I had pole position. For the first day's practice there had been thick fog on the circuit at Watkins Glen—the surface was pretty wet and nobody got down to any decent times at all until the very end when it started to dry out. On the second day everybody started whittling down their times and eventually Jimmy did a 1 minute 06.07 seconds which

looked to be about the quickest. Then right at the very end I
went out and did a 1 minute 05.48 seconds which was very
satisfying as it won me 1,000 dollars for the fastest lap in practice.

On our lap times, Jimmy and I were half a second better
than the next two competitors, Gurney in the Eagle-Weslake
and Amon in the Ferrari, who looked like being our main opposition. It seemed as though Jimmy and I had more or less got
the race between us. That night, I remember, Walter Hayes
called a meeting in Colin's room; Walter is a director of English
Ford and the mainspring behind the Ford interest in Grand
Prix racing. With Harley Copp, the Technical Director of Ford,
who supplied the practical support, he must be congratulated for Ford's extremely successful efforts. It is also Walter
who, with Henry Taylor, was jointly responsible for me joining
Team Lotus. It would never have occurred to me had they not
planted the seed, and it was Walter's idea to have two drivers of
equal status in the team in case anything went wrong with one
car or one engine. Originally a journalist, he has certainly
made his mark with Ford public relations and also in motor
racing.

There were four of us in Colin's room—Colin Chapman,
Walter Hayes, Jimmy and myself. Although this was an English
Ford enterprise and nothing whatsoever to do with American
Ford, Walter was particularly anxious that we should do well in
the United States Grand Prix and, therefore, he didn't want
the two of us jeopardising the race by scrapping together. We
agreed that the fairest thing to do was to toss a coin to decide
who should cross the line first if the two of us ended up dicing
in front of the field; the one who lost would have the privilege,
assuming we were both in front, of winning the Mexican Grand
Prix.

I won the toss and so, if we were sufficiently far in front of the
field that we could then go round at our own speed without
scrapping, it fell to me to win the American Grand Prix. This
was just team tactics—though they didn't quite work out in
practice; there was no sense in the two of us blowing ourselves
up. This was actually the first occasion on which we had any
discussion about team tactics before a race, but we realised
the importance of this race to Ford, and it was up to the drivers
to do their best for Lotus and Ford.

I made quite a good start and took the lead with Clark second and Gurney third. It wasn't long after the start that I began to experience trouble with the clutch and I was having difficulty changing gear. There was a synchromesh cone fitted on the ZF gearboxes we were using—not really necessary on a racing gearbox—and of course if the clutch goes this makes it more difficult to change gear. I was having a bit of trouble and I couldn't go quite as quickly as I had anticipated. Eventually Clark went by me and began to draw out a little bit of a lead and I got pressed by Amon in the Ferrari.

By this time I had got quite a severe vibration due to the clutch and something having got slightly out of balance—it was all a little bit worrying and I was gradually dropping back behind Clark. However, every now and then the car would work all right and, during this struggle with Amon, I set up fastest lap with 1 minute 6.0 seconds which was then the lap record.

Just at the very end of the race Clark also had trouble when his top wishbone bolt came adrift or broke and the rear wheel leant in at a drunken angle. He had another two laps to do and managed to continue in this state though at a slightly reduced pace. Of course, I was not aware of any of this until I saw him at the very last moment as I crossed the line just six seconds behind him. He had won the race and I was second, giving Lotus and Ford their one-two—but only just!

At the Mexican Grand Prix, Clark and Amon were on the front row of the grid with Gurney and myself on the second row. There was a bit of confusion at the start—Jimmy was taken unawares by the starter—and I managed to take the lead on the first lap. In fact, Gurney hit Jimmy up the backside when he didn't get away and Jimmy's exhaust pipe went into Dan's radiator—so that put Dan Gurney out of the race straight away; it must have been very disappointing for him.

Jimmy Clark took the lead and went on to win the race quite comfortably. He had, earlier on, made the decision to drive the Mark 49/I car instead of the 49/II, which is a slightly later one; a Mexican driver ran the 49/II in the end and that was the car that retired in the race, so it was a lucky choice for Jimmy. My own race terminated when the crucifix broke in the half-shaft and one of the couplings on the driveshaft then flailed around and took off the suspension unit—all of which gave me quite a moment. I was able to coast back to the pits and we pushed the car away in preparation for shipment back to England; when the mechanics came to drain off all the fluids, they found that there was hardly any water left—apparently the radiator had been leaking. So it didn't look as if I was due to finish that race anyway.

This was the last race of the season; Jack Brabham came second behind Jimmy, and Denny Hulme came third in the race to win the Championship. It must have been very satisfying for Denny whom I remember coming over from New Zealand with a friend and racing around Europe for many years before he went into Grand Prix racing.

There seems to be quite a spate of New Zealand drivers in Grand Prix racing at the moment, if anything outnumbering the English and more than twenty per cent of the total numbers —an extraordinarily large percentage from such a small country with only two and a half million people.

CHAPTER FOURTEEN

1968

The 1968 season started off in a bloody rush. The first race was on the 1st January, the South African Grand Prix at Kyalami, and we did very well. Jimmy Clark came in first and I was second. It was to be Jimmy's last Championship victory.

We were using the same cars as last year, the Mark 49 with a 3-litre Ford V8 engine, fuel-injected. Mine was the same car that I had driven at the end of 1967, but Clark's was a new one, though it was otherwise the same as mine. The new cars, the 49Bs, were not quite ready.

The South African circuit is quite a fast one with very nice sweeping turns, a couple of hairpins and quite a long straight. It's more or less on the side of a hill—you go rushing down one side on rather a fast old corner, up the other side and round a hairpin into the straight. It's quite an interesting circuit—a little bit narrow—but the weather is always very good. Except at five o'clock. It always rains at five; you see a damn great black cloud coming up from nowhere which just hits the circuit and drops its lot. And there you are, all wet and 'orrible. It's amazing what an effect it has on the cars. The trouble is that the circuit is well over 5,000 feet up and the air is a bit thin. On the Lotus we had to use a special cam for the fuel injection and run the engine a bit lean—you don't want to put in the usual amount of fuel if you're not getting the normal amount of air. The funny thing is that you can start practice, say about two o'clock, with one setting on the fuel injection cam, and by the time this great black cloud comes along, you've got to alter it because the air gets so much more humid. It affects things so much that you have to change the mixture.

Anyway, none of this gave us too much trouble—our cars seemed to be happier than most of the others. Kyalami is a nice place to be in January; but the altitude has some effect on the drivers as well—you can get a bit breathless if you over-exert yourself—and my hotel didn't have any lifts; it didn't have a second storey either.

We all stayed at a place called Kyalami Ranch, just about a mile from the circuit; we could lie by the hotel swimming pool and watch a part of the circuit which climbed just above the ranch. In fact, when someone had a special training session up there—I think both Honda and Matra had a few—I could wallow by the pool and time their laps: very amusing, except when they put in a fast lap which somehow wasn't quite as funny. You have to be careful, because you get sunburned very quickly. There is no muck in the air and the old ultra-violet rays come through pretty smartly. You can get sunstroke quite easily and find yourself unable to race.

Anyway, the race went according to plan and I felt the year had got off to a good start. My next Grand Prix, the Spanish, went even better. This was in May and was run on a new circuit at Jarama, which had only just been built. We had run in a Formula 1 race there in the previous November—just Lotus and a few locals. We came first and second, but there wasn't much opposition; most of the other cars were Formula 2 anyway.

It is a twisty circuit, very tight with only one little straight. I got myself into trouble because I told the Spaniards I thought the circuit was a bit Mickey Mouse; of course, they didn't understand what I meant and I spent an embarrassing hour trying to describe what a Mickey Mouse circuit is.

Anyway, the circuit is not bad at all, but you spend a lot of time in very low gear so the car takes a hell of a pounding in the engine and transmission departments, with the revs rising very quickly and then backing off in a low gear—winding everything up the other way. You can do a lot of damage with that sort of treatment very easily.

In the race itself, I was very lucky. Chris Amon was running away with it in the Ferrari and had built up a lead of over twenty seconds, when he packed up out on the circuit—his fuel pump gave up. I couldn't have done too much about him, although I was trying very hard; I was being pestered the whole way by Denny Hulme. Denny and I had a really fabulous race together, though fortunately I came out on top and won the race. If Amon had not retired, though, I am quite sure I couldn't have caught him; but that's the luck of the game.

I was delighted to have won—it was my first Grand Prix win since the American Grand Prix of 1965 so it was a long time since I had seen the chequered flag. I was a little worried that I would not know what it looked like, but in fact I did recognise it and that was that.

It had been a very tough race—the temperature was very high, the circuit was a difficult one and most of us felt pretty whacked by the end of the race. I think it was almost as tough as Monte Carlo for the drivers—it is very easy to make a mistake on a tight little circuit like Jarama and race-day certainly had been hot.

.   .   .   .   .

In April we went to Hockenheim for the Formula 2 race; Jimmy had a new car which I'd done some testing in and it seemed quite nice—an improvement over the old car. We didn't feature all that well in practice, but then the Lotus never did brilliantly on a very fast circuit. Hockenheim really is an odd sort of circuit with a massive stadium and a little twiddly, very twisty piece of track in front of it and then the course goes out into the woods and disappears for miles with one long sweeping bend at the end of it and then there are miles and miles of straight back to the twiddly bit again.

On race day it was raining and I can remember soldiering on in about eighth place or thereabouts and every time I came into the infield I could see Jimmy in front of me on one of the twisty bits of track; then he disappeared—I thought perhaps he had gained a bit on me, or lost a bit, and was just in a different part of the circuit. About the same time I also noticed on the back straight, on one of the fastest bits of the circuit, that there were some skid marks going off the track and into the trees.

I realized straight away that whoever had gone off there was in serious trouble, but it never occurred to me that it might have been Jimmy.

When I came into the pits at the end of the race, one of the mechanics told me that it was Jimmy who had crashed; all the mechanics were in a pretty shocked state, but I knew at once that he must have been killed—he would have gone straight into the trees at near maximum speed. My reactions at the time were a bit odd—I don't think I really took in what had happened. It was as if someone had told me it was a fine day—I heard what they had said but I didn't twig what it meant. It took a while to register that that was the last time we were going to see Jimmy.

Why he went off, I don't think anyone knows; the car was in several pieces, but nothing could be found wrong with it that didn't look as if it had happened in the accident.

I think it is pretty certain that it wasn't Jimmy's fault; there is a gentle curve at this point of the circuit but it doesn't require any particular skill to negotiate—all the drivers on the circuit were taking it flat out—and it had stopped raining, though the track was still wet. The car itself was pretty well brand new so there was no question of old age having crept in; it was a very nice car, in fact, and identical to mine except for one or two small refinements.

Jim Clark had all the requirements for his profession to a very high degree: he was a natural athlete; he had very good muscular and mental coordination; he had a very good eye—he could hit a ball well—his timing was extremely good and so were his reactions. To be any good in motor racing you've got to be a very competitive person and this he certainly was; in his driving he could be aggressive too, but he didn't take undue risks. You can be aggressive and competitive; you can also be boorish, aggressive to the point of being dangerous—and this he was not. In fact you could say that he was a safe driver in that his judgement of situations was particularly good.

You win races by taking as few chances as possible; it's a calculated risk, and you have to calculate on your car's performance and your own performance. Now Jimmy's skill made him, I think, a very safe driver because he had the skill to control his car in a relaxed fashion.

This was in complete contrast to his character, really. I would describe him as a rather nervous, highly-strung person —and he was a very bad passenger—but once behind the wheel of a car he was completely confident and relaxed. We had occasion just recently to drive from Cologne to Monte Carlo and back in a Ford car for a publicity stunt. Part of the time he slept in the car, but when he was awake he would be biting his nails and saying, 'Christ, watch out!' We were completely different; he could never understand how I could just sit there when he was making the odd mistake and getting a bit near the edge. He'd turn round and say, 'Well, for Christ's sake say something'. I was more relaxed than he was, or he was more nervous than I am—it's difficult to know which way to put it.

But he enjoyed his life and he always made the best of it.

Basically he was a very shy person and he had to make an obvious effort to submerge his shyness and emerge as a character, a personality—which he did, but he did find it difficult. He made no bones about it, he didn't like making speeches but he had to do it and I saw him—as did everyone else in motor racing—getting better and better at making speeches as he became better adjusted to his role as a public figure.

He had the will to win, this tremendous urge to win, which you've just got to have. Some people have it more than others and he had it more than most. He was a fighter whom you could never shake off and whom you never dared underestimate. He invariably shot off in the lead and just killed the opposition, set up a lead and just sat there, dictating the race.

He was an ideal racing driver.

.   .   .   .   .

We all moved to Monte Carlo to prepare for the Monaco Grand Prix on the 26th May. This time we were running the new cars—the 49Bs, one for me and one for Jackie Oliver who had joined the team. They had a slightly longer wheelbase, wings on the front and a rather curious wedge shape to the body at the rear. This was our first venture into aerodynamics —which is a very technical term for streamlining—and the idea was that it would form a rear spoiler.

The gearbox was brand new. Up till now we had used a German ZF box—it is a particularly good one, in fact—but this time we went to Hewland. It was actually the Hewland Formula 2 box, a great deal smaller and lighter than the ZF, and designed to take a lot less torque. The drive shaft was also new; it came out of the Morris 1800 and incorporated a special type of constant velocity joint which used a great many minute ball bearings.

Altogether we were a bit worried as to whether this light-weight gearbox would last the course, because Monte Carlo is a particularly tight circuit and very low-geared. The maximum speed is only about 132 mph as we come out of the tunnel approaching the chicane, and most of the time we are running a good bit slower than that. You use first gear quite a lot, too, whereas on most circuits, particularly with a 3-litre, you practically only use it to get off the line.

The other main difference was a revised suspension layout, which reduced the camber changes as the wheels moved up and down.

One new car had actually been sent out to Spain and was sitting in the pits during the Grand Prix but, following Jim Clark's fatal accident, Colin Chapman did not come out for the race and sent instructions that we were not to use it. He did not want it to run without his being there as there were a few things which he wanted sorted out.

So this was the debut of the 49B and we won first time out, more or less repeating what Jimmy had done at Zandvoort when the Mark 49 made its bow.

The race itself developed into a big battle between myself and Richard Attwood, who drove, I think, the best race he has ever driven. I must say he gave me a lot of trouble. It really was a very good race and I thoroughly enjoyed it. I would have liked a bigger gap, but I just didn't want to take too much out of the car. I was very conscious of all those new bits and the transmission was getting quite a testing, so I played it very very cool, or tried to, and just stayed in front of him.

I think I could have played it the other way and stormed out in front to build up a large comfortable lead—it might have given him less incentive to keep attacking me. But knocking half a second off your time puts a lot of extra strain on the car. I didn't think it was worth the risk and as long as I didn't get rattled I felt I could pull out that little bit extra when necessary. And I could set my own pace.

It worked very well, of course, but it was close—just 2.2 seconds after 2 hours of racing. It was an interesting race and I thoroughly enjoyed winning it again. I am particularly fond of the Monaco Grand Prix; it's a lovely place in May and there is a tremendous amount of atmosphere—you're inside the race as soon as you get there. You can sit at a cafe on the track and anyone can walk or drive round the circuit. The whole place is filled with people who have just come for the race—the Monday after, it is quite empty. I remember I had to stay on one year after the meeting; I went out on the Monday evening and there wasn't a soul around—it was like a ghost town.

At Monte Carlo, as I have said, we used aerodynamics for the first time, but it wasn't much of a place to find out about these things. I had the wings on the front of the car and the wedge-shaped tail, but I did not mess about with them because I did not think I was going fast enough for them to have much effect.

The next Grand Prix was the Belgian at Spa and this is a very fast circuit indeed, about five miles round, and we were putting in 150 mph laps. And aerodynamics begin to mean a lot at this sort of speed.

I didn't get very much practice, because as I set off on the first day, I motored about ten yards and there was a sudden clonk and the rear wheels locked up. We had the whole gearbox out on the pit road and messed around with it. I forget what the trouble was, but we got it sorted out. I just did a complete lap—and that was enough to tell us that the engine was missing. I didn't really get any more practice that day.

The next day it poured with rain. So there I was, flogging around in the wet, trying to sort the car out on a circuit that was entirely different from Monte Carlo—and it was only my second time out in the car, because there had not been any chance to test it between races.

I wasn't happy about the car, I rather got the feeling that it wasn't going too fast in a straight line. When race day came I still hadn't really tested the wings and the spoiler on the rear at high speed and I thought I would do better without them. I asked Colin if I could leave them off and run the car as it had been the year before; although the suspension was different, I felt that like that I would know where I was. Jackie Oliver chose to run with the aerodynamic appendages.

In the end my race didn't run too long. I was fairly well placed at the beginning, but then on lap 6 the drive shaft went: the grease had escaped from the constant velocity joints and they got so hot that all the little ball bearings welded together and seized up solid. I parked the car and walked back. That was my Belgian Grand Prix.

Before the Dutch Grand Prix at Zandvoort on the 23rd June we were able to get in a bit of development work and I found that the aerodynamics really did work. The car felt better through the corners and we were getting more grip. Unfortunately, this didn't stop me going off the track twice during the race—and this was rather sad because it cost me three championship points and a lot of self-respect, as well as earning me a few black looks.

When the race started, it was pouring with rain and I was having a bit of thrash when Stewart went by as if I had been tied to a post. It was a bit disturbing. He just disappeared in a cloud of spray and I never saw him again until he lapped me: very unfair. Anyway, there I was flogging along in second place until I went straight on at the end of the straight . . .

The track at Zandvoort runs through the sand dunes and there is always a bit of sand on the track. With all the water sloshing around, there was a good bit of sand flying around as well and it was getting sucked into the air intake of the fuel injection system. Now the throttle slides are machined to pretty fine tolerances—and the sand was getting drawn into them, causing the slides to stick slightly and preventing them from fully closing; this meant that a small amount of power was being maintained to the wheels. So I would be braking for a corner quite nicely and then, in the last twenty yards, whoops, I would stop slowing. This would only happen at the last second and then I would have to run quickly through the gears and teeter around the outside of the corner. I didn't twig at first what was happening—I thought I was just getting my braking wrong, braking a bit late or something. It was a bit of a puzzle. The first time it happened, I was caught unawares and just went straight on.

I clobbered a wire fence, but I didn't do much damage (or, at least, I didn't think so) and I backed the car out and carried on. The only trouble was my steering wheel had turned through about thirty degrees. Oh Lord, I thought, I've bent it. But it looked all right; I leant out and had a good look and I also tried wiggling it. Well, it was all very awkward, because I like to hook my thumbs over the top of the spokes and I couldn't. The car was a tight fit anyway and I was having a bit of trouble getting my hands past my thighs on lock. So I carried on, thinking to myself that I'd better watch it.

Then it started to rain again. It kept on changing its mind —suddenly it would come down a lot harder but you would only know this because you could see it bouncing in front of you on the road. Sometimes it got very difficult to see but you could not really feel much because nowadays we all wear face masks. Puddles start appearing in front of you and then the water shines back at you as if you are at sea. Then suddenly you start to aquaplane—and that's 'orrible. Anyway, the rain kept coming and going and I was now running fourth after my little excursion.

Then I did it again. On lap eighty-one I went straight on at the same place—only this time I knocked a wheel off. It was so stupid and I was very cross. I had to walk back to the pits and tell them I had shunted it; the ignominy!

Colin didn't even say goodbye; it was understandable, I suppose.

I was a bit happier again when we set off for Rouen and the French Grand Prix, though we didn't do very well in practice. It was the first time that we used the aerodynamic wing on the back. This is much the same as an aeroplane wing except that the aeroplane wing gives you lift and ours, being upside down, gives negative lift—or downward load, which increases the faster you go, and presses the wheels onto the ground. Unfortunately, you never get something for nothing and there is a lot of drag from the wing which means you go slower on the straight. The problem is to work out the angle so that you get the maximum grip without too much drag. You don't want to lose on the straight all the time that you have gained on the corners. So the wings are a bit of a compromise, but they certainly help on the majority of circuits which I've driven on. The car is a little bit more comfortable to drive and you certainly get through corners quicker because of the extra grip.

Colin never thinks in half-measures and so our wings were the largest ever seen in motor racing. They took a bit of adjusting, but they were very, very effective. On the other hand, we were at this stage losing a bit too much time on the straights. It is very tiresome to get out a lead on someone and then find they go past you on the straight and you can't even keep up with them. Anyway, we were gradually getting the hang of it. Of course, the next thing was that all sorts of little gadgets started to appear to make the wings go flat on the straight. Ferrari produced a highly sophisticated arrangement with little electric solenoids—worked off the brake, the throttle pedal and off the gear lever, with manual switches as well, a tremendous box of tricks. To digress a bit, it was very amusing to watch

Jacky Ickx's Ferrari at Monza in the Italian Grand Prix—he would come out of the long South Curve and one lap he'd come by with the wings up and then the next time round they'd be flat. The Ferrari mechanics would go rushing out to signal him that they should be flat on the straight—a very difficult message to get over and they all got very excited. It was quite a pantomime. The only unfortunate thing about it was that I had found myself in a position to be a spectator.

To return to Rouen—the Rouen circuit is a good one with a very fast downhill section with a load of curves which you take at speeds varying from 120 to 160 mph, a hairpin which calls for first gear, and quite a fast main straight. It runs through woods, very picturesque, and a real road circuit. It is fast; demands a certain amount of courage, a good car and very good roadholding.

Just as the race started, down came the rain and there was only one bloke in the race on rain tyres—Jacky Ickx, who had had the foresight to put on rain tyres after the warming up lap. The rest of the field had normal dry tyres and were therefore at an equal disadvantage. Stewart had really scored over us at Zandvoort; he had had a fabulous compound for the wet and had just left us. This time he was in the same boat as the rest of us.

I can remember working up through the field (I had been well to the back of the grid) and happily passing Jackie Stewart without too much bother, whereas at Zandvoort he had just left me for cold. It is quite an indication of the value of a good wet tyre.

It didn't last, though: my half-shaft went—I couldn't understand it because I had absolutely no grip. Anyway, it actually sheared in the middle as I left the hairpin and so I had rather a damp race watching everyone else. I am not sure that I wasn't quite pleased to be out of it because it was a particularly nasty race under those conditions. So that was my race.

I walked down to the hairpin and watched the race from there. I could tell immediately when Stewart, in the Matra-Ford, called at the pits and changed his tyres. He came out of the hairpin just as if it was dry—it was fantastic. Before, there had been quite a lot of wheelspin on gentle throttle application; now, the car came out of the hairpin and went off like a rocket.

It certainly opened my eyes. Stewart had lost a lot of time going into the pits and he still came second.

Jacky Ickx drove one of the best races of his life under appalling conditions and won the race for Ferrari and himself. It was a good race and showed how much Ferrari had improved in the last year or two. I never really reckoned their cars too much on roadholding, but they had certainly come back to the fore now—they had got a very competitive car and they have certainly always known how to make engines.

The British Grand Prix was at Brands Hatch in July. Our two cars went very well in practice—I got pole position with Jackie Oliver beside me and Jo Siffert's 49B entered by Rob Walker was just behind. It was all very satisfactory because we won a hundred bottles of bubbly for the fastest lap in practice and I was having a party on the night after the race, which all tied in very nicely.

The race also went very nicely until lap 26; I had a reasonably comfortable lead and then, coming along the bottom straight, a knuckle joint in the final drive went and set the half shaft whirling round to wipe off the suspension. By this time, we had changed the constant velocity joint, the Morris type, and gone back to one that we had used quite successfully the year before. In spite of all that, the wheel fell in and it was all a bit of a drama. At least I was able to come into the pits and retire the car quite gracefully without a long walk. But it was a shame really because I had never won a British Grand Prix and it is the one race I would like to win, especially at Brands Hatch, because that's where I had my first race.

Oliver now took over the lead until lap 43 when his car seized a bearing and Jo Siffert went on to a brilliant win. It was very nice to see Rob Walker chalk up a win. He hadn't had much success since Stirling drove for him back in 1961, but he had pressed on. I always think of him as a true amateur, in the peculiar sense of the word as applied to motor racing—we all take money from various sources so there are really no amateurs and nobody cares anyway. But Rob Walker really does it because he enjoys it. Throughout motor racing he is universally respected as the private entrant who is battling against the manufacturers and of course is liked by everyone for his sportsmanship and imperturbable affability. I am glad to be able to count him among my friends.

From Brands Hatch, we went to the Nurburgring and the German Grand Prix, due to take place on the 4th of August. It was possibly the most miserable race of its kind that anybody had ever seen. Throughout the meeting, the whole place was shrouded in mist and cloud—it's fairly high up there, in the Eifel Mountains, and we were in cloud most of the time. During practice we would start off from the pits, the highest point on the circuit, in all this mist and fog, and then, as we got a bit lower, it would clear and the road would just be wet, until we climbed again and found ourselves back in the cloud.

The actual course is about 14 miles round and it rises and falls something like a thousand feet; there are 187 corners, roughly half and half left-hand and right-hand; the circuit varies, with different degrees of banking, and some of it, where it is patched, is very slippery. And all this matters a lot more in the wet—you have got to try and know the circuit like the back of your hand. You must know where the puddles form and where streams are liable to run across the track. And then you can become airborne very easily because the track rises and falls, running over little bridges and humps. It isn't only hard on the driver. The suspension takes a hell of a pounding and so does the chassis.

In theory, a chassis cannot hit the ground. When a car is built, you take all the springs off, let it down on its suspension and set the rubber bump stops so that the chassis won't hit the ground with four heavy blokes jumping on it—you would think that that would do it. But you can still take the car to Nurburgring and after the first lap all the bottom of the car is worn away. You come down so hard on your springs and rubbers, that you flatten them and the tyres as well, and your chassis hits the ground after all. A car has got to be very tough to stand this sort of thing, though of course running the race in the wet would take some of the loads off because the speeds would be down.

The practices weren't all that much fun in these conditions and the organisers were very worried. They had various meetings with the Grand Prix Drivers' Association to find out what we thought about it—they were worried as to whether we should race or not. They went a long way to make things better for us and laid on an extra practice, whereas normally they are a bit too inclined to follow the book over there. When race day came I went round the track in a sports car and then they asked Jo Bonnier and me if we thought we could race. We said that we thought we could—we didn't think it was very nice, but with a quarter of a million people there to watch, there really wasn't much option. We felt we just had to get on with it.

Jackie Stewart fairly romped away at the start and I had a good old dice with Chris Amon. It was very difficult—the rain was sometimes hard, sometimes light; part of the time we were aquaplaning. And I had Amon breathing down my neck the whole bloody race—it's bad enough on your own, without having a car in your mirror all the time!

And so it went on for twelve laps—there are only fourteen laps in all, because of the length of the circuit—with Stewart way out in front, me second, with Amon pacing me hard and Jochen Rindt not very far behind us in fourth place. On lap 12 it started to rain really hard and I came sailing over the top of a hill blind and plunged downhill into a little stream running across the road. I simply did not see it at all—it hadn't been there the last time round. I hit it with a wallop and the car spun round like a top. Suddenly, there I was slap in the middle of the road: Oh Lord, I thought, where's Amon? I was trying to keep an eye out for him and also to get the car out of the way. It wouldn't start on the starter and I had to get out and push it, thinking that Amon was going to hit me at any moment.

Actually, Chris had gone into the ditch at North Curve some ten miles back and I simply hadn't noticed. He was out of the race with a badly damaged car.

I managed to get my car moving at last and I pushed the starter as it rolled down the slope, so it was all legal and above board. I was away again. A couple of seconds later there was old Rindt breathing down my neck instead of Amon. I had Jochen up my chuff for the remaining two laps.

When you have had a bit of a spin you've got to be very careful that you don't get rattled—getting out of the car, pushing it and then getting back in, breaks your rhythm. I had moved the bit of rubber at my back and I wasn't quite comfortable—silly little things, but they put you off a bit and upset your concentration. You have to be very careful not to make the same mistakes again. This is a lesson I learned very early on, at Brands Hatch, as I think I have already mentioned . . . .

Anyway, you have to be very careful for the next few corners and sort of play yourself in. This time all went well and I managed to draw out a few seconds on the last lap and come in second. Jackie Stewart had won, of course, but this was the first race I had finished since Monte Carlo and I was quite pleased.

For Monza in September we had entered three cars—Jackie Oliver's, mine, and a third for Mario Andretti, but in the end Andretti was not allowed to start in the race because he had been to a meeting in America less than twenty-four hours before —it was a shame because he went very well in practice on the first day before rushing to America for a race on the Saturday.

I got away to a good start in the race, and led for a bit, but I was soon overwhelmed; it's a great race for slipstreaming and we were all flogging around, picking up a tow from each other. It is a fast circuit with very difficult corners—there are two at Lesmo, with about a quarter of a mile between them, which you can take at about 110 and 130 mph; the South Turn just before the pits, a fairly tight one, but you still do over 80 or 90 there; and then there is the Curva Grande, which gets its name because it is one of the most difficult corners in racing. I was coming out of there at 160 mph. It's a very, very hairy old corner, and, if you get it right, very satisfying.

After about nine laps Chris Amon lost it on some oil. He spun round and Surtees, trying to avoid him, jammed on his brakes, hit the oil and slammed into the barrier. Chris's car hit the barrier backwards, flipped over and disappeared into the trees. It was a bit of a nasty old sight. Then there were just three or four of us battling on. On the next lap, a back wheel came off my car as I was coming through second Lesmo. I didn't know what had happened but I hit the barrier with a right thwack and ran along it for a bit before I could stop the car.

You don't have too much braking if you lose a back wheel, because the opposite front one gets cocked up in the air and you've only got one front brake and one back; the other front brake just locks up and doesn't do anything. You stop rather gradually and while all this was going on I saw my missing wheel flashing by on the other side. Then I twigged what had happened, though it couldn't do much to help matters. I just parked it and cadged a lift back to the pits, taking the broken wheel as evidence.

It was obvious that the McLaren-Fords were going extremely fast. They had the same engine as us but, boy, they were quick. On a fast track like Monza the McLaren was a very fast car indeed.

There was a big race going on between Siffert and Stewart and the McLaren-Fords. Bruce McLaren's own car went out with an oil leak and Denny Hulme gradually pulled away to win the Italian Grand Prix. He had not been having too good a season till then, but this put him back into the reckoning. I was still leading the Championship table, with Stewart in second place.

Jacky Ickx was the unlucky one—he had come very near to taking second place at Monza and then had been passed at the last moment by Servoz-Gavin when the Ferrari engine suddenly faltered. You can imagine the effect. Ickx emerged from the last corner, in front, and all the thousands of Italians went barmy—they stood up cheering and waving—and then the next second Servoz-Gavin flashed by and all the cheering turned to moans as everyone dropped back in their seats. The Italians get terribly excited over racing; they really enjoy it and it's delightful to see. And after all, it was the Italian Grand Prix.

Ickx's luck was still out for the Canadian Grand Prix. His throttle stuck during practice and his car went into a bank. His leg was broken and that took him right out of the battle.

The Saint Jovite circuit, which was host for the second Canadian Grand Prix, is very tight and bumpy, it plays hell with the transmission. Chris Amon went extremely well, but he and Ferrari were unlucky again. He was driving really well; his car was a good one; and then the transmission went on lap seventy-two after he had pulled out a lead of nearly a lap over everyone else.

I was running about fourth spot when I started getting a clonk; every time I accelerated or changed gear, there was a great clonk and the car was handling very queerly. I couldn't understand it, so I began to eyeball everything around and take a look at the suspension. Then I pulled the mirror down to have a look at the rear suspension and, I thought, Do you know that's a bit odd: I could see the exposed rod connecting the rear suspension to the plunger of the shock-absorber, and

I had a pretty good idea of how much of the rod should show under normal conditions; on the left side, the rod hardly showed at all—which meant that the shock-absorber was almost fully compressed—whereas on the other side I could see almost the whole rod. It just didn't make sense and all the time there was this awful clonking and an 'orrible vibration. The car was going down the straight with a great big dart and weave and every time I went over a bump the car just floated off and the wheel did a spin. It really began to get a bit nasty and everything was getting steadily worse—the weaving, the vibration and the handling.

Well, I thought, this is stupid; I'd better go in and look at it. But I was very loath to stop. Anyway, good sense prevailed and I called in at the pits. 'There's something broken at the rear,' I told them.

They all went round it, everyone was poring over it pulling at this and that. Then they came back to me and said: 'It's fine, nothing wrong with it at all.'

I didn't say anything, actually. I got out of the car and had a look myself and I must say I couldn't see anything.

'Right,' I said, 'I'll get back and start it up and you can just put your hand on the car.'

They had the car up on a jack with the wheels in the air, so I put it in gear and opened it up; as I opened it up, so the chassis opened up as well. When I backed off, the chassis closed again, and there was a great clonk and a lot of vibration.

'Bloody hell!' they all said. 'Look at that!'—and everybody's eyes popped out on stalks. I thought I had better have a look too.

Now the thing about this car is that the engine itself forms part of the chassis. There is the monocoque bit where I sit, which has the fuel tanks in it, and the engine is bolted straight onto the back of this with four bolts, one to each corner; the rear suspension is simply hung on to the back of the engine. So, as I said, the engine is really part of the chassis.

Now what had happened was that the bolts holding the two top corners had fretted, worked loose and broken. With only the two bottom bolts holding the whole car was like a hinge and, as I accelerated, the car just opened in the middle.

I had often wondered what would happen if the engine blew up and the whole thing came apart—well of course it hasn't actually happened yet—but I hadn't thought of the car just bending at the middle.

They started to wheel it away but I said 'Look, now I know what's wrong, I'll just go out and see how I get along.'

It was diabolical. I had already had one or two moments earlier; at one stage I had thought I was sitting a bit lower than usual—a little nearer the ground—and I seemed to be looking uphill at everything. Most peculiar. But that was exactly what I was doing.

So off I went, changing gear very slowly and backing off very slowly, so that the car didn't break up on me. I only changed gear when I had to and I couldn't brake too hard either. The cornering was a bit queer, because the front half of the car would be trying to go one way and the rear half the other way. Anyway, it was drivable and then I began to get the scent of Rodriguez, also in trouble, in front of me. I started pressing on a bit harder and I was beginning to catch him—he was in third place and I was fourth, with Vic Elford in company. There were only three laps to go, when the handling began to get worse and I thought I might not finish at all, so I slacked off a bit and came in fourth. We had been pretty lucky, really, to get home. And I got some more valuable points for the Championship.

As far as I could see we just weren't quick enough for the American Grand Prix. We did reasonably well in practice and Andretti went very well indeed, but we weren't quick enough down the straight. Everyone was getting away from us. I accelerated off up the hill at the start all right and I was just getting into third gear when all of a sudden the engine died; Oh God, I thought, that's it, finish—I'm out! I had only done a hundred yards—but it picked up and I carried on somewhat puzzled but relieved. I never really worked out what it was until after the race that evening; I happened to be talking to Chris Amon and he said, 'You should have seen your car at the start, the fuel was fairly pouring out the breather at the back of your neck.'

What had happened was that with full tanks the fuel was pouring out under acceleration and going straight down the air intakes, loading up the engine with fuel so that it was so rich that it just couldn't work. Anyway, the engine picked up again and by the time I had reached the end of the straight I was down to fourth place. I put the brakes on and, as you brake, you tend to go forward a bit; this time the whole steering wheel went bonk and pushed straight down into the dashboard, which wasn't so bad, except that it trapped my fingers between the wheel and dashboard. This is all right when you are going in a straight line but I was starting to turn the corner. I still wanted to be in the race so I forced the wheel round and of course my hands were so close to the dash that I knocked all the switches off. The engine stopped and there I was, in the middle of a corner with a pack of snarling cars all around me with the engine switched off. I lost quite a bit of ground but I got it going and I began to pull away again.

I had to pull the wheel back pretty carefully because I didn't quite know what it was up to—if I pulled too hard, it might come right out. Even so, I couldn't stop it moving, so one minute I'd be driving along like a bus-driver and the next minute like Farina—straight-armed. This went on for the whole race, but eventually I got things more or less sorted out so that I didn't push on the wheel too much—but once you start getting in amongst other cars, you forget and push on the wheel again—and down it goes. At the end of it all I picked up a very beautiful second place, behind Jackie Stewart, so it was well worth the skinned knuckles.

After the American Grand Prix we went to Mexico; the Olympic Games were all over and the athletes had gone home a couple of weeks before, so we missed all that. The Mexican Grand Prix was going to be the needle match in the Championship. Denny Hulme had won in Canada and at Monza, so he was a contender with 33 points; Jackie Stewart had 36 points, and I had the best start with 39. But if Stewart won the race, he would win the Championship. Even if I came second to him, he would still get it, because although our scores would have been equal at 45, he would have won more races than I and so would get the Championship. It really boiled down to this —I had to go out and beat both of them by winning the race myself.

We turned up on the Thursday to get in some unofficial practice, but there was nothing doing as the officials couldn't seal off the circuit, which is in a park. Monday had been the last chance for unofficial practice. And that canny Scotsman Jackie Stewart had been there on Monday doing just that while

I had been flogging around Rome in a Formula 2 race. Matra hadn't gone to Rome, so they told me, because they weren't offered enough starting money—and all the time they were out in Mexico practising. Even so, I enjoyed the race in Rome, but I only came in seventh. I don't know what the Italians made of it when I won the Championship a few days later. Must have been a carve-up!

Mexico, of course, is very high up and so we had all our usual problems over the fuel mixture and loss of power. The course is a bit tight and twisty, very flat but with quite a lot of twisting—for which you need power; we were about twenty-five per cent down on power, and this affects your handling. And our wings were only of real use when you were trying to transmit full power to the road.

Lotus had three cars out there. One was for Jackie Oliver and I was to take my pick of the other two; whichever I didn't choose would be driven by Moises Solana, a local Mexican driver. We had one car without wings, just to see what effect they had and also to baffle the opposition—'Now why are Lotus running without wings? Perhaps we ought to try!'—the idea was to baffle them a bit without baffling ourselves, which was all too easy.

It was understood that Solana wouldn't get a car until after I had made my decision, which would be towards the end of practice. He was always in the background hoping to hop into a car. The Press down there are of course pretty pro-Mexican and when it was seen that Solana wasn't going to get in a car while I was driving it they began to get a bit nasty. Colin's face was getting a bit grim and so Jackie volunteered to share his car with Solana, who actually went very well.

I settled for the car with the wings in the end and we got down to making it work; it was a new adjustable type of wing with a Bowden cable connected to a pedal in the cockpit by which I could flatten it. In its normal position it was set to give the correct down-load for cornering; after I had come off the banking after the pits, and had finished all my gear-changing, I could put my foot on the pedal and keep it there, bringing the wing down to a flat position and reducing the drag on the straight. The cockpit was narrow and only just had room for the clutch, brake and accelerator pedals, so the wing pedal was mounted above the clutch.

When I first went out, the wing didn't work at all—it went
flat on its own after about 10 mph. The pressure was in the
wrong place in relation to the pivot point. We had to re-make
the wing—it was beautifully constructed, real aircraft stuff.
When we tried it the next day, it was better, but it still went
flat when the wind pressure built up. We were using Bungee
rubber cord to hold it down and we went on adding to the
thickness until at last we got it strong enough. There was a
bit of an odd moment each time I pushed the pedal—it would
need a pretty strong shove and then the wing would flip through
top dead centre and the pedal would go soft, as the wing went
flat. I never quite understood how it did that, but it worked
quite well. If I took my foot off, it would go back to the down-
load position—which is very important. The brakes are set up
to work with the wing pressing on the back wheels, and, if it
isn't, the braking ratio between front and rear is thrown out,
your back wheels lock up and your car goes all over the road—
very nasty.

I had clobbered a kerb or something at the end of practice,
which meant changing the wheel, and when I did my warming-
up lap just before the race I realised that the new wheel was out
of balance; as I came back to the pits, the *Wheelbase* film unit
took a shot of me—you can see my mouth working quite clearly,
but not a sound can be heard until I come out at the end with
'. . . out of balance.' I imagine quite a lot must have been cut
out.

I made a flying start for the race; we rolled forward from the
dummy grid to the start, beckoned on by the Mexican starter,
and then he dropped his flag almost immediately. I never take
my eyes off the starter and I made a fabulous start, with Surtees'
Honda coming up beside me like a rocket—the Honda has a
fantastic amount of power. It's a heavy car and doesn't handle
well, but boy! it's got power.

Anyway, Surtees went flashing by and steamed into the first
corner too quickly. I got him coming out of the next one and I
never saw him again. But Jackie came through, came through
very well and then we had a big ding-dong.

On the third lap, as I came into the straight, I pushed the
pedal to flatten the wing—and the pedal went light. Crumbs, I
thought, we're in trouble. I turned my mirror—I always have
them mounted fairly loose—and had a look: there was the old

Bungee rubber band waving in the breeze. I had a look in the other mirror, slightly despairing, because if that one was gone, I was sunk. Without the rubber bands to pull the wing into the maximum downward load position, the car oversteers like a pig, but it was all right and it held all through the race. With only one rubber Bungee, it couldn't come back to the maximum download position for braking at the end of the straight when I let off the pedal, but, as the speed dropped, it came into the right position of its own accord and stayed there. It was all a bit hairy under braking, but it held.

The race developed into a battle between the three of us— Jackie Stewart, Jo Siffert, who was really going extremely well, and myself. This year the Mexicans had done away with their old markers—half-tyres stuck in concrete which the drivers were not too keen on—and had funny little kerbs, about two inches high with a hard standing on the far side, so it looked a bit like the M1. When I went round during practice I thought the kerbs looked a bit ineffective. I've got to watch this one, I said to myself. Some fellows are going to cut the corners across these kerbs—and I watched to see where I could use a short-cut to best advantage.

As I was in the lead on the first lap I drove round the track the proper way; Jackie Stewart was very impressed—he told me afterwards that I had driven just like a gentleman on the first lap. So there I was, setting a good example. But when I looked in my mirror I could see everyone carving straight across all the corners. When Jackie started attacking, I thought: Blow this!—the only trouble was that I was a bit worried because these little bumps can damage the transmission—so I fixed things so that I could change gear as I went over the kerbs, which would take the load off the transmission.

Things built up into a real battle royal with Jackie and he managed to get past me. I sat on his tail for about four laps, but I just couldn't get by him on the straight. I don't know whether it was the wing—but we hadn't been all that fast on the straight without it.

I didn't want to lose him on the straight, because I needed his tow, but I could hold him round the corners. I started to be a little unkind to him—I would pull out one side to make a pass, and then go back and pull out the other. I could see him looking in his mirror—thinking: Where's the bugger now?

You can press on someone a bit this way and it worked. He made a bit of a mistake and ran onto the dirt. Out of the next corner I was alongside him and we went down the straight side by side, but I was on the inside, and I got through. We went round most of the way pretty well nose to tail, but I could just pull out enough on the twisty bits so that there was a bit of a gap as we went into the straight; he just couldn't get up and pass me before the end of the straight.

I had to do this every lap, and I didn't want to take too much out of the car early on. Then I saw that Jo Siffert was only four or five seconds behind, and I thought it would be much better if Siffert took the lead and Jackie went back to third place, even if I had to be second. This would help me contain Jackie.

I managed to keep the pace down a bit and Jo duly came up past Stewart, and after a bit went past me. I sat on his tail and we both began to draw away from Jackie. Siffert's car was a little bit quicker than mine on the straight; I think this was because he had a much smaller wing, mounted lower down. But this might not have been the case—Jo's car was fitted with an engine that had arrived with a little note from Cosworth, telling him to make sure to fit this particular engine (I've never had a little note like that!). All I do know is that Jo's car was really flying.

I went down the straight faster behind Jo than I could on my own and we were drawing out nicely. It was lovely and Jackie was getting smaller and smaller in my mirror. And then Siffert packed up—his throttle linkage had come adrift. That's nice, I thought, here we are back to square one—all my plans ruined. And it was very bad luck for Siffert, too.

Then I really had to pile the pressure on—I wanted to maintain a little bit of advantage just to dissuade Jackie. I put in a few fast laps, but it takes a bit of doing when you can perhaps only make a fifth of a second each lap. And then, all of a sudden, Jackie disappeared. That's a bit of luck, I thought, and I hope he keeps it up. I was suddenly pulling out three seconds a lap, so he was obviously in trouble. I began to ease up a fraction, but not too much; I wanted to work up a nice big gap without too much effort.

Jackie had apparently got fuel feed trouble. Some rubber stuff from the tank had come adrift and got stuck in the injection unit, which slowed him up a bit. It got steadily worse and then Bruce McLaren moved up into second place.

Denny Hulme, the other Championship contender, was right out of it too—he had had an accident coming off the banking. A rear shock absorber broke—the eye at the top snapped off and it collapsed—which sent his car out of control. He bounced off a barrier on one side of the track and then slammed into the barrier on the other side. His car slid along the rails and caught fire just by the pits. Denny got out quite all right and the fire was put out fairly easily too—the car was not very badly damaged. Altogether, it was a very nicely contained accident.

On the last laps, I eased off still more and drove pretty slowly. I had already lapped Rodriguez and Oliver who were battling for third place behind Bruce McLaren and, with two or three laps to go, they were gradually catching me. Oliver of course was my team-mate so I thought I would hold position to the last lap and then, if Oliver was in front, I would cross the line ahead of him, but if he was not, I would let both cars pass me before the finish so that Oliver would have one more lap to catch Rodriguez.

So I eyeballed all this and then I saw Rodriguez slip through. Well, I thought, that's it, he's through and now I had better let them pass and give Oliver another lap to try to regain third place.

The big drama came as I went into the hairpin. Out of the corner of my eye I could see Rodriguez arriving with tyres smoking. I did a big swerve and he just missed me, leaving me scrabbling round the outside of the corner. Oliver slipped through as well, but it had been a near thing.

And I had been robbed of the Championship on that very corner four years before—someone had knocked me round, bending my exhaust pipes, so that I had had to make a pit stop which had cost me the race. And now the same thing had very nearly happened again.

Cor, I thought, that's enough of this caper. I'm not taking any more chances. Pedro Rodriguez was running on his home ground and the crowd was obviously getting a bit excited.

Anyway, I let them through. Oliver did get his third place and I won the Championship. It was a very nice way to finish the race with two cars so well up. The season had had its ups and downs, but it had finished up well!

Directly after my return from Mexico I was right in the thick
of it; I was attending every kind of function, making speeches
and presentations, and receiving a few as well. But undoubtedly
the highlight of this very hectic couple of months was the day
upon which I went with Bette, Brigitte and Damon to Buckingham Palace to receive the Order of the British Empire from
Her Royal Highness Queen Elizabeth the Queen Mother. It
was a superb occasion, beautifully staged in the magnificent
ballroom of the palace. The Queen Mother could not have
been nicer and seemed genuinely pleased that I had won the
Championship.

Naturally I felt proud and also grateful to the sport for the
recognition and honour it had brought me. This was again
brought home to me on the night of the BBC *Sportsview* Personality of the Year contest when I came second to David
Hemery, the Olympic Gold Medallist.

CHAPTER FIFTEEN

1969

1969 was the first year that I did the whole Tasman Series—the four races in New Zealand and three more in Australia. I had never done the complete Series before and now I was able to see what the other races that I had missed were like. I enjoyed the trip, though it took rather a long time, and in between the races I took up golf. Jochen Rindt, Piers Courage, Frank Gardner and I had some pretty fierce needle matches; Frank was a first-class player, and it must have been very boring for him, but the others had only taken it up shortly before. I went round teaching myself from a small book of tips on golfing by Jack Nicklaus and I was reading it and learning how to play whilst I was playing. I really got hooked on golf and when I got home I rang up Dick Jeffries at Dunlop and ordered up a complete set of golf clubs and a bag and started to take proper lessons.

Jochen had just joined me in the Lotus team to replace Jackie Oliver who had left to go to BRM; Piers Courage was out there driving for Frank Williams, an English private entrant; Frank Gardner was driving the Mildren-Alfa for Alec Mildren.

The racing itself from my point of view was nothing much to speak about; we went out with slightly modified Mark 49 Formula 1 cars with $2\frac{1}{2}$-litre Ford engines which we had used the previous year, but Jochen's car got written off after the second race—as things turned out this paid off nicely, though the experience must have been a bit traumatic, because they sent him out a 49B car that I had been using during 1968 in the Championship races and this was an advantage. The main opposition came from Chris Amon in a Ferrari and of course Chris went on to win the whole series—a very fine effort.

The Grand Prix season started off quite well, but with our

decision to produce the four-wheel drive car—and we all hoped that this was going to be the answer for the year—our efforts were somewhat spread. We were assuming that we would convert completely to the four-wheel drive cars for the Grands Prix and then we were entering a car for Indianapolis in May —and this, too, was to prove detrimental to our Formula 1 hopes; consequently the year as a whole was a disappointing one.

The Lotus four-wheel drive car was designated the Type 63 and had a Lotus-designed four-wheel drive system manufactured by ZF. It was certainly one of the best thought out racing car designs that I have ever seen and it was a disappointment that it never fulfilled its promise.

The World Championship went, of course, to Jackie Stewart and the Matra Ford, with Ken Tyrrell as the team manager and master tactician behind the effort. It was a tremendous achievement for Ken to come into Grand Prix racing and win the Championship on this scale— they had a most successful season. They had a lot of backing from Matra but nevertheless it was they who had to do it; they ran the cars themselves and they tackled it in what I would say was a very professional manner. Jackie drove brilliantly, the cars themselves were beautifully prepared—this was largely because they did a great deal of testing—and they thoroughly deserved their success.

Other drivers who showed up well during the year were Jochen Rindt, my team-mate, who drove particularly fast, got pole position on many occasions only to be robbed of a chance of finishing well by mechanical failure; Jackie Ickx came up and showed that he too is a driver with a lot of potential— his win at Nurburgring was undoubtedly one of the races of the year and really marked him as a future champion; and Denny Hulme was another driver who did well—he won the Mexican Grand Prix quite convincingly to show the same form which had won him the Championship in 1967.

I only won one Grand Prix, but that was Monte Carlo— always a good one to win! Naturally, I would like to have done better. We were mostly running the two-year-old 49Bs which were still competitive, though we were perhaps scratching a bit towards the end of the year.

·   ·   ·   ·   ·

The season started in South Africa on the Kyalami Circuit outside Johannesburg. There weren't many new cars—most of us were using last year's cars because the new cars weren't ready. The race was at the beginning of March, the cars had to be sent out by boat, which took about a month, so it was more convenient for most teams to send out the cars they'd been using the year before. We had three 49Bs, one for me, one for Jochen Rindt, and one for Mario Andretti, who had been brought over from America. We had one innovation with our front wings, somewhat similar to the way Brabham's had run their wings the year before: they were attached to the front uprights as opposed to the body. A further advance was to have these wings movable so that the driver could flatten both front and rear wings going down the straight. This meant employing roughly the same system that we had used at Mexico in 1968, but then of course only on the rear wing. It was proving a little bit difficult to work because of the load on the cables—the load was so great that the cables were stretching and were no longer flattening the wings. A further problem came when both the wings on Jochen's car and that of Mario Andretti broke in practice; we then had to cut down the height of the uprights so that they were under less load—but were also much less effective.

For the race I chose to run with this new set-up and so did Jochen, but Mario elected to run with the little side wings mounted on the body—and I think he was probably right. As the race progressed, my cables stretched, and I was not able to flatten my wings, so the car went slower down the straight.

Just before the start of the race some enormous black clouds had come up over the city of Johannesburg and there was tremendous speculation as to whether to go onto rain tyres or not. I reckoned that with any luck the storm should just pass by the circuit and not quite catch us and that's what happened. I was able to run on dry tyres throughout the race.

The race started off with Stewart, Brabham, Rindt and myself in that order with the rest of the field behind; it wasn't long before Brabham went out with one of his wings broken and then Jochen had a spot of trouble with his car, because I passed him and found myself chasing Stewart. I was able to hold him for some time at about seven seconds, but then, as the cars got lighter, he gradually drew away. I managed to maintain my position in second place, however, and finished the race this way with Stewart winning the first race of 1969.

The BARC* Easter Monday meeting was held at Thruxton this year for the second time running—having lost Goodwood, the BARC were now developing Thruxton into a major circuit —and it was for Formula 2 cars. It is a pleasant circuit with some very fast high-speed corners and ideally suited for Formula 2. Jochen and I were both there driving the new Lotus Formula 2 cars for Winkelmann, a private team managed by Alan Rees. It was the first time out with these cars and we were looking forward to trying our new mounts. We did quite well; I was in the first heat with Stewart and made rather a poor start, but then eventually I got by Beltoise, who put up a good fight, and started gaining on Stewart quite well until I spun in the Esses. My Lotus was a bit of a tight fit and the steering wheel fouled my thighs—I got a bit crossed up on opposite lock and my hand caught my leg; I was not able to turn the wheel and consequently I spun round. This was pretty well exactly what had happened to me in Oporto in 1959 and the remedy was exactly the same; we got the car back to the works, they just sawed off the dashboard bulkhead, lifted it up one and a half inches to give me a bit more clearance and welded it back in again. We then had to mess about with the screen to give my hands a bit of clearance round the wheel, but otherwise it was no problem.

Jochen Rindt was leading his heat quite handsomely until he had a puncture and had to come in to change the wheel, so he finished quite well down.

The start of the final saw myself on the front row, having finished third, and Jochen on about the eighth row; as the starter dropped his flag, I found I couldn't disengage the clutch and I wasn't able to select a gear—I got no further than the first corner. The clutch was ruined—for some reason or other it had seized on the shaft. Jochen carved his way through the field in grand style and eventually he caught and passed Jackie Stewart to win quite easily—the first Formula 2 race of the season and the first time out with the Lotus Formula 2 car. Once again he showed his mastery of Formula 2 racing; he seems to be almost unbeatable in this and he is always the man

* British Automobile Racing Club.

to beat. He has not had anywhere near the same luck in Formula 1 racing, but he is undoubtedly a very fast driver indeed and must eventually be a winner in Grand Prix racing.

.   .   .   .   .

The Spanish Grand Prix at Barcelona was the next Championship race after the South African and it took three and a half hours to fly there. Practice went quite well—in fact Jochen finished up in pole position with 1 minute 25.7 seconds and I was third with 1 minute 26.6 seconds. Colin had made some alterations to our wings, increasing the length and also adding a lip along the back to make them much more effective—it certainly paid off because it brought our times down quite considerably.

The course itself is a very tricky one, round a park on the outskirts of Barcelona, quite hilly and in places fairly bumpy. This year, at the special request of the GPDA, the organizers had put up a double Armco barrier round most of the circuit —the year before, for a Formula 2 race there, they had only had straw bales; as things turned out, this was to prove a godsend.

The race started with Rindt, Amon, Siffert and myself in the lead; eventually I got past Siffert and set off to try and catch Amon. I was cresting the highest point of the circuit, a bit of a bump just before the hairpin, and was doing about 150 mph when the car suddenly went out of control and hit the guardrail on the left. I spun round and round like a top and then went straight across the road and spun into the guardrail on the other side. The car did a sort of horizontal cartwheel down the barrier on the other side of the road, with bits falling off and being knocked off all the way along. I just sat in the cockpit, firmly tied down by my lapstraps, hanging onto the wheel. There was absolutely nothing I could do— the car was completely out of control. Eventually it came to a stop and I was able to get out, thanking my lucky stars that I was all right and nothing had happened to me.

There were bits of car scattered over a couple of hundred yards, all over the road, and it really looked like a tremendous shunt. It appears that when I crested the rise—and the cars actually take off at this point—the strain on the wing had been too much and it had collapsed, putting the car out of

control, although I did not of course realise this at the time; I
thought that perhaps a wheel had come off. The first thing I
did was to get the car well to the side of the track and get most
of the bits picked up. Then I had a good look round the car
to see what had happened—I was expecting to find evidence
of a rear wheel falling off or the rear suspension broken before
the shunt. But I had a good look around and I couldn't see
anything at all—nothing looked as if it had been broken before
the accident.

Having drawn a blank with my car, I started to have a good
look at Jochen's to see if his was all right—I wanted to make
sure that nothing happened to him. And suddenly, as he
flashed past, I noticed a crease appearing in the underside of
his rear wing—just very slight. By this time the mechanics had
arrived from the pits so I sent one of them running back to
Colin for him to call Jochen in; I started to run down to the
hairpin to see if I could warn him—this is a pretty slow point
on the circuit and he might just have seen my signals.

Jochen only came by once more and then exactly the same
thing happened to him as it had to me—the wing collapsed,
just folded in half, and he went right out of control. The car
shot across the road and slid down the barrier into my parked
car, which catapulted his car over the top of mine so that it
ended up upside down. I saw the whole thing and rushed
straight to it; I got the people round to turn the car the right
way up but it was terribly difficult to get Jochen out; the car
was more or less like a banana bent up double with its steering
wheel pressed against Jochen's lap—I can remember standing
on the car and wrenching the wheel up as far as I could so
that we could pull Jochen clear. It was a very nasty situation;
there was petrol pouring out of the car and running down the
gutters and there were hundreds of people all round—one of
them might at any moment toss a lighted fag-end into the
gutter and send the lot of us up.

Anyway, after what seemed an age we got him out and into
an ambulance. I kept talking to him the whole time to reassure
him, but I couldn't tell how badly hurt he was. His face was
covered in blood, but I thought this could be a nosebleed; he
was obviously a bit dazed. Back at the hospital his injuries
turned out to be a broken cheekbone and a hairline fracture of
the skull. He was very lucky to have got away with such slight

injuries after what had been a monumental shunt. His escape proved the strength of the monocoque body and how much of an aid to safety it can be. Our mishaps also fully justified the expense to which the organizers had gone in erecting the safety barriers—if they had not been there, there is no doubt about it, neither Jochen nor I would be alive today, and nor would a large number of spectators; there was a very large crowd lining the whole length of the circuit and, without the guardrails, the two cars would certainly have mown down an appalling number of spectators. All in all we had much for which to be thankful.

The other people to have trouble with wings at Barcelona were the Brabham team—they had made up wings of fibreglass and one in fact had broken right in front of the grandstands, right in front of the CSI* representatives—they were able to walk out into the middle of the road and pick up the bits so obviously they were not terribly impressed with the wing situation. It looked as if they were bound to do something about them, but of course they acted rather slowly and they did not hold a meeting before the Monaco Grand Prix.

In the meantime we had to go to Indy to start training there for the race at the end of May, but the cars weren't ready so our trip was a bit wasted. We only arrived back in Europe, in Monte Carlo, about half an hour before practice started on the Thursday and we found ourselves right in the middle of a row about wings. Apparently there had been an almighty fuss about them—whether they should be worn or not.

For the first day of practice, we all had the wings on—just as we had at Barcelona. There were moves being made and meetings held before practice was over and during the evening; the next day the CSI came out and said they must ban wings that weren't part of the bodywork, which meant the rear wings only—so we could leave the front wings on if we wanted. There was a tremendous row about this, but there wasn't much that we could do about it. All the practice times for the first day were cancelled—so we'd all been practising for nothing —and we started again at 8.15 on the Friday morning without the rear wings to see if we could get our cars resorted.

Team Lotus, of course, had had enough trouble in finding

* Commission Sportive Internationale, the governing body of international motor racing.

cars in any case after losing two at Barcelona. Jochen was not
fit, but they had scrambled up two ex-Tasman cars, suitably
upgraded, for Dickie Attwood and myself.

We all found it a bit strange without the wings, but gradually
we managed to get the cars sorted to go round reasonably
quickly. On the second day of practice I was only .2 seconds
slower than my time with wings, so there wasn't too much in
it—but then Monte Carlo is a slow-speed circuit and not ideal
for wings anyway. Gradually it transpired that we were allowed
to have spoilers up to a certain height above the ground and
for the race itself I had one fitted, though I hadn't worn it in
practice—there hadn't been time.

I felt that the whole decision had been taken far too late and
not to have made up their minds until after the first practice
seemed ludicrous, but there we were. Although I had been
closely involved in the accidents at Barcelona, I felt the ban
was a retrograde step—the wings were a positive aid to suspension and made the cars go quicker. In the end a compromise was reached and we were allowed to run wings if they
were attached to the chassis; they had to be within a certain
width and height from the ground. And this was a fairly accept-
able compromise; although wings on the chassis were not as
effective as those mounted on the wheel hubs, they were safer
because they were part of the sprung weight and considerably
lower.

The Monaco Grand Prix started with Stewart and Amon
streaking out in front. Now I knew that in practice Beltoise in
the sister car to Stewart's had had a halfshaft go; also that
Amon had had two gearboxes go. So I rather felt that both
their transmissions were a little bit on the weak side—come
to that, I knew mine also was a bit suspect—and Monte Carlo
is extremely tough on transmissions. So I resisted the temptation to try and battle it out with them at the beginning, though
it was a terrible feeling to watch them going away. I just felt
that I must conserve my car and particularly when it was
carrying a full load of fuel.

And of course Amon's gearbox did give trouble and Stewart
went out with a broken halfshaft, the same complaint from
which Beltoise had suffered in practice.

Courage and Ickx were having a tremendous duel behind
me, but I managed to keep them at a distance, somewhere

between 14 and 20 seconds. Piers Courage challenged me two or three times but I was always able to answer him and open up the gap again.

It had been a hell of a gamble, but it had paid off and I was able to win my fifth Monaco Grand Prix, which gave me a tremendous amount of satisfaction. I don't think that any one Grand Prix has ever been won by a driver five times so that added to the pleasure.

Colin Chapman came straight over from Indianapolis on the Sunday for the day of the race, as he was busy there getting our Indy cars sorted, so it was a very nice day's trip for him, just to pop over and see his car win the race. And then I went back with him the next day.

We got back in time for running on the Tuesday but the cars were not ready; we were having quite a bit of trouble getting all the bits over and of course the cars were quite a lot more complicated. We were using the turbo-charged Ford 2.8-litre engine as opposed to the turbine engine that we had used last year. Mario had done some running that week and was going quite quickly, but coming out of Turn 4 one day he had a very unpleasant accident—a hub broke on the right-hand rear wheel and he spun off and wrote the car off against a wall. This put our cars under suspicion and the technical inspection team were round immediately to check our hubs. The cars had to be stripped down to see what the matter was with our hubs. A close examination of the broken pieces from Mario's car made it look as if it could have been a heat treatment problem—there were definite signs of this near the radius of the hubs. Colin got on the phone back to the works every night and they spent hours going over their calculations—eventually they decided the hubs could possibly be on the weak side. They started to make some new ones at the works, but this of course meant that we couldn't run the cars.

Our programme was now considerably delayed and we missed the first period for qualification. Mario had got his back-up car which he had used in the Championship series in America and he was able to go out in this car, putting up some very creditable times. We had this drama for all that week and in the meantime Jochen turned up, having recovered from his shunt in Barcelona; we were able to reheat-treat some of the hubs and get in a bit of practice that way, but Colin wasn't too keen on our running the cars too much until we had the new hubs.

In the end it got down to the final week of qualification and we were having brand new hubs made—then the machine broke down and that more or less put paid to our hopes of getting the hubs in time. Colin telephoned me at about 8.30 on the Sunday morning, which was the last day of qualification, to tell me that he was withdrawing the cars completely. There was nothing else he could do. I remember going down to the track and finding everyone very dejected, the mechanics were absolutely worn out and morale was low.

It was very hard on Colin who had spent so much time getting the cars built and had produced such a brilliant design. There didn't seem to be anything else for us to drive so Jochen and I returned to Europe. It was all a tremendous disappointment.

.   .   .   .   .

Team Lotus turned up for the Dutch Grand Prix with two four-wheel drive cars and two 49Bs—the idea being to give each car a bit of a run and see how they went. As usual of course we didn't get enough time to do much development work and we had a few changes to cope with on the 49Bs; we had come out with new deflectors or spoilers on the backs of the cars, instead of the improvised wings which were being displayed by most of the other cars. After viewing the opposition, Colin flew back to England and brought back a couple of panel-beaters and some of our old wings; overnight, they made up an improvised wing for the 49Bs which we attached to the bodywork and the chassis so as to be in line with everyone else.

For practice, my 49B was not quite ready as they hadn't finished one section of the wing, so I went out in the four-wheel drive car. It was raining, so I was quite interested to see how the car would go in the wet. I found that I could get round just about as quickly as everyone else in the wet but I did not seem to be any quicker, so there really did not seem to be much advantage. However, looking back now, I remember that I was gauging my time against Denny Hulme and I think that he had some particularly good wet weather tyres on his car; I was running on completely standard tyres, so perhaps the comparison was not quite fair to the four-wheel drive car;

in any case, it felt quite nice going round Zandvoort in the wet
and I enjoyed driving it.

For the start Rindt was on pole, Stewart was next and I was
beside him, but I made the best start of the three of us and got
into the lead. Somehow or other, my 49B did not seem to be
handling all that well and I think this was perhaps due to the
new wing arrangement and the fact that we hadn't strength-
ened up the springs on the rear. The car was bottoming out and
I had some particularly nasty moments. Gradually I dropped
back and at one stage I called in at the pits—the car was
handling so badly that I felt something must have broken,
though it hadn't in fact. This delay of course dropped me
well back and eventually I finished sixth or seventh—it wasn't
a particularly good race for me.

Jochen went out with a broken halfshaft and Stewart won
the race quite comfortably.

The French Grand Prix was even worse; it was one of those
Grands Prix that I just prefer to forget. Again there seemed to
be something wrong with the car and it didn't handle; we just
could not find out what was the matter during practice and I
had some very nasty moments in the race.

The race was run at Clermont Ferrand, on the side of a
mountain in the middle of France—a very pretty circuit, very
twisty, with all sorts of corners; it's like a miniature Nurburgring, rather narrow and an interesting circuit. The stars of the
race were Stewart who came first and Beltoise who came in
second after just pipping Ickx, so the French Matras scored a
one-two in the French Grand Prix—France really had a
holiday. It was quite something for them and it was rather nice
to see.

Jochen didn't fare too well—he wasn't at all well and the
circuit was so twisty and hilly that it made him feel sick; he
eventually retired feeling very ill indeed. John Miles who had
now joined the team drove the four-wheel drive car and he also
retired with some sort of bother on the fuel injection—the belt
driving the mechanical pump broke and so he had no fuel
pressure. As you have to remove the engine to mend the belt,
there was no way that he could be got back into the race.

The British Grand Prix was held at Silverstone this year—
a very fast circuit, the fastest in Great Britain, with lap speeds of
around 130 mph; the slowest corners are about 80 mph and

the fastest around 150 mph. A pretty fast old circuit. And I had the feeling that of all the circuits Silverstone was the most ideal for the four-wheel drive car, but even here it did not show up to any great advantage.

Our cars did not turn up for the first practice period on Thursday morning so I wandered around feeling a bit spare. Ron Tauranac had arrived with two Brabhams but no drivers— Jack Brabham had damaged his foot in an accident and Jackie Ickx had been delayed somewhere. He came up and asked me if I would like to try the Brabham and I agreed to as I hadn't got a car. I thought it wouldn't be a bad idea to see what the opposition was like, so there I was jumping into a Brabham. I thoroughly enjoyed it; I didn't go tremendously fast but I suggested one or two changes to the car like the rear spring and roll-bar settings and in the end I got it going reasonably well. Towards the end of practice Jackie turned up and took over the car; and he went quicker in that car than he did in his own. Of course, speculation was rife at seeing me going round in a Brabham and all sorts of rumours started. They were completely unfounded, but the real explanation seemed a bit too simple. I was very grateful for the chance to drive a Brabham and glad of a drive on that particular morning.

Our cars turned up in the afternoon and I discovered that I hadn't got a 49B as mine had been provisionally sold to John Love, the chap who had come so near to winning the South African Grand Prix in 1967; all that turned up was a 49B for Jochen and a couple of four-wheel drive cars. I did a couple of laps in the four-wheel drive but it wasn't running perfectly and I couldn't do much practice—it was not particularly fast anyway and, at this stage, it didn't seem too competitive.

The next day Jo Bonnier turned up with a 49B—it was the car that Richard Attwood had driven at Monte Carlo and the one that I had driven in the Tasman Series; it had been upgraded from a 49A to full 49B specification. Jo very kindly agreed to let me have the car for the British Grand Prix; he agreed to take the four-wheel drive car. I thought this was extremely generous of him, particularly as a Swedish television company had come over to cover the race and the Swedes would obviously be keen to see Jo doing well.

Unfortunately, things still didn't go too well because I went out in practice and only did a couple of laps before the front wheels started to wobble. There was trouble with the bearings and two laps were enough to damage the hubs; Colin flew back to the works to pick up some spare hubs and he got back in time for the afternoon practice. Out I went again and then I had a bit of trouble with the water-pipe which broke and let all the water out; then the fuel pressure went so I hardly got any practice laps in at all.

On Saturday morning the organisers announced that they would allow half an hour's practice, untimed, for anyone who cared to take advantage of the offer. I was quite keen to give the car a run to make sure that everything was finally all right, but when we came to start the car, it just wouldn't go. We couldn't start it and I missed that practice as well. There was nothing for it but to change the engine. The mechanics set to and they changed the engine there and then—they did the whole job in two hours, fifty minutes which was a pretty good time. And the car was got ready, just in time for the race, though without too much practice, I was well down on the grid.

The race started and I got involved with Amon, Siffert, Courage and Rodriguez in a tremendous battle; Stewart and Rindt had gone out into the lead, followed by Ickx and Hulme, though Denny Hulme was to drop out soon afterwards with some sort of bother. Anyway, we four had a terrific battle which went on for most of the race.

Soon after the start, I noticed that my car was over-steering badly, and I was a bit puzzled as to why—I never discovered until after the race what the problem was. In fact, one of the front wings had got itself lifted up into rather an acute angle, which of course gave me a tremendous amount of grip at the front—and so the back was over-steering badly. The car was quite a handful, with bags of over-steer when, in fact, at Silverstone you want a trace of under-steer if anything.

And then towards the end of the race, both Jochen and I ran out of fuel; there must have been a miscalculation and we both had to make pit stops. Jochen finished fourth but I only came in seventh and well out of the hunt.

John Miles had a good run until he lost his gears with gear selection trouble, but he managed to finish. All in all, a disappointing race for Team Lotus and for myself.

The other big disappointment was the overall failure of four-wheel drive. The four-wheel drive cars had arrived in force for this race; Cosworth turned up with a most interesting looking car and there were also the four-wheel drive cars of McLaren, Matra and Lotus. Jackie Stewart was some two seconds slower in his four-wheel drive car than he was in the two-wheel drive car; Beltoise actually drove the four-wheel drive Matra in the race—Stewart took over his car after his own had been wrecked in practice following a puncture—but it didn't show much promise.

After the race, Bette and I gave a party at our home in Mill Hill—we had put up a marquee in the garden and about two hundred people turned up. Bette and I thoroughly enjoyed it and I think the guests did as well—they did not leave until the early hours of the morning. We hadn't got much to celebrate, but the party went with a swing.

A few days later we took the entire family to the German Grand Prix. We stayed for a couple of days before the race with Prince Metternich and his charming wife at Schloss Johannisberg on the Rhine near Rudesheim. They have got some wonderful wine cellars there and some of the best wine in Germany—so we were able to have some very fine evenings tasting them. We had a wonderful time and from there we went on to the Ring.

The German Grand Prix at Nurburgring was held in better weather than last year when mist and cloud covered the circuit for the race and the two days of practice. This year the weather was quite kind. The surprise in practice was the speed of Jackie Ickx in the Brabham—he was quicker than anybody else and seemed to be fairly comfortable doing it.

The organisers were running some Formula 2 cars in the race to make up the field because as the circuit is fourteen miles long you need quite a few cars to keep the spectators interested —a car only comes round about once every eight minutes. Before the race there was a spectacular display by the Red Arrows aerobatics team of the RAF—they gave everyone a bit of a fright and especially the few spectators who had positioned themselves in the tops of some trees; one of them was seen to fall out when the Red Arrows almost took off the top branches of his particular tree. It was really most impressive.

Stewart and Rindt made pretty good starts, but Ickx made a very bad one and had to pick up a lot of ground. I remember on the very first lap I saw him coming up in my mirror and I moved right over to get out of his way—I realised that he was going considerably quicker than myself and I didn't want to impede his progress. I think he found that practically everyone gave him the same treatment. He certainly was flying. His knowledge of the Ring and his driving ability combined to make him invincible. The Brabham is an extremely good-handling car—it might not have the ultimate in traction, perhaps not as much as the Lotus, but it can be thrown about with impunity and this gives the driver a lot of confidence at a place like Nurburgring. Ickx was certainly making full use of it and it wasn't long before he got into the lead and drew away from Stewart. He won the race quite easily.

I had some trouble with my gear-box and eventually I couldn't engage fourth gear at all, which was a bit of a disadvantage; the gear selector had broken off. But I managed to finish fourth, which was not too astounding, but at least I had finished and I had picked up three points in the Championship stakes. Stewart was second and McLaren third; Jochen dropped out with engine trouble. For this race, Colin had brought over Mario Andretti to drive the four-wheel drive car, but unfortunately he went off on the very first lap when the car grounded heavily. He flew off the road, knocked a couple of wheels off and poor Vic Elford, who happened to be following, hit one of the errant wheels. This took Vic off into the trees and he broke his arm in three places which put him out of racing for the rest of the season.

The German Grand Prix was undoubtedly Ickx's race and he won it in the most brilliant fashion.

.   .   .   .   .

The Gold Cup meeting at Oulton Park came up next on the 16th August. The field was a bit mixed—it was a Formula 1 race but with some Formula 5000* and Formula 2 cars thrown in. Jochen was driving one of the four-wheel drive cars but the other one had been damaged in the German Grand Prix so that put paid to my chances of a four-wheel drive car for this particular race; we had intended to enter both four-wheel drive cars just to see how competitive they were. However, I persuaded Alan Rees to enter a Formula 2 car for me, though of course I

* For single-seater cars with stock V-8 engines of 5 litres capacity and open to ungraded drivers.

didn't stand much chance against the Formula 1 or Formula 5000 cars. I thought it would be a bit of fun—I like Oulton Park and I like racing in England generally; I felt it was worth the effort. I had quite a good race but just before the end, as I was lying in fifth position, the seal on the oil filter broke—all the oil came out onto the exhaust pipe and I went round in a cloud of smoke looking rather like the *Torrey Canyon*. Eventually the oil pressure began to drop so I had to switch off and retire the car.

Jackie Ickx won, his second Formula 1 win in two weeks; Stewart was put out of contention when a battery lead came adrift and Jochen Rindt finished second with the four-wheel drive car running reliably for about the first time, albeit some way behind Ickx.

Directly after the race my Formula 2 car was loaded up in the transporter and the lads set off straight down to Enna— it's a long drive from Oulton Park to Sicily and they were anxious to get started immediately. I was going to meet them there the following weekend; I spent a couple of days in England catching up with my correspondence and then, with three friends on board for a bit of sun, I flew down to Sicily stopping the night at Nice on the way down. When we reached Sicily, we flew low over the hotel where we were going to stay to let them know we had arrived and then landed at the airport at Catania near Mount Etna.

For the Formula 2 race at Enna we brought down two cars, one for myself and one for John Miles. Jochen was driving in a race in Finland that weekend and was working this in with his holiday up there.

Enna is a very fast road circuit round a lake in the middle of Sicily. The lake is actually full of snakes, so it is not the sort of place where you want to do too much swimming, and the road gets pretty dusty—it isn't used normally—and this means that the cars get absolutely shot-blasted. The drivers have to wear extra screens over their visors so that they can tear them off during the race, because they get so peppered with stones that they become opaque and you can't see a thing.

In the first heat the clutch wouldn't disengage and I couldn't get into gear; eventually I managed to get it into second gear and got the car moving, but by this time everyone had fled the scene and I set off on my own. I managed to work my way through the field and I came in about seventh. For the final, I managed to tag on to the leading group and we had a tremendous tussle—it was slip-streaming par excellence; there are just about two corners where you back off and the rest of the circuit is a flat-out blind. With all the cars having very close performances, it was almost impossible for anyone to make a break. I worked it out so that I knew when I had to make a bit of a challenge and in the meantime I was quite happy to run along at the back of the field, watching points, seeing where I could pick up a bit of time and checking the best places for slip-streaming. With about seven or eight laps to go, I started to make my effort. By the time we got to the last lap and the last bend before the finish, I was all set. I took the whole of the leading group on the outside of the last corner—quite hair-raising—and I thought I had made it. I had managed to open up a gap which I'd hoped was enough to get me across the line first, but I hadn't reckoned on Piers Courage in his Brabham; it must have been one of the fastest cars on the circuit. He just came by me as if I was tied to a post, but, anyway, I managed to finish second and that was a lot better than I had expected. The Lotus is not noted as a particularly quick car in a straight line. It was a most enjoyable race and an interesting weekend.

After the prize-giving, Robin Widdows and I left to drive back to Taormina, Robin driving; he was staying at the same hotel. Robin had also been racing at Enna and had done very well. Somehow we got lost and we found ourselves on a very winding, twisty road instead of the straight main road which runs through to Taormina. We were flogging along through the night—it was about one o'clock in the morning—and at one stage we passed some soldiers. About a quarter of an hour later, as we drove into the outskirts of a village we heard the most terrible noise from behind. The next minute a police car shot by us with sirens wailing, gongs going and guns being brandished out of the windows. Good Lord, we thought, we seem to be in a spot of bother. We stopped and Robin got out to see what was going on. The 'police' car, in fact, was full of soldiers and they leaped out with machine-guns, surrounded the car and refused to let Robin approach them. I thought I'd better get out as well and see what the trouble was. They were all looking pretty wild and apparently we had driven through a road block; they thought we were some sort of banditti. Luckily, as soon as I got out of the car, one of the soldiers recognised me and the next minute we were all friends. The whole thing was forgotten as everyone shook hands with everyone else—but it had been quite a scary moment. It never ceases to amaze me when I am recognised in the most outlandish places. Here we were in the middle of the night in the centre of Sicily and someone knew who I was. It's a good indication of the international popularity of motor racing and the power of television and the press.

The family and I had a short holiday in Sicily after the race, which was a great success. It was wonderful to get away with the children and just to play with them in the sea—they were all swimming like fishes, even Samantha who was only four. We had a marvellous time, swimming and fishing and snorkelling, and then a friend of ours came over from Malta with his family in a yacht so we were able to take the children out sailing as well. All in all we had a splendid time and the children got as brown as berries.

.   .   .   .   .

In September I went to Monza for the Italian Grand Prix. We had two 49Bs for the race, one for Jochen and one for myself, and a four-wheel drive car for John Miles. Practice didn't go too well; on the second day when the fast times are made I only did a few laps and then my engine broke—so I just sat there and watched myself being gradually pushed further back down the grid until I finished on about the fifth row. I wasn't too unhappy because on the first day I had managed to get the car fairly well sorted and I knew exactly how I wanted it set up. As long as I did not lose the leading group, I would not be in too bad a position—provided, that is, I made a reasonably good start. We decided to run without wings in the race as we found that the cars were in fact faster down the straight without the wings and we didn't seem to be losing too much round the corners, so that appeared to be the better arrangement. Stewart also ran without wings though the McLarens ran with them. Everyone seemed slightly undecided on the subject, though I personally was quite sure that I would be better off without them.

The race started and I managed to get on to the tail end

of the leading group; we had been going for a couple of laps when I noticed that my exhaust note had changed. Crumbs, I thought, the engine's blowing up! I looked in my mirror to see where everyone else was and then I saw that one of the tail pipes was sticking up at a very odd angle—apparently it was beginning to fall off and it did eventually fly away. In fact, it hit Surtees—or rather, Surtees hit it—and it bent his front wishbone, bounced off the top of his helmet and knocked out one of his electrical coils, which put his car right out of the picture. Of course, he was very lucky that it didn't do him any more damage, because if the tailpipe had hit him in the face at 160 mph it would certainly have put *him* right out of the picture. Anyway, it was very unfortunate for him and I was very sorry, though there was nothing I could do about it—of course I was not even aware of all this until after the race.

With one tailpipe missing my engine went a little bit flat and didn't seem to accelerate too well as a result. Then, about this time, Jack Brabham who was immediately in front of me in the leading group began to have a bit of trouble and lose oil at a fast and furious pace. The oil seal on his filter had blown and he was blowing out oil all over the place—as I was the next car to come along, I was getting the full benefit of all this oil on the track. I was slipping and sliding all over the place. And then of course I began to drop back.

Jack eventually brought his car into the pits, but by then I had lost about ten seconds on the leading group and it rather looked as if that was that—to lose the leading group at Monza, which is pure slip-streaming, more or less puts you out of the race. But I wasn't going to let it go at that and I put in a very determined bid; very, very slowly and gradually, driving at ten-tenths through the Curva Grande, the Lesmos and the Parabolica, I managed very gradually to pull them back. At last, I could see the group coming into view and slowly but surely I managed to get back on to their tail. I think this was probably one of my finer efforts: I've never seen that done before at Monza. And I was missing a tail pipe which meant that on one side I just had four stub exhausts; this, of course, affected the power curve somewhat and dropped me down on power.

Once I was up with the leaders, I was able to tag on to them and worked myself up into second spot behind Stewart.

In fact, I managed to pass Stewart occasionally at the end of the pit straight and then lead him through the Lesmos, but he could always get me going down the back straight and put himself back in the lead by the time we had got back to the pits again. But I was quite happy with the situation. Like everyone else, I was trying to work out a method of winning the race and in which position I would have to be when we started the last lap, and where and when and how I was going to make a move. It was a question of in what position to be as we entered the Parabolica so as to win the race; I had worked out what I thought was quite a good scheme, provided it wasn't messed up by somebody else—and of course this is always the big if.

Unfortunately it never came to that. With five laps to go my halfshaft broke. One of the rubber grease-retaining cups had come adrift, all the grease came out, the joint seized and so the halfshaft broke. That was that and I just coasted down to Parabolica and parked the car on the grass.

I remember getting a terrific reception from the crowd as I walked back—it was just as if I had won the race. Very sporting of them. As it was, I got to the pits just in time to see the breathtaking finish. Stewart was just leading from Rindt, who was just leading from Beltoise and he was just leading from McLaren; there were only nineteen hundredths of a second between the four cars, after a race of something like 280 miles. A very stirring finish to a very stirring race; the Italians certainly got their money's worth—the only thing that marred the race from their point of view was that Ferraris' were not at full strength; Rodriguez was driving one of last year's cars, but it was not in the hunt, it just wasn't quick enough. Chris Amon should have been driving a new flat-12 car but, during testing the day before, it had broken and he couldn't run at all. So there was no red car in the front of the race, and no Ferrari challenge on Italian home ground.

Anyway, the race was one of the most exciting ever seen at Monza, one of the most exciting of the year. Stewart certainly had an uncommonly fast car; whether it was a case of correct design or an extremely good engine I don't really know, but it was incredibly fast. He had the legs of everyone in that race.

·   ·   ·   ·   ·

The next race on the calendar was the following weekend, a Formula 2 race down at Albi in the South of France. We flew down in a Piper Aztec taking one or two of the lads— John Coombs, Paul Watson and one or two others. We made our way to Toulouse, where the Concorde is being built, which has a brand-new and incredibly long runway. I landed very short on the runway, thinking that I would help the Controller by turning off at the first intersection and getting out of the way as quickly as possible. No sooner had I landed than he came through and said, 'I'd like to tell you that the runway here is eleven thousand feet long.'

Well, blow you, I thought—so I took off again and flew the whole length of the runway, landed at the far end and taxied in to clear Customs. No sooner had we done that than we were told that we could not fly on to Albi because the runway there was under repair. So there we were stuck; practice was due to start at 2 o'clock and it was already twelve; there was no question of motoring there and getting there in time. Then we discovered that there was a little light plane with a very short field performance which could take us, but they wouldn't let us in with the Aztec—although I knew very well I could get it down pretty well anywhere. We hired the plane which was a bit of an old rattle-trap and it took us about half-an-hour to get to Albi.

By this time I had got the most terrible sinus headache and was really feeling sick. I had taken about twelve aspirins and there didn't seem to be much else I could do about it. To crown it all, when we finally landed at Albi, we could quite easily have landed the Aztec alongside the main runway which is what the local flying club was doing. But the French are very strict about their rules and Toulouse just wouldn't let us take off to land there.

I duly went out to practice, but I wasn't feeling too good. However, I set up joint second fastest lap with Jackie Stewart, and Jochen was a tenth of a second quicker. I was pretty fortunate, for the following day it rained all day and nobody went any quicker, so that left us on the front rows of the grid. The race started and Stewart, Rindt and myself immediately drew away from the rest of the field; once again Stewart seemed to have a very quick motor or else the Lotus were a bit slow down the straight. He was certainly motoring very quickly but I found I could just about hang on by slip-streaming all around the circuit. In fact I had boobed—on the first day of practice there had been quite a strong following wind and I had been getting about 9,800 down the straight; I felt that this was just a bit too high, particularly if we were going to do some slip-streaming, so I put in a taller top gear. I wasn't able to check this on the following day's practice because it rained. Well, of course, on race day itself the wind was not quite as strong. My car would not pull more than 9,000 and I never got on to the power range at all. Most of the power comes in at 9,600 and I was even slower down the straight than I had been before.

However, I just managed to hold on to Stewart for a bit and then, coming out of the hairpin, I missed a gear change and that was it—Stewart was off. Just that one little mistake was enough for me to lose the tow and he was gone. In the meantime Jochen had gone straight down one of the escape roads; he was in a bit of trouble with his brakes, and so he got left behind. There I was trailing Stewart and leading the rest of the field. Eventually Stewart had some trouble with the engine and that left me in the lead. I was able to come home and win my first Formula 2 race for something like five years —a long time. I wasn't the only one who was surprised—all the motoring press remarked upon it. Of course it was very pleasant to win.

For the Canadian Grand Prix it was the same as Monza— two 49Bs for Rindt and myself and the four-wheel drive car for John Miles. In practice John really excelled himself and put up some very creditable times. He clocked a time of 1 minute 20.7 seconds which I thought was very fast indeed for the four-wheel drive car on that circuit. It was the first time it had really showed some potential and he did very well. The highlight of practice was Jackie Ickx who managed to turn in a time of 1 minute 17.4 seconds—quite a lot quicker than anybody else. It seemed pretty certain that he was going to be the man to beat in the race.

Rindt made a superb start but was eventually passed by Stewart and then Ickx; these two then drew away from the rest of the field. I was lying somewhere around seventh or eighth after the start and I managed to work my way through the field up to about fourth place. Then I began a tremendous dice with Jack

Brabham; Jack eventually passed me and, with me hanging on to him, we began to pick off Rindt. At one stage we had been about twelve seconds behind Rindt and we managed to whittle this down to about two seconds—and then one of my camshafts must have gone because there was a frightening noise from the engine and I switched it off quickly. I parked my car just behind John Miles—he had stopped just a couple of laps earlier with some obscure trouble.

Ickx and Stewart had touched cars at one point, as Ickx was trying to take Stewart, and both cars had spun; Stewart went off the track and damaged his car so as not to be able to continue, but Ickx went on in the race and came in comfortably first. In the meantime, Brabham had managed to get by Rindt and so the Brabhams came home in a one-two—a tremendous finish for them. It really looked as if things were looking up for Brabham's because there had been rumours that they were going to pack up for next year; now, with this sort of result, I am sure that they will be able to find a sponsor to back them for the coming year.

And then came the American Grand Prix at Watkins Glen. Jochen and I had our usual 49Bs, but this time Mario Andretti was brought in to drive the four-wheel drive car in place of John Miles. The first day's practice was wet and miserable—everyone thought that perhaps this was where the four-wheel drive car would come into its own, but in fact it was slower than the two-wheel drive cars. I did a reasonable amount of practice in the wet, getting the car set up for these conditions just in case it was going to rain on race day. Jack Brabham ended up the quickest on that day, but times rather depended on when exactly you went out, because the track would begin to dry, then it would drizzle again, making it wet, and times went down again. It really did not matter as long as it did not go and rain again on the following day.

Practice the next day was dry, but it was a bit windy and gusty. Jackie Ickx broke a wing on one of the fastest sections of the circuit, on the back straight leading to the pits, and made three monumental spins. He ended up on the side of the track unhurt. Jochen managed to set up the fastest lap, with Denny Hulme second, Stewart third and myself fourth. They have a two-two grid at Watkins Glen so Rindt and Hulme were on the first row and Stewart and myself on the second. Hulme made a

particularly bad start and I had to go round him on the outside into third place just behind Rindt and Stewart.

I had on some experimental tyres that Firestone had given
us and they had been a bit worried just before the start that
the new tyres might chunk a bit on the inside of the shoulder
due to overheating, so they asked me to take some camber off
the rear wheels. I was a bit loath to do this, but rather than have
the tyres chunking I decided to do as they asked. So I was
running with the new tyres and I had taken off half a degree
of camber. This of course affected the car's road-holding and it
didn't seem to be handling too well; apart from this I didn't think
that the new tyres were all that hot either. Apparently Rodriguez
was even more worried; he had on the same type of tyres, but
came in to have them changed to standard tyres after 20 laps or
so. A long pit stop like that puts you right out of the running.

I was carrying on, but with the car's handling not at its best
I gradually dropped back and towards the end of the race I was
lying in fifth place. Somebody dropped some oil on the far side
of the circuit and I spun round on this, which rather surprised
me for I had seen the oil and was taking care. The engine of
course stalled. It wouldn't start on the starter so I had to climb
out and push it as far as a little downhill section where I could
get it rolling and jump back in. When I got out to push it, I
noticed that the rear tyres were bald and had been chunking—
which gave me the reason for my spin and also caused me a little
concern. Shortly after the spin, I thought I noticed something
slightly odd about the handling and, thinking of the bald tyres, I
knew I should have to indicate to the pits that I must make a
pit stop for a change of tyres. As I went by the pits I pointed to
the rear tyres so that they would be ready for the tyre change.

I never made it. Going down the straight on that particular
lap, the right-hand rear tyre collapsed and the car went out
of control. It veered off the track, hit a bank, shot me out and
rolled over. I carried on rolling along the ground. The car
ended up upside down.

When I had got out of the car following my spin I had had to
undo my seatbelts, but I couldn't do them up myself due to the
narrowness of the cockpit and I have to get one of the mechanics
to do them up for me—so of course my seatbelts were not done
up when the car crashed. I shall never know whether this was a
good or bad thing. . . .

Jochen Rindt went on to win the race which was the richest Grand Prix that's ever been held—the first prize was 50,000 dollars. The American organisers certainly ought to be congratulated on being able to raise such a colossal purse.

I had broken my right knee just on the joint, dislocated the left one and torn all the ligaments. Fortunately, the nerves were not too badly damaged. I was taken to the Arnott Ogden Memorial Hospital in Elmira, where I received excellent treatment. Their main concern was to get me well enough to stand the journey home and this took a little longer than anticipated due to my having a very high fever for a couple of days and a very low blood count. I had five pints of blood stuffed into me before I was well enough for the trip. Naturally I wanted to get home as soon as possible: Bette had flown out immediately and she was as anxious as I was to get home, although we were both extremely well taken care of, and my treatment was first rate.

I could remember very little of the accident, except going backwards at high speed. I must have been a bit dozy in hospital because I can remember some of the lads coming to see me directly after the race and I told them to tell Bette that I wouldn't be dancing for a while. I also remember asking the doctor, while he was about it, to try and straighten my left leg—which had been bandy since my motorcycle accident twenty-one years ago—so as to make life easier for my tailor.

For my flight home Cameron Argetsinger, the organiser of the United States Grand Prix, very kindly arranged for a light aircraft, a Cessna 402, to fly me in from Elmira to New York Airport to meet up with the 11.30 pm TWA flight to London, arriving at 10.30 am the next morning. I had a hell of a shock when TWA asked me to pay for four first class seats upon which they had made my bed. I suggested that they might do the same thing down the other end of the aircraft in the tourist section—but due to the seating arrangement this was impossible. David Frost happened to be on the same flight making one of his weekly trips to the States. The most hazardous part of the trip was the constant swapping of stretchers and the danger of my being dropped. I have never felt so helpless.

The reception at London Airport was tremendous; they really did me proud—it was much better than when I won the Championship. All the press and television companies, plus loads of friends, were there—it did me heart good to see 'em all.

Fords had laid on their own ambulance and driver and everyone mucked in to load me up. Walter Hayes of Ford had very kindly arranged for the best team of surgeons for the operation and I was whisked off to the University College Hospital to be placed in their care. I was very impressed when they suggested operating on the Sunday morning and thereby forfeited their weekend. They certainly worked hard for I was in the operating theatre for four-and-a-half hours.

At the moment I am in hospital recovering from the operation which I hope is going to prove a success. The surgeons are apparently very pleased with the way things went and now it's just a question of time to get the plasters off and learn to walk again.

The nurses are gorgeous and have been responsible for the most pleasurable part of my stay in hospital; four or five times a day they pop in to 'do' my back which entails rubbing cream onto my bottom; this apparently prevents bed sores, but it really brightens up my day—what luxury!

Apart from these pleasures my days are filled with visits from my family, relatives, friends, business associates, all fitted in between the kind and efficient medical treatment that I am receiving. I must add at this point that my most persistent visitor has been my solicitor who forced me to remove great chunks of material from this book for reasons of libel—hence some of the gaps and the reason for my leaving unsaid all those things that I ought to have said. The surgeons, matrons, sisters, nurses and administration have been more than helpful —they have even allowed me out to attend the occasional function. I have been inundated with 'get well' cards, cables and letters, some of them funny and some extremely rude but equally funny. My secretary has typed her fingers to the bone answering all my correspondence. I can honestly say that I haven't been bored once.

My accident of course meant that I missed going to the Formula 2 race in Rome and to the Mexican Grand Prix—the first Grand Prix that I have ever missed through injury and only the second that I have missed in the entire course of my professional driving career. It was a particularly sad occasion for me, but of course from one point of view I must be thankful that the accident occurred at the end of a season and I did not miss too many races.